Analogies and Theories

The Lipsey Lectures

The Lipsey Lectures offer a forum for leading scholars to reflect upon their research. Lipsey lecturers, chosen from among professional economists approaching the height of their careers, will have recently made key contributions at the frontier of any field of theoretical or applied economics. The emphasis is on novelty, originality, and relevance to an understanding of the modern world. It is expected, therefore, that each volume in the series will become a core source for graduate students and an inspiration for further research.

The lecture series is named after Richard G. Lipsey, the founding professor of economics at the University of Essex. At Essex, Professor Lipsey instilled a commitment to explore challenging issues in applied economics, grounded in formal economic theory, the predictions of which were to be subjected to rigorous testing, thereby illuminating important policy debates. This approach remains central to economic research at Essex and an inspiration for members of the Department of Economics. In recognition of Richard Lipsey's early vision for the Department, and in continued pursuit of its mission of academic excellence, the Department of Economics is pleased to organize the lecture series, with support from Oxford University Press.

Analogies and Theories

Formal Models of Reasoning

Itzhak Gilboa, Larry Samuelson,
and David Schmeidler

OXFORD
UNIVERSITY PRESS

OXFORD
UNIVERSITY PRESS

Great Clarendon Street, Oxford, OX2 6DP,
United Kingdom

Oxford University Press is a department of the University of Oxford.
It furthers the University's objective of excellence in research, scholarship,
and education by publishing worldwide. Oxford is a registered trade mark of
Oxford University Press in the UK and in certain other countries

First Edition published in 2015

Published in the United States of America by Oxford University Press
198 Madison Avenue, New York, NY 10016, United States of America

British Library Cataloguing in Publication Data
Data available

Library of Congress Control Number: 2014956892

ISBN 978–0–19–873802–2

Acknowledgments

We are grateful to many people for comments and references. Among them are Daron Acemoglu, Joe Altonji, Dirk Bergemann, Ken Binmore, Yoav Binyamini, Didier Dubois, Eddie Dekel, Drew Fudenberg, John Geanakoplos, Brian Hill, Bruno Jullien, Edi Karni, Simon Kasif, Daniel Lehmann, Sujoy Mukerji, Roger Myerson, Klaus Nehring, George Mailath, Arik Roginsky, Ariel Rubinstein, Lidror Troyanski, Peter Wakker, and Peyton Young. Special thanks are due to Alfredo di Tillio, Gabrielle Gayer, Eva Gilboa-Schechtman, Offer Lieberman, Andrew Postlewaite, and Dov Samet for many discussions that partly motivated and greatly influenced this project. Finally, we are indebted to Rossella Argenziano and Jayant Ganguli for suggesting the book project for us and for many comments along the way.

We thank the publishers of the papers included herein, The Econometric Society, Elsevier, and Springer, for the right to reprint the papers in this collection. (Gilboa and Schmeidler, "Inductive Inference: An Axiomatic Approach" *Econometrica*, 71 (2003); Gilboa and Samuelson, "Subjectivity in Inductive Inference", *Theoretical Economics*, 7, (2012); Gilboa, Samuelson, and Schmeidler, "Dynamics of Inductive Inference in a Unified Model", *Journal of Economic Theory*, 148 (2013); Gayer and Gilboa, "Analogies and Theories: The Role of Simplicity and the Emergence of Norms", *Games and Economic Behavior*, 83 (2014); Di Tillio, Gilboa and Samuelson, "The Predictive Role of Counterfactuals", *Theory and Decision*, 74 (2013) reprinted with kind permission from Springer Science+Business Media B.V.) We also gratefully acknowledge financial support from the European Research Council (Gilboa, Grant no. 269754), Israel Science Foundation (Gilboa and Schmeidler, Grants nos. 975/03, 396/10, and 204/13), the National Science Foundation (Samuelson, Grants nos. SES-0549946 and SES-0850263), The AXA Chair for Decision Sciences (Gilboa), the Chair for Economic and Decision Theory and the Foerder Institute for Research in Economics (Gilboa).

Contents

1

Introduction

1.1 Scope

This book deals with some formal models of reasoning used for inductive inference, broadly understood to encompass various ways in which past observations can be used to generate predictions about future eventualities. The main focus of the book are two modes of reasoning and the interaction between them. The first, more basic, is *case-based*,[1] and it refers to prediction by analogies, that is, by the eventualities observed in similar past cases. The second is *rule-based*, referring to processes where observations are used to learn which general rules, or theories, are more likely to hold, and should be used for prediction. A special emphasis is put on a model that unifies these modes of reasoning and allows the analysis of the dynamics between them.

Parts of the book might hopefully be of interest to statisticians, psychologists, philosophers, and cognitive scientists. Its main readership, however, consists of researchers in economic theory who model the behavior of economic agents. Some readers might wonder why economic theorists should be interested in modes of reasoning; others might wonder why the answer to this question isn't obvious. We devote the next section to these motivational issues. It might be useful first to delineate the scope of the present project more clearly by comparing it with the emphasis put on similar questions in fellow disciplines.

1.1.1 *Statistics*

The use of past observations for predicting future ones is the bread and butter of statistics. Is this, then, a book about statistics, and what can it add to existing knowledge in statistics?

[1] The term "case-based reasoning" is due to Schank (1986) and Schank and Riesbeck (1989). As used here, however, it refers to reasoning by similarity, dating back to Hume (1748) at the latest.

While our analysis touches upon statistical questions and methods at various points, most of the questions we deal with do not belong to statistics as the term is usually understood. Our main interest is in situations where statistics typically fails to provide well-established methods for generating predictions, whether deterministic or probabilistic. We implicitly assume that, when statistical analysis offers reliable, agreed-upon predictions, rational economic agents will use them. However, many problems that economic agents face involve uncertainties over which statistics is silent. For example, statistical models typically do not attempt to predict wars or revolutions; their success in predicting financial crises is also limited. Yet such events cannot be ignored, as they have direct and non-negligible impact on economic agents' lives and decisions. At the personal level, agents might also find that some of the weightiest decisions in their lives, involving the choice of career paths, partners, or children, raise uncertainties that are beyond the realm of statistics.

In light of the above, it is interesting that the two modes of reasoning we discuss, which originated in philosophy and psychology, do have close parallels within statistics. Case-based reasoning bears a great deal of similarity to non-parametric methods such as kernel classification, kernel probabilities, and nearest-neighbor methods (see Royall, 1966, Fix and Hodges, 1951–2, Cover and Hart, 1967). Rule-based reasoning is closer in spirit to parametric methods, selecting theories based on criteria such as maximum likelihood as well as information criteria (such as the Akaike Information Criterion, Akaike, 1974) and using them for generating predictions. Case-based reasoning and kernel methods are more likely to be used when one doesn't have a clear idea about the underlying structure of the data generating process; rule-based reasoning and likelihood-based methods are better equipped to deal with situations where the general structure of the process is known. Viewed thus, one may consider this book as dealing with (i) generalizations of non-parametric and parametric statistical models to deal with abstract problems where numerical data do not lend themselves to rigorous statistical analysis; and (ii) ways to combine these modes of reasoning.

It is important to emphasize that our interest is in modeling the way people think, or should think. Methods that were developed in statistics or machine learning that may prove very successful in certain problems are of interest to us only to the extent that they can also be viewed as models of human reasoning, and especially of reasoning in the type of less structured problems mentioned above.

1.1.2 *Psychology*

If this book attempts to model human reasoning, isn't it squarely within the realm of psychology? The answer is negative for several reasons. First, following the path-breaking contributions of Daniel Kahneman and Amos Tversky, psychological research puts substantial emphasis on "heuristics and biases", that is, on judgment and decision making that are erroneous and that clearly deviate from standards of rationality. There is great value in identifying these biases, correcting them when possible and accepting them when not. However, our focus is not on situations where people are clearly mistaken, in the sense that they can be convinced that they have been reasoning in a faulty way. Instead, we deal with two modes of reasoning that are not irrational by any reasonable definition of rationality: thinking by analogies and by general theories. Not only are these modes of reasoning old and respectable, they have appeared in statistical analysis, as mentioned above. Thus, while our project is mostly descriptive in nature, trying to describe how people think, it is not far from a normative interpretation, as it focuses on modes of reasoning that are not clearly mistaken.

Another difference between our analysis and psychological research is that we view our project not as a goal in itself, but as part of the foundations of economics. Our main interest is not to capture a given phenomenon about human reasoning, but to suggest ways in which economic theorists might usefully model the reasoning of economic agents. With this goal is mind, we seek generality at the expense of accuracy more than would a psychologist. We are also primarily interested in mathematical results that convey general messages. In contrast to the dominant approach in psychology, we are not interested in accurately describing specific phenomena within a well-defined field of knowledge. Rather, we are interested in convincing fellow economists which paradigms should be used for understanding the phenomena of interest.

1.1.3 *Philosophy*

How people think, and even more so, how people should think, are questions that often lead to philosophical analysis. More specifically, how people should be learning from the past about the future has been viewed as a clearly philosophical problem, to which important contributions were made by thinkers who are considered to be primarily philosophers (such as David Hume, Charles Peirce, and Nelson Goodman, to mention but a few). As in other questions, whereas psychology tends to take a descriptive approach, focusing on actual human reasoning and often on its faults and flaws, philosophy puts a greater emphasis on normative questions. Given that our main interest also has a more normative flavor than does mainstream psychological research, it stands to reason that our questions would have close parallels within philosophy.

There are some key differences in focus between our analysis and the philosophical approach. First, philosophers seem to be seeking a higher degree of accuracy than we require. As economic theorists, we are trained to seek and are used to finding value in definitions and in formal models that are not always very accurate, and that have a vague claim to be generalizable without a specific delineation of their scope of applicability. (See Gilboa, Postlewaite, Samuelson, and Schmeidler, 2013, where we attempt to model one way in which economists sometimes view their theoretical models.) Thus, while philosophers might be shaken by a paradox, as would a scientist be shaken by an empirical refutation of a theory, we would be more willing to accept the paradox or the counter-example as an interesting case that should be registered, but not necessarily as a fatal blow to the usefulness of the model. The willingness to accept models that are imperfect should presumably pay off in the results that such models may offer. Our analysis thus puts its main emphasis on mathematical results that seem to be suggesting general insights.

Another distinction between our analysis and mainstream analytical philosophy is that the latter seems to be focusing on rule-based reasoning almost entirely. In fact we are not aware of any formal, mathematical models of case-based reasoning within philosophy, perhaps because this mode of reasoning is not considered to be fully rational. We maintain that there are problems of interest in which one has too little information to develop theories and select among them in an objective way. In such problems, it might be the case that the most rational thing to do is to reason by analogies. Hence we start off with the assumption that both rule-based and case-based reasoning have a legitimate claim to be "rational" modes of reasoning, and seek models that capture both, ideally simultaneously.

1.1.4 *Conclusion*

There are other fields in which inductive inference is studied. Artificial intelligence, relying on philosophy, psychology, and computer science, offers models of human reasoning in general and of induction in particular. Machine learning, a field closer to statistics, also deals with the same basic fundamental question of inductive inference. Thus, it is not surprising that the ideas discussed in the sequel have close counterparts in statistics, machine learning, psychology, artificial intelligence, philosophy linguistics, and so on.

The main contribution of this work is the formal modeling of arguments in a way that allows their mathematical analysis, with an emphasis on the ability to compare case-based and rule-based reasoning. The mathematical analysis serves a mostly rhetorical purpose: pointing out to economists strengths and weaknesses of formal models of reasoning that they may be using in their own modeling of economic phenomena. With this goal in mind, we seek insights that appear to be generally robust, even if not necessarily perfectly accurate. We hope that the mathematical analysis reveals some properties of models that are not entirely obvious a priori, and may thereby be of help to economists in their modeling.

1.2 Motivation

Economics studies economic phenomena such as production and consumption, growth and unemployment, buying and selling, and so forth. All of these phenomena relate to human activities, or decision making. It might therefore seem very natural that we would be interested in human reasoning: presumably if we knew how people reason, we would know how they make decisions, and, as a result, which economic phenomena to expect.

This view is also consistent with a reductionist approach, suggesting that economics should be based on psychology: just as it is argued biology can be (in principle) reduced to chemistry, economics can be (in principle) reduced to psychology. From this point of view, it would seem very natural that economists would be interested in the way people think and perform inductive inference.

Economists have not found this conclusion obvious. First, the alleged reduction of one scientific discipline to another seldom implies that all questions of the latter should be of interest to the former. Chemistry need not be interested in high-energy physics, and biologists may be ignorant of the chemistry of polymers. Second, psychology has not reached the same level of success of quantitative predictions as have the "exact" sciences, and thus it may seem less promising as a basis for economics as would, say, physics be for chemistry. And, perhaps more importantly, in the beginning of the twentieth century the scientific nature of psychology was questioned. While the philosophy of science was dominated by the Received View of logical positivism (Carnap, 1923), and later by Popper's (1934) thought, psychology was greatly influenced by Freudian psychoanalysis, famously one of the targets of Popper's critique. Thus, psychology was not only considered to be an "inexact" or a "soft" science; many started viewing it as a non-scientific enterprise.[2]

In response to this background, many economists sought refuge in the logical positivist dictum that understanding how people think is unnecessary for understanding how they behave. The revealed preference paradigm came

[2] See Loewenstein (1988).

to the fore, suggesting that all that matters is observed behavior (see Frisch, 1926, Samuelson, 1938). Concepts such as tastes and beliefs were modeled as mathematical constructs—a utility function and a probability measure—which are defined solely by observed choices. Economists came to think that how people think, and how they form their beliefs, was, by and large, of no economic import. Or, to be precise, the beliefs of rational agents came to be modeled by probability measures which were assumed to be updated according to Bayes's rule with the arrival of new information. It became accepted that, beyond the application of Bayes's rule for obtaining conditional probabilities, no reasoning process was necessary for understanding people's choices and resulting economic phenomena.

This view of economic agents as "black boxes" that behave *as if* they were following certain procedures paralleled the rise of behaviorism in psychology (Skinner, 1938). Whereas, however, in psychology, strict behaviorism was largely discarded in favor of cognitive psychology (starting in the 1960s), in economics the "black box" approach survives to this day. (See, for instance, Gul and Pesendorfer, 2008.) Indeed, given that the subject matter of economics is people's economic activities, it is much easier to dismiss mental phenomena and cognitive processes as irrelevant to economics than it is to do so when discussing psychology. And, importantly, axiomatic treatments of people's behavior, and most notably Savage's (1954) result, convinced economists that maximizing expected utility relative to a subjective probability measure is the model of choice for descriptive and normative purposes alike. This model allows many degrees of freedom in selecting the appropriate prior belief, but beyond that leaves very little room for modeling thinking. Presumably, if we know how people behave and make economic decisions, we need not concern ourselves with the way people think.

We find this view untenable for several reasons. First, Savage's model is hardly an accurate description of people's behavior. In direct experimental tests of the axioms, a non-negligible proportion of participants end up violating some of them (see Ellsberg, 1961, and the vast literature that followed). Moreover, many people have been found to consistently violate even more basic assumptions (see Tversky and Kahneman, 1974, 1981). Further, when tested indirectly, one finds that many empirical phenomena are easier to explain using other models than they are using the subjective expected utility hypothesis. Hence, one cannot argue that economics has developed a theory of behavior that is always satisfactorily accurate for its purposes. It stands to reason that a better understanding of people's thought processes might help us figure out when Savage's theory is a reasonable model of agents' behavior, and how it can be improved when it isn't.

Second, Savage's result is a powerful rhetorical device that can be used to convince a decision maker that she would like to conform to the subjective expected utility maximization model, or even to convince an economist that economic agents might indeed behave in accordance with this model, at least in certain domains of application. But the theorem does not provide any guidance in selecting the utility function or the prior probability involved in the model. Since tastes are inherently subjective, theoretical considerations may be of limited help in finding an appropriate utility function, whether for normative or for descriptive purposes. However, probabilities represent beliefs, and one might expect theory to provide some guidance in finding which beliefs one should entertain, or which beliefs economic agents are likely to entertain. Thus, delving into reasoning processes might be helpful in finding out which probability measures might, or should capture agents' beliefs.

Third, Savage's model follows the general logical positivistic paradigm of relating the theoretical terms of utility and probability to observable choice. But these choices often aren't observable in practice, and sometimes not even in principle. For example, in order to capture possible causal theories, one needs to construct the state space in such a way that it is theoretically impossible to observe the preference relation in its entirety. In fact, observable choices would be but a fraction of those needed to execute an axiomatic derivation. (See Gilboa and Schmeidler, 1995, and Gilboa, Postlewaite, and Schmeidler, 2009, 2012.) Hence, for many problems of interest one cannot rely on observable choice to identify agents' beliefs. On this background, studying agents' reasoning offers a viable alternative to modeling beliefs.

In sum, we believe that understanding how people think might be useful in predicting their behavior. While in principle one could imagine a theory of behavior that would be so accurate as to render redundant any theory of reasoning, we do not believe that the current theories of behavior have achieved such accuracy.

1.3 Overview

The present volume consists of six chapters, five of which have been previously published as separate papers. The first two of these deal with a single mode of reasoning each, whereas the rest employ a model that unifies them. Chapter 2[3] focuses on case-based reasoning. It offers an axiomatic approach to the following problem: given a database of observations, how should different eventualities be ranked? The axiomatic derivation assumes that observations in a database may be replicated at will to generate a new database, and that it would be meaningful to pose the same problem for the

[3] Gilboa and Schmeidler, 2003.

new database. For example, if the reasoner observes the outcomes of a roll of a die, and has to predict which outcome is more likely to occur on the next roll, we assume that any database consisting of finitely many past observations can be imagined, and that the reasoner should be able to respond to the ranking question given each such database. The key axiom, *combination*, roughly suggests that, should eventuality a be more likely than another eventuality b, given two disjoint databases, then a should be more likely than b also given their union. Ranking outcomes by their relative frequencies clearly satisfies this axiom: if one outcome has appeared more often than another in each of two databases, and will thus be considered more likely given each, so it will be given their union. Coupled with a few other, less fundamental assumptions, the combination axiom implies that the reasoner would be ranking alternative eventualities by an additive formula. The formula can be shown to generalize simultaneously several known techniques from statistics, such as ranking by relative frequencies, kernel estimation of density functions (Akaike, 1945), and kernel classification. Importantly, the model can also be applied to the ranking of theories given databases, where it yields an axiomatic foundation for ranking by the maximum likelihood principle.[4] The chapter also discusses various limitations of the combination axiom. Chief among them are situations in which the reasoner engages in second-order induction, learning the similarity function to be used when performing case-to-case induction,[5] and in learning that involves both case-to-rule induction and (rule-to-case) deduction. These limitations make it clear that, while the combination axiom is common to several different techniques of inductive inference, it by no means encompasses all forms of learning.

Chapter 3[6] deals with rule-based reasoning. It offers a model in which a reasoner starts out with a set of theories and, after any finite history of observations, needs to select a theory. It is assumed that the reasoner has a subjective a priori ranking of the theories, for example, a "simpler than" relation. Importantly, we assume that there are countably many theories, and for each one of them there are only finitely many other theories that are ranked higher. Given a history, the reasoner rules out those theories that have been refuted by the observations, and selects a maximizer of the subjective ranking among those that have not been refuted, that is, chooses one of the simplest theories that fit the data. A key insight is that, in the absence of a subjective ranking, the reasoner would not be able to learn effectively: she would be unable to consistently choose among all possible theories that are consistent with observed history. Hence, even if the observations happen to

4 A sequel paper, Gilboa and Schmeidler (2010), generalizes the model to allow for an additive cost attached to a theory's log-likelihood, as in Akaike Infomation Criterion.

5 See Gilboa, Lieberman, and Schmeidler, 2006.

6 Gilboa and Samuelson, 2012.

fit a simple theory, the reasoner will not conclude that this theory is to be used for prediction, as there are many other competing theories that match the data just as well. By contrast, when a subjective ranking—such as simplicity—is used as an additional criterion for theory selection, the reasoner will learn simple processes: at some point all theories that are simpler than the true one (but not equivalent to it) will be refuted, and from that point on the reasoner will use the correct theory for prediction. Thus, the preference for simplicity provides an advantage in prediction of simple processes, while incurring no cost when attempting to predict complex or random processes. This preference for simplicity does not derive from cognitive limitations or the cost of computation; simplicity is simply one possible criterion that allows the reasoners to settle on the correct theory, should there be one that is simple. In a sense, the model suggests that had cognitive limitations not existed, we should have invented them.

Chapter 4[7] offers a formal model that captures both case-based and rule-based reasoning. It is also general enough to describe Bayesian reasoning, which may be viewed as an extreme example of rule-based reasoning. The reasoner in this model is assumed to observe the unfolding of history, and, at each stage t, after observing some data, x_t, to make a single-period prediction by ranking possible outcomes in that period, y_t. The reasoner uses *conjectures*, which are simply subsets of states of the world (where each state specifies (x_t, y_t) for all t). Each conjecture is assigned a non-negative weight a priori, and after each history those conjectures that have not yet been refuted are used for prediction. As opposed to Chapter 3, here we do not assume that the reasoner selects a single "most reasonable conjecture" in each period for generating predictions; rather, all unrefuted conjectures are consulted, and their predictions are additively aggregated using their a priori weights. (The model also distinguishes between relevant and irrelevant conjectures, though the ranking of eventualities in each period is unaffected by this distinction).

The extreme case in which all weight is put on conjectures that are singletons (each consisting of a single state of the world) reduces to Bayesian reasoning: the a priori weights are then the probabilities of the states, and the exclusion of refuted conjectures boils down to Bayesian updating. The model allows, however, a large variety of rules that capture non-Bayesian reasoning: the reasoner might believe in a general theory that does not make specific predictions in each and every period, or that does not assign probabilities to the values of x_t. More surprisingly, the model allows us to capture case-based reasoning, as in kernel classification, by aggregating over appropriately defined "case-based conjectures". Beyond providing a unified framework for these modes of reasoning, this model also allows one to ask

[7] Gilboa, Samuelson, and Schmeidler, 2013.

how the relative weights of different forms of reasoning might change over time. We show that, if the reasoner does not know the structure of the underlying data generating process, and has to remain open-minded about all possible eventualities, she will gradually use Bayesian reasoning less, and shift to conjectures that are not as specific. The basic intuition is that, because Bayesian reasoning requires that weight of credence be specified to the level of single states of the world, this weight has to be divided among pairwise disjoint subsets of possible histories, and the number of these subsets grows exponentially fast as a function of time, t. If the reasoner does not have sharp a priori knowledge about the process, and hence divides the weight of credence among the subsets in a more or less unbiased way, the weight of each such subset of histories will be bounded by an exponentially decreasing function of t. By contrast, conjectures that allow for many states may be fewer, and if there are only polynomially many of them (as a function of t), their weight may become relatively higher as compared to the weight of the Bayesian conjectures. This result suggests that, due to the fact that Bayesian approach insists on quantifying *any* source of uncertainty, it might prove non-robust as compared to modes of reasoning that remain silent on many issues and risk predictions only on some.

Chapter 5[8] uses the same framework to focus on case-based vs. rule-based reasoning. Here, the latter is understood to mean theories that make predictions (regarding y_t) at each and every period (after having observed x_t), so, in this model theories cannot "pick their fights", as it were. They differ from Bayesian conjectures in that the latter are committed to predict not only the outcome y_t but also the data x_t. Yet, making predictions about y_t at each and every period is sufficiently demanding to partition the set of unrefuted theories after every history, and thereby to generate an exponential growth of the number of subsets of theories that may be unrefuted at time t. In this chapter it is shown that, under certain reasonable assumptions, should reality be simple, that is, described by state of the world that conforms to a single theory, the reasoner will learn it. The basic logic of this simple result is similar to that of Chapter 3: it suffices that the reasoner be open-minded to conceive of all theories and assign some weight to them. Should one of these simple theories be true, sooner or later all other theories will be refuted, and the a priori weight assigned to the correct theory will become relatively large. Moreover, in this chapter we also consider case-based conjectures, and show that their weight diminishes to zero. As a result, not only is the correct theory getting a high weight relative to other theories, the entire class of rule-based conjectures becomes dominant as compared to the case-based ones. That is, the reasoner would converge to be rule-based.

[8] Gayer and Gilboa, 2014.

However, in states of the world that are not simple, that is, that cannot be described by a single theory, under some additional assumptions the converse is true: similarly to the analysis of Chapter 4, case-based reasoning would drive out rule-based reasoning. Chapter 5 also deals with situations in which the phenomenon observed is determined by people's reasoning, that is, that the process is endogenous rather than exogenous. It is shown that under endogenous processes rule-based reasoning is more likely to emerge than under exogenous ones. For example, it is more likely to observe people using general theories when predicting social norms than when predicting the weather.

Finally, Chapter 6[9] applies the model of Chapter 4 to the analysis of counterfactual thinking. It starts with the observation that, while counterfactuals are by definition devoid of empirical content, some of them seem to be more meaningful than others. It is suggested that counterfactual reasoning is based on the conjectures that have not been refuted by actual history, h_t, applied to another history, $h'_{t'}$, which is incompatible with h_t (hence counterfactual). Thus, actual history might be used to learn about general rules, and these can be applied to make predictions also in histories that are known not to be the case. This type of reasoning can make interesting predictions only when the reasoner has non-Bayesian conjectures: because each Bayesian conjecture consists of a single state of the world, a Bayesian conjecture that is unrefuted by the actual history h_t would be silent at the counterfactual history $h'_{t'}$. However, general rules and analogies that are unrefuted by h_t might still have non-trivial predictions at the incompatible history $h'_{t'}$. The model is also used to ask what counterfactual thinking might be useful for, and to rule out one possible answer: a rather trivial observation shows that, for an unboundedly rational reasoner, counterfactual prediction cannot enhance learning.

1.4 Future Directions

The analysis presented in this volume is very preliminary and may be extended in a variety of ways. First, in an attempt to highlight conceptual issues, we focus on simple models. For example, we assume that theories are deterministic; and that case-based reasoning takes into account only the similarity between two cases at a time. In more elaborate models, one might consider probabilistic theories, analogies that involve more than two cases, more interesting hybrids between case-based and rule-based theories, and so forth.

[9] Di Tillio, Gilboa, and Samuelson, 2013.

Our analysis deals with reasoning, and does not say anything explicit about decision making. At times, it is quite straightforward to incorporate decision making into these models, but this is not always the case. For example, the unified model (of Chapters 4–6) is based on a credence function that is, in the language of Dempster (1967) and Shafer (1976), a "belief function", and therefore a capacity (Choquet, 1953–4). As such, it lends itself directly to decision making using Choquet expected utility (Schmeidler, 1989). However, single-period prediction does not directly generalize to single-period decision making: while prediction can be made for each period separately, when making decisions one might have to consider long-term effects, learning and experimentation, and so forth.

We believe that the models presented herein can be applied to a variety of economic models. For example, it is tempting to conjecture that agents' reasoning about stock market behavior shifts between rule-based and case-based modes: at times, certain theories about the way the market works gain ground, and become an equilibrium of reasoning: the more people believe in a theory, other things being equal, the more it appears to be true. But from time to time an external shock will refute a theory, as happens in the case of stock market bubbles. At these junctures, where established lore is clearly violated, people may be at a loss. They may not know which theory should replace the one just dethroned. They may also entertain a healthy degree of doubt about the expertise of pundits. It is then natural to switch to a less ambitious mode of reasoning, which need not engage in generalizations and theorizing, but will rely more on simple analogies to past cases. Indeed, one may conjecture that psychological factors affect the choice of rule-based vs. case-based reasoning, with a greater degree of self-confidence favoring the former, whereas confusion and self-doubt induce a higher relative weight of the latter.

More generally, the relative weight assigned to case-based and rule-based reasoning might be affected by a variety of factors. Gayer, Gilboa, and Lieberman (2007) empirically compare the fit of case-based and rule-based models to asking prices in real-estate markets. They find that case-based reasoning is relatively more prevalent than rule-based reasoning in a rental market as compared to a purchase market. The explanation for this result is that rules are more concise and are therefore easier to coordinate on; hence, a speculative market that needs a higher degree of coordination (such as the purchase market) would tend to be more rule-based than would a market of a pure consumption good (such as the rental market). This conclusion reminds one of the comparison between exogenous and endogenous processes in Chapter 5. Thus, coordination games might favor rule-based, as compared to case-based reasoning. Gayer, Gilboa, and Lieberman (2007) also speculate that statistical considerations, such as the size of the database, might affect the relative importance of the two modes of reasoning, with rule-based reasoning being typical of databases that are large enough to develop rules, but not sufficiently so to render them useless.

We hope and believe that formal models of modes of reasoning will be developed and used for the analysis of economic phenomena. Economics probably cannot afford to ignore human thinking. Moreover, the interaction between economics and psychology should not be limited to biases and errors, documented in psychology and applied in behavioral economics. Economics too can benefit from a better understanding of human thinking, and perhaps mostly when applied to rational prediction and decision making. Both analogies and general theories should play major roles in understanding how economic agents think.

1.5 References

Akaike, H. (1954), "An Approximation to the Density Function", *Annals of the Institute of Statistical Mathematics*, **6**: 127–32.

Akaike, H. (1974), "A new look at the statistical model identification". *IEEE Transactions on Automatic Control*, **19**(6), 716–23.

Carnap, R. (1923), "Uber die Aufgabe der Physik und die Andwednung des Grundsatze der Einfachstheit", *Kant-Studien*, **28**: 90–107.

Choquet, G. (1953), "Theory of Capacities", *Annales de l'Institut Fourier*, 5: 131–295.

Cover, T. and P. Hart (1967), "Nearest Neighbor Pattern Classification", IEEE *Transactions on Information Theory*, **13**: 21–7.

Dempster, A. P. (1967), "Upper and Lower Probabilities Induced by a Multivalued Mapping", *Annals of Mathematical Statistics*, **38**: 325–39.

Di Tillio, A., I. Gilboa, and L. Samuelson (2013), "The Predictive Role of Counterfactuals", *Theory and Decision*, **74**: 167–82.

Ellsberg, D. (1961), "Risk, Ambiguity and the Savage Axioms", *Quarterly Journal of Economics*, **75**: 643–69.

Fix, E. and J. Hodges (1951), "Discriminatory Analysis. Nonparametric Discrimination: Consistency Properties". Technical Report 4, Project Number 21-49-004, USAF School of Aviation Medicine, Randolph Field, TX.

Fix, E. and J. Hodges (1952), "Discriminatory Analysis: Small Sample Performance". Technical Report 21-49-004, USAF School of Aviation Medicine, Randolph Field, TX.

Frisch, R. (1926), "Sur un probleme d'economie pure", *Norsk Matematisk Forenings Skrifter*, **16**.

Gayer, G. and I. Gilboa (2014), "Analogies and Theories: The Role of Simplicity and the Emergence of Norms", *Games and Economic Behavior*, **83**: 267–83.

Gayer, G., I. Gilboa, and O. Lieberman (2007), "Rule-Based and Case-Based Reasoning in Housing Prices", *BE Journals in Theoretical Economics*, **7**.

Gilboa, I., O. Lieberman, and D. Schmeidler (2006), "Empirical Similarity", *Review of Economics and Statistics*, **88**: 433–44.

Gilboa, I., A. Postlewaite, L. Samuelson, and D. Schmeidler (2013), "Economic Models as Analogies", *The Economic Journal*, **124**: F513–33.

Gilboa, I., A. Postlewaite, and D. Schmeidler (2009), "Is It Always Rational to Satisfy Savage's Axioms?", *Economics and Philosophy*, **25**: 285–96.

Gilboa, I., A. Postlewaite, and D. Schmeidler (2012), "Rationality of Belief", *Synthese*, **187**: 11–31.

Gilboa, I. and L. Samuelson (2012), "Subjectivity in Inductive Inference", *Theoretical Economics*, **7**: 183–215.

Gilboa, I., L. Samuelson, and D. Schmeidler (2013), "Dynamics of Inductive Inference in a Unified Model", *Journal of Economic Theory*, **148**: 1399–432.

Gilboa, I. and D. Schmeidler (1995), "Case-Based Decision Theory", *Quarterly Journal of Economics*, **110**: 605–39.

Gilboa, I. and D. Schmeidler (2001), *A Theory of Case-Based Decisions*. Cambridge: Cambridge University Press.

Gilboa, I. and D. Schmeidler (2003), "Inductive Inference: An Axiomatic Approach", *Econometrica*, **71**: 1–26.

Gilboa, I. and D. Schmeidler (2010), "Likelihood and Simplicity: An Axiomatic Approach", *Journal of Economic Theory*, **145**: 1757–75.

Gul, F. and W. Pesendorfer (2008), "The Case for Mindless Economics", in *The Foundations of Positive and Normative Economics*, by Andrew Caplin and Andrew Shotter (eds.). Oxford University Press.

Hume, D. (1748), *Enquiry into the Human Understanding*. Oxford: Clarendon Press.

Loewenstein, G. (1988), "The Fall and Rise of Psychological Explanations in the Economics of Intertemporal Choice", in *Choice over Time*, edited by G. Loewenstein and J. Elster. Russell Sage Foundation: New York.

Popper, K. R. (1934), *Logik der Forschung;* English edition (1958), *The Logic of Scientific Discovery*. London: Hutchinson and Co. Reprinted (1961), New York: Science Editions.

Riesbeck, C. K. and R. C. Schank (1989), *Inside Case-Based Reasoning*. Hillsdale, NJ: Lawrence Erlbaum Associates, Inc.

Royall, R. (1966), *A Class of Nonparametric Estimators of a Smooth Regression Function*. Ph.D. Thesis, Stanford University, Stanford, CA.

Samuelson, P. (1938), "A Note on the Pure Theory of Consumer Behavior", *Economica*, **5**: 61–71.

Savage, L. J. (1954), *The Foundations of Statistics*. New York: John Wiley and Sons.

Schank, R. C. (1986), *Explanation Patterns: Understanding Mechanically and Creatively*. Hillsdale, NJ: Lawrence Erlbaum Associates.

Schmeidler, D. (1989), "Subjective Probability and Expected Utility without Additivity", *Econometrica*, **57**: 571–87.

Shafer, G. (1976), *A Mathematical Theory of Evidence*. Princeton: Princeton University Press.

Skinner, B. F. (1938), *The Behavior of Organisms: An Experimental Analysis*. Cambridge, Massachusetts: B. F. Skinner Foundation.

Tversky, A. and D. Kahneman (1974), "Judgment under Uncertainty: Heuristics and Biases", *Science*, **185**: 1124–31.

Tversky, A. and D. Kahneman (1981), "The Framing of Decisions and the Psychology of Choice", *Science*, **211**: 453–8.

2

Inductive Inference

An Axiomatic Approach

2.1 Introduction

Prediction is based on past cases. As Hume (1748) argued, "From causes which appear similar we expect similar effects. This is the sum of all our experimental conclusions". Over the past decades Hume's approach has found reincarnations in the artificial intelligence literature as reasoning by analogies, reasoning by similarities, or case-based reasoning (See Schank (1986) and Riesbeck and Schank (1989)). Many authors accept the view that analogies, or similarities to past cases hold the key to human reasoning, and that moreover, the literature on machine learning and pattern recognition deals with using past cases, or observations, for predicting or classifying new data. (See, for instance, Forsyth and Rada (1986) and Devroye, Gyorfi, and Lugosi (1996)). But how should past cases be used? How does, and how should one resolve conflicts between different analogies? To address these questions, let us first consider a few examples.

Example 1: A die is rolled over and over again. One has to predict the outcome of the next roll. As far as the predictor can tell, all rolls were made under identical conditions. Also, the predictor does not know of any a-priori reason to consider any outcome more likely than any other. The most reasonable prediction seems to be the mode of the empirical distribution, namely, the outcome that has appeared most often in the past. Moreover, empirical frequencies suggest a plausibility ranking of all possible outcomes, and not just a choice of the most plausible ones.[1]

Example 2: A physician is asked by a patient if she predicts that a surgery will succeed in his case. The physician knows whether the procedure

[1] The term "likelihood" in the context of a binary relation, "at least as likely as", has been used by de Finetti (1937) and by Savage (1954). It should not be confused with "likelihood" in the the context of likelihood functions, also used in the sequel. At this point we use "likelihood" and "plausibility" informally and interchangeably.

succeeded in most cases in the past, but she will be quick to remind her patient that every human body is unique. Indeed, the physician knows that the statistics she read included patients who varied in terms of age, gender, medical condition, and so forth. It would therefore be too naive of her to quote statistics as if the empirical frequencies were all that mattered. On the other hand, if the physician considers only past cases of patients that are identical to hers, she will probably end up with an empty database.

Example 3: An expert on international relations is asked to predict the outcome of the conflict in the Middle East. She is expected to draw on her vast knowledge of past cases, coupled with her astute analysis thereof, in forming her prediction. As in Example 2, the expert has a lot of information she can use, but she cannot quote even a single case that was identical to the situation at hand. Moreover, as opposed to Example 2, even the possible eventualities are not identical to outcomes that occurred in past cases.

We seek a theory of prediction that will permit the predictor to make use of available information, where different past cases might have differential relevance to the prediction problem. Specifically, we consider a prediction problem for which a set of possible eventualities is given. This set may or may not be an exhaustive list of all conceivable eventualities. We do not model the process by which such a set is generated. Rather, we assume the set given and restrict attention to the problem of qualitative ranking of its elements according to their likelihood.

The prediction rule Consider the following prediction rule for Example 2. The physician considers all known cases of successful surgery. She uses her subjective judgment to evaluate the similarity of each of these cases to the patient she is treating, and she adds them up. She then does the same for unsuccessful treatments. Her prediction is the outcome with the larger aggregate similarity value. This generalizes frequentist ranking to a "fuzzy sample": in both examples, likelihood of an outcome is measured by summation over cases in which it occurred. Whereas in Example 1 the weight attached to each past case is 1, in this example this weight varies according to the physician's subjective assessment of similarity of the relevant cases. Rather than a dichotomous distinction between data points that do and those that do not belong to the sample, each data point belongs to the sample to a certain degree, say, between 0 and 1.

The prediction rule we propose can also be applied to Example 3 as follows. For each possible outcome of the conflict in the Middle East, and for each past case, the expert is asked to assess a number, measuring the degree of support that the case lends to this outcome. Adding up these numbers, for all known cases and for each outcome, yields a numerical representation of the likelihood ranking. Thus, our prediction rule can be applied also when there is no structural relationship between past cases and future eventualities.

Formally, let M denote the set of known cases. For each $c \in M$ and each eventuality x, let $v(x, c) \in \mathbb{R}$ denote the degree of support that case c lends to eventuality x. Then the prediction rule ranks eventuality x as more likely than eventuality y if and only if

$$\sum_{c \in M} v(x, c) > \sum_{c \in M} v(y, c). \tag{1}$$

Axiomatization The main goal of this chapter is to axiomatize this rule. We assume that a predictor has a ranking of possible eventualities given any possible memory (or database). A memory consists of a finite set of past cases, or stories. The predictor need not envision all possible memories. She might have a rule, or an algorithm that generates a ranking (in finite time) for each possible memory. We only rely on qualitative plausibility rankings, and do not assume that the predictor can quantify them in a meaningful way. Cases are not assumed to have any particular structure. However, we do assume that for every case there are arbitrarily many other cases that are deemed equivalent to it by the predictor (for the prediction problem at hand). For instance, if the physician in Example 2 focuses on five parameters of the patient in making her prediction, we can imagine that she has seen arbitrarily many patients with particular values of the five parameters. The equivalence relation on cases induces an equivalence relation on memories (of equal sizes), and the latter allows us to consider replication of memories, that is, the disjoint union of several pairwise equivalent memories.

Our main assumption is that prediction satisfies a *combination axiom*. Roughly, it states that if an eventuality x is more likely than an eventuality y given two possible disjoint memories, then x is more likely than y also given their union. For example, assume that the patient in Example 2 consults two physicians who were trained in the same medical school but who have been working in different hospitals since graduation. Thus, the physicians can be thought of as having disjoint databases on which they can base their prediction, while sharing the inductive algorithm. Assume next that both physicians find that success is more likely than failure in the case at hand. Should the patient ask them to share their databases and re-consider their predictions? If the inductive algorithm that the physicians use satisfies the combination axiom, the answer is negative.

We also assume that the predictor's ranking is *Archimedean* in the following sense: if a database M renders eventuality x more likely than eventuality y, then for every other database N there is a sufficiently large number of replications of M, such that, when these memories are added to N, they will make eventuality x more likely than eventuality y. Finally, we need an assumption of *diversity*, stating that any list of four eventualities may be ranked, for some conceivable database, from top to bottom. Together, these assumptions necessitate that prediction be made according to the rule suggested by the formula (1) above. Moreover, we show that the function v in (1) is essentially unique.

This result can be interpreted in several ways. From a descriptive viewpoint, one may argue that experts' predictions tend to be consistent as required by our axioms (of which the combination is the most important), and that they can therefore be represented as aggregate similarity-based predictions. From a normative viewpoint, our result can be interpreted as suggesting the aggregate similarity-based predictions as the only way to satisfy our consistency axioms. In both approaches, one may attempt to measure similarities using the likelihood rankings given various databases.

Observe that we assume no a priori conceptual relationship between cases and eventualities. Such relationships, which may exist in the predictor's mind, will be revealed by her plausibility rankings. Further, even if cases and eventualities are formally related (as in Example 2), we do not assume that a numerical measure of distance, or of similarity is given in the data.

Our decision rule generalizes several well-known statistical methods, apart from ranking eventualities by their empirical frequencies. Kernel methods for estimation of a density function, as well as for classification problems, are a special case of our rule. If the objects that are ranked by plausibility are general theories, rather than specific eventualities, our rule can be viewed as ranking theories according to their likelihood function. In particular, these established statistical methods satisfy our combination axiom. This may be taken as an argument for this axiom. Conversely, our result can be used to axiomatize these statistical methods in their respective set-ups.

Methodological remarks The Bayesian approach (Ramsey (1931), de Finetti (1937), and Savage (1954)) holds that all prediction problems should be dealt with by a prior subjective probability that is updated in light of new information via Bayes's rule. This requires that the predictor have a prior probability over a space that is large enough to describe all conceivable new information. We find that in certain examples (as above) this assumption is not cognitively plausible. By contrast, the prediction rule (1) requires the evaluation of support weights only for cases that were actually encountered. For an extensive methodological discussion, see Gilboa and Schmeidler (2001).

Since the early days of probability theory, the concept of probability serves a dual role: one relating to empirical frequencies, and the other—to quantification of subjective beliefs or opinions. (See Hacking (1975).) The Bayesian approach offers a unification of these roles employing the concept of a subjective prior probability. Our approach may also be viewed as an attempt to unify the notions of empirical frequencies and subjective opinions. Whereas the axiomatic derivations of de Finetti (1937) and Savage (1954) treat the process of the generation of a prior as a black box, our rule aims to make a preliminary step towards the modeling of this process.

Our approach is thus complementary to the Bayesian approach at two levels: first, it may offer an alternative model of prediction, when the information available to the predictor is not easily translated to the language of a prior probability. Second, our approach may describe how a prior is generated. (See also Gilboa and Schmeidler (2002)).

The rest of this chapter is organized as follows. Section 2 presents the formal model and the main results. Section 3 discusses the relationship to kernel methods and to maximum likelihood rankings. Section 4 contains a critical discussion of the axioms, attempting to outline their scope of application. Finally, Section 5 briefly discusses alternative interpretations of the model, and, in particular, relates it to case-based decision theory. Proofs are relegated to the appendix.

2.2 Model and Result

2.2.1 *Framework*

The primitives of our model consist of two non-empty sets X and $\mathbb{C}$. We interpret X as the set of all conceivable *eventualities* in a given prediction problem, p, whereas $\mathbb{C}$ represents the set of all conceivable *cases*. To simplify notation, we suppress the prediction problem p whenever possible. The predictor is equipped with a finite set of cases $M \subset \mathbb{C}$, her *memory*, and her task is to rank the eventualities by a binary relation, "at least as likely as".

While evaluating likelihoods, it is insightful not only to know what has happened, but also to take into account what could have happened. The predictor is therefore assumed to have a well-defined "at least as likely as" relation on X for many other collections of cases in addition to M itself. Let $\mathbb{M}$ be the set of finite subsets of $\mathbb{C}$. For every $M \in \mathbb{M}$, we denote the predictor's "at least as likely as" relation by $\succsim_M \subset X \times X$.

Two cases c and d are *equivalent*, denoted $c \sim d$, if, for every $M \in \mathbb{M}$ such that $c, d \notin M$, $\succsim_{M\cup\{c\}} = \succsim_{M\cup\{d\}}$. To justify the term, we note the following.

Observation: $\sim$ is an equivalence relation.

Note that equivalence of cases is a subjective notion: cases are equivalent if, in the eyes of the predictor, they affect likelihood rankings in the same way. Further, the notion of equivalence is also context-dependent: two cases c and d are equivalent as far as a specific prediction problem is concerned.

We extend the definition of equivalence to memories as follows. Two memories $M_1, M_2 \in \mathbb{M}$ are equivalent, denoted $M_1 \sim M_2$, if there is a bijection

$f : M_1 \to M_2$ such that $c \sim f(c)$ for all $c \in M_1$. Observe that memory equivalence is also an equivalence relation. It also follows that, if $M_1 \sim M_2$, then, for every $N \in \mathbb{M}$ such that $N \cap (M_1 \cup M_2) = \varnothing$, $\precsim_{N \cup M_1} = \precsim_{N \cup M_2}$.

Throughout the discussion, we impose the following structural assumption.

Richness Assumption: For every case $c \in \mathbb{C}$, there are infinitely many cases $d \in \mathbb{C}$ such that $c \sim d$.

A note on nomenclature: the main result of this chapter is interpreted as a representation of a prediction rule. Accordingly, we refer to a "predictor" who may be a person, an organization, or a machine. However, the result may and will be interpreted in other ways as well. Instead of ranking eventualities one may rank *decisions, acts,* or a more neutral term, *alternatives*. Cases, the elements of $\mathbb{C}$, may also be called *observations* or *facts*. A memory M in $\mathbb{M}$ represents the predictor's *knowledge* and will be referred to also as a *database*.

2.2.2 *Axioms*

We will use the four axioms stated below. In their formalization let $\succ_M$ and $\approx_M$ denote the asymmetric and symmetric parts of $\succsim_M$, as usual. $\succsim_M$ is *complete* if $x \succsim_M y$ or $y \succsim_M x$ for all $x, y \in X$.

A1 Order: For every $M \in \mathbb{M}$, $\succsim_M$ is complete and transitive on X.

A2 Combination: For every disjoint $M, N \in \mathbb{M}$ and every $x, y \in X$, if $x \succsim_M y$ $(x \succ_M y)$ and $x \succsim_N y$, then $x \succsim_{M \cup N} y (x \succ_{M \cup N} y)$.

A3 Archimedean Axiom: For every disjoint $M, N \in \mathbb{M}$ and every $x, y \in X$, if $x \succ_M y$, then there exists $l \in \mathbb{N}$ such that for any l-list $(M_i)_{i=1}^{l}$ of pairwise disjoint M_i's in $\mathbb{M}$, where for all $i \leq l$, $M_i \sim M$ and $M_i \cap N = \emptyset$, $x \succ_{M_1 \cup \ldots \cup M_l \cup N} y$ holds.

Axiom 1 simply requires that, given any conceivable memory, the predictor's likelihood relation over eventualities is a weak order. Axiom 2 states that if eventuality x is more plausible than eventuality y given two disjoint memories, x should also be more plausible than y given the union of these memories. Axiom 3 is states that if, given the memory M, the predictor believes that eventuality x is strictly more plausible than y, then, no matter what is her ranking for another memory, N, there is a number of "repetitions" of M that is large enough to overwhelm the ranking induced by N.

Finally, we need a diversity axiom. It is not necessary for representation of likelihood relations by summation of real numbers. Theorem 1 below is an equivalence theorem, characterizing precisely which matrices of real numbers will satisfy this axiom.

A4 Diversity: For every list (x, y, z, w) of distinct elements of X there exists $M \in \mathbb{M}$ such that $x \succ_M y \succ_M z \succ_M w$. If $|X| < 4$, then for any strict ordering of the elements of X there exists $M \in \mathbb{M}$ such that $\succ_M$ is that ordering.

2.2.3 *Results*

For clarity of exposition, we first state the sufficiency result.

Theorem 1 Part I–Sufficiency: *Let there be given X, $\mathbb{C}$, and $\{\succsim_M\}_{M \in \mathbb{M}}$ satisfying the richness assumption as above. Then (i) implies (ii(a)):*

(i) *$\{\succsim_M\}_{M \in \mathbb{M}}$ satisfy A1–A4;*

(ii(a)) *There is a matrix $v : X \times \mathbb{C} \to \mathbb{R}$ such that:*

$$\begin{cases} \text{for every } M \in \mathbb{M} \text{ and every } x, y \in X, \\ x \succsim_M y \quad \text{iff} \quad \sum_{c \in M} v(x, c) \geq \sum_{c \in M} v(y, c), \end{cases} \tag{2}$$

In other words, axioms A1–A4 imply that $\{\succsim_M\}_{M \in \mathbb{M}}$ follow our prediction rule for an appropriate choice of the matrix v. Not all of these axioms are, however, necessary for the representation to obtain. Indeed, the axioms imply special properties of the representing matrix v. First, it can be chosen in such a way that equivalent cases are attached identical columns. Second, every four rows of the matrix satisfy an additional condition. Existence of a matrix v satisfying these two properties together with (2) does imply axioms A1–A4. Before stating the necessity part of theorem, we present two additional definitions.

Definition: A matrix $v : X \times \mathbb{C} \to \mathbb{R}$ *respects case equivalence* (with respect to $\{\succsim_M\}_{M \in \mathbb{M}}$) if for every $c, d \in \mathbb{C}$, $c \sim d$ iff $v(\cdot, c) = v(\cdot, d)$.

When no confusion is likely to arise, we will suppress the relations $\{\succsim_M\}_{M \in \mathbb{M}}$ and will simply say that "v respects case equivalence".

The following definition applies to real-values matrices in general. It will be used for the matrix $v : X \times \mathbb{C} \to \mathbb{R}$ in the statement of the theorem, but also for another matrix in the proof. It defines a matrix to be diversified if no row in it is dominated by an affine combination of any other three (or less) rows. Thus, if v is diversified, no row in it dominates another. Indeed, the property of diversification can be viewed as a generalization of this condition.

Definition: A matrix $v : X \times Y \to \mathbb{R}$, where $|X| \geq 4$, is *diversified* if there are no distinct four elements $x, y, z, w \in X$ and $\lambda, \mu, \theta \in \mathbb{R}$ with $\lambda + \mu + \theta = 1$ such that $v(x, \cdot) \leq \lambda v(y, \cdot)) + \mu v(z, \cdot) + \theta v(w, \cdot)$. If $|X| < 4$, v is diversified if no row in v is dominated by an affine combination of the others.

We can finally state

Theorem 1 Part II – Necessity: *(i) also implies*
(ii(b)) the matrix v is diversified; and
(ii(c)) the matrix v respects case equivalence.
Conversely, (ii(a,b,c)) implies (i).

Theorem 1 Part III – Uniqueness: *If (i) [or (ii)] hold, the matrix v is unique in the following sense: v and u both satisfy* (2) *and respect case equivalence iff there are a scalar $\lambda > 0$ and a matrix $\beta : X \times \mathbb{C} \to \mathbb{R}$ with identical rows (i.e., with constant columns), that respects case equivalence, such that $u = \lambda v + \beta$.*

Observe that, by the richness assumption, $\mathbb{C}$ is infinite, and therefore the matrix v has infinitely many columns. Moreover, the theorem does not restrict the cardinality of X, and thus v may also have infinitely many rows.

Given any real matrix of order $|X| \times |\mathbb{C}|$, one can define for every $M \in \mathbb{M}$ a weak order on X through (2). It is easy to see that it will satisfy A1 and A2. If the matrix also respects case equivalence, A3 will also be satisfied. However, these conditions do not imply A4. For example, A4 will be violated if a row in the matrix dominates another row. Since A4 is not necessary for a representation by a matrix v via (2) (even if it respects case equivalence), one may wonder whether it can be dropped. The answer is given by the following.

Proposition: Axioms A1, A2, and A3 do not imply the existence of a matrix v that satisfies (2).

Some remarks on cardinality are in order. Axiom A4 can only hold if the set of types, $\mathbb{T} = \mathbb{C}/\sim$, is large enough relatively to X. For instance, if there are two distinct eventualities, the diversity axiom requires that there be at least two different types of cases. However, six types suffice for X to have the cardinality of the continuum.[2]

Finally, one may wonder whether (2) implies that v respects case equivalence. The negative answer is given below.

Remark: Condition (2) does not imply that v respects case equivalence.

2.3 Related Statistical Methods

2.3.1 *Kernel estimation of a density function*

Assume that Z is a continuous random variable taking values in $\mathbb{R}^m$. Having observed a finite sample $(z_i)_{i \leq n}$, one is asked to estimate the density function of Z. Kernel estimation (see Akaike (1954), Rosenblatt (1956), Parzen

[2] The proof is omitted for brevity's sake.

(1962), Silverman (1986), and Scott (1992) for a survey) suggests the following. Choose a (so-called "kernel") function $k : \mathbb{R}^m \times \mathbb{R}^m \to \mathbb{R}_+$ with the following properties: (i) $k(z, y)$ is a non-increasing function of $\|z - y\|$; (ii) for every $z \in \mathbb{R}^m$, $\int_{\mathbb{R}^m} k(z, y)dy = 1$.[3] Given the sample $(z_i)_{i \leq n}$, estimate the density function by $f(y|z_1, \ldots, z_n) \equiv \frac{1}{n} \sum_{i \leq n} k(z_i, y)$.

Consider the estimated function f as a measure of likelihood: $f(y) > f(w)$ is interpreted as saying that a small neighborhood around y is more likely than the corresponding neighborhood around w. With this interpretation, kernel estimation is clearly a special case of our prediction rule, with $v(y, z) = \frac{1}{n} k(z, y)$. Observe that kernel estimation presupposes a notion of distance on $\mathbb{R}^m$, whereas our theorem derives the function v from qualitative rankings alone.

2.3.2 *Kernel classification*

Kernel methods are also used for classification problems. Assume that a classifier is confronted with a data point $y \in \mathbb{R}^m$, and it is asked to guess to which member of a finite set A it belongs. The classifier is equipped with a set of examples $M \subset \mathbb{R}^m \times A$. Each example (x, a) consist of a data point $x \in \mathbb{R}^m$, with a known classification $a \in A$. Kernel classification methods would adopt a kernel function as above, and, given the point y, would guess that y belongs to a class $a \in A$ that maximizes the sum of $k(x, y)$ over all x's in memory that were classified as a.

Our general framework can accommodate classification problems as well. As opposed to kernel estimation, one is not asked to rank (neighborhoods of) points in $\mathbb{R}^m$, but, *given* such a point, to rank classes in A. Assume a point $y \in \mathbb{R}^m$ is given, and, for a case $(x, a) \in M$, define $v_y(b, (x, a)) = k(x, y)1_{a=b}$ (where $1_{a=b}$ is 1 if $a = b$ and zero otherwise). Clearly, the ranking defined by v_y boils down to the ranking defined by kernel classification.

As above, this axiomatization can be viewed as a normative justification of kernel methods, and also as a way to elicit the "appropriate" kernel function from qualitative ranking data. Again, our approach does not assume that a kernel function is given, but derives such a function together with the kernel classification rule.

A popular alternative to kernel classification methods is offered by nearest neighbor methods. (See Fix and Hodges (1951, 1952), Royall (1966), Cover and Hart (1967), Stone (1977), and Devroye, Gyorfi, and Lugosi (1996)). It is easily verified that nearest neighbor approaches do not satisfy the Archimedean axiom. Moreover, for $k > 1$ a majority vote among the k-nearest

[3] More generally, the kernel may be a function of transformed coordinates. The following discussion does not depend on assumptions (i) and (ii) and they are retained merely for concreteness.

neighbors violates the combination axiom. Thus, our axioms offer a normative justification for preferring kernel methods to nearest neighbor methods.

2.3.3 *Maximum likelihood ranking*

Our model can also be interpreted as referring to ranking of theories or hypotheses given a set of observations. The axioms we formulated apply to this case as well. In particular, our main requirements are that theories be ranked by a weak order for every memory, and that, if theory x is more plausible than theory y given each of two disjoint memories, x should also be more plausible than y given the union of these memories.

Assume, therefore, that Theorem 1 holds. Suppose that, for each case c, $v(x,c)$ is bounded from above. (This is the case, for instance, if there are only finitely many theories to be ranked.) Choose a representation v where $v(x,c) < 0$ for every theory x and case c. Define $p(c|x) = \exp(v(x,c))$, so that $\log\left(p(c|x)\right) = v(x,c)$.

Our result states that, for every two theories x, y:

$$x \succsim_M y \text{ iff } \sum_{c \in M} v(x,c) \geq \sum_{c \in M} v(y,c),$$

which is equivalent to

$$\exp\left(\sum_{c \in M} v(x,c)\right) \geq \exp\left(\sum_{c \in M} v(y,c)\right) \text{ or to}$$

$$\prod_{c \in M} p(c|x) \geq \prod_{c \in M} p(c|y).$$

In other words, if a predictor ranks theories in accordance with A1–A4, there exist conditional probabilities $p(c|x)$, for every case c and theory x, such that the predictor ranks theories as if by their likelihood functions, under the implicit assumption that the cases were stochastically independent.[4] On the one hand, this result can be viewed as a normative justification of the likelihood rule: any method of ranking theories that is not equivalent to ranking by likelihood (for *some* conditional probabilities $p(c|x)$) has to violate one of our axioms. On the other hand, our result can be descriptively interpreted, saying that likelihood rankings of theories are rather prevalent. One need not consciously assign conditional probabilities $p(c|x)$ for every case c given every theory x, and one need not know probability calculus in order to generate predictions in accordance with the likelihood criterion. Rather, whenever

[4] We do not assume that the cases that have been observed (M) constitute an exhaustive state space. Correspondingly, there is no requirement that the sum of conditional probabilities $\sum_{c \in M} p(c|x)$ be the same for all x.

one satisfies our axioms, one may be ascribed conditional probabilities $p(c|x)$ such that one's predictions are in accordance with the resulting likelihood functions. Thus, relatively mild consistency requirements imply that one predicts *as if* by likelihood functions.

Finally, our result may be used to elicit the subjective conditional probabilities $p(c|x)$ of a predictor, given her qualitative rankings of theories. However, our uniqueness result is somewhat limited. In particular, for every case c one may choose a positive constant β_c and multiply $p(c|x)$ by β_c for all theories x, resulting in the same likelihood rankings. Similarly, one may choose a positive number α and raise all probabilities $\{p(c|x)\}_{c,x}$ to the power of α, again without changing the observed ranking of theories given possible memories. Thus there will generally be more than one set of conditional probabilities $\{p(c|x)\}_{c,x}$ that are consistent with $\{\succsim_M\}_{M\in\mathbb{M}}$.

The likelihood function relies on independence across cases. Conceptually, stochastic independence follows from two assumptions in our model. First, we have defined $\{\succsim_M\}_{M\in\mathbb{M}}$ where each M is a set. This implicitly assumes that only the number of repetitions of cases, and not their order, matters. This structural assumption is reminiscent of de Finetti's exchangeability condition (though the latter is defined in a more elaborate probabilistic model). Second, our combination axiom also has a flavor of independence. In particular, it rules out situations in which past occurrences of a case make future occurrences of the same case less likely.[5]

2.4 Discussion of the Axioms

The rule we axiomatize generalizes rankings by empirical frequencies. Moreover, the previous section shows that it also generalizes several well-known statistical techniques. It follows that there is a wide range of applications for which this rule, and the axioms it satisfies, are plausible.

But there are applications in which the axioms do not appear compelling. We discuss here several examples, trying to delineate the scope of applicability of the axioms, and to identify certain classes of situations in which they may not apply.

In the following discussion we do not dwell on the first axiom, namely, that likelihood relations are weak orders. This axiom and its limitations have been extensively discussed in decision theory, and there seems to be no special arguments for or against it in our specific context.

We also have little to add to the discussion of the diversity axiom. While it does not appear to pose conceptual difficulties, there are no fundamental

[5] See the clause "mis-specified case" in the next section.

reasons to insist on its validity. One may well be interested in other assumptions that would allow a representation as in (2) by a matrix v that is not necessarily diversified.

The Archimedean axiom is violated when a single case may outweigh any number of repetitions of other cases. For instance, a physician may find a single observation, taken from the patient she is currently treating, more relevant than any number of observations taken from other patients.[6] In the context of ranking theories, it is possible that a single case c constitutes a direct refutation of a theory x. If another theory y was not refuted by any case in memory, a single occurrence of case c will render theory x less plausible than theory y regardless of the number of occurrences of other cases, even if these lend more support to x than to y.[7] In such a situation, one would like to assign conditional probability of zero to case c given theory x, or, equivalently, to set $v(x, c) = -\infty$. Since this is beyond the scope of the present model, one may drop the Archimedean axiom and seek representations by non-standard numbers.

We now turn to the combination axiom. As is obvious from the additive formula in (2), our rule implicitly presupposes that the weight of evidence derived from a given case does not depend on other cases. It follows that the combination axiom is likely to fail whenever this "separability" property does not hold. We discuss here several examples of this type. We begin with those in which re-definition of the primitives of the model resolves the difficulty. Examples we find more fundamental are discussed later.

Mis-specified cases Consider a cat, say Lucifer, who every so often dies and then may or may not resurrect. Suppose that, throughout history, many other cats have been observed to resurrect exactly eight times. If Lucifer had died and resurrected four times, and now died for the fifth time, we'd expect him to resurrect again. But if we double the number of cases, implying that we are now observing the ninth death, we would not expect Lucifer to be with us again. Thus, one may argue, the combination axiom does not seem to be very compelling.

Obviously, this example assumes that all of Lucifer's deaths are equivalent. While this may be a reasonable assumption of a naive observer, the cat connoisseur will be careful enough to distinguish "first death" from "second death", and so forth. Thus, this example suggests that one has to be careful in the definition of a "case" (and of case equivalence) before applying the combination axiom.

Mis-specified theories Suppose that one wishes to determine whether a coin is biased. A memory with 1,000 repetitions of "Head", as well as a

[6] Indeed, the nearest neighbor approach to classification problems violates the Archimedean axiom.

[7] This example is due to Peyton Young.

memory with 1,000 repetitions of "Tail" both suggest that the coin is indeed biased, while their union suggests that it is not. Observe that this example hinges on the fact that two rather different theories, namely, "the coin is biased toward Tail" and "the coin is biased toward Head" are lumped together as "the coin is biased". If one were to specify the theories more fully, the combination axiom would hold.[8]

Theories about patterns A related class of examples deal with concepts that describe, or are defined by patterns, sequences, or sets of cases. Assume that a single case consists of 100 tosses of a coin. A complex sequence of 100 tosses may lend support to the hypothesis that the coin generates random sequences. But many repetitions of the very same sequence would undermine this hypothesis. Observe that "the coin generates random sequences" is a statement about *sequences* of cases. Similarly, statements such as "The weather always surprises" or "History repeats itself" are about sequences of cases, and are therefore likely to generate violations of the combination axiom.

Second-order induction An important class of examples in which we should expect the combination axiom to be violated, for descriptive and normative purposes alike, involves learning of the similarity function. For instance, assume that one database contains but one case, in which Mary chose restaurant x over y.[9] One is asked to predict what John's decision would be. Having no other information, one is likely to assume some similarity of tastes between John and Mary and to find it more plausible that John would prefer x to y as well. Next assume that in a second database there are no observed choices (by anyone) between x and y. Hence, based on this database alone, it would appear equally likely that John would choose x as that he would y. Assume further that this database does contain many choices between other pairs of restaurants, and it turns out that John and Mary consistently choose different restaurants. When combining the two databases, it makes sense to predict that John would choose y over x.

This is an instance in which the similarity function is learned from cases. Linear aggregation of cases by fixed weights embodies learning *by* a similarity function. But it does not describe how this function *itself* is learned. In Gilboa and Schmeidler (2001) we call this process "second-order induction" and show that the additive formula cannot capture such a process.

Combinations of inductive and deductive reasoning Another important class of examples in which the combination axiom is not very

[8] Observe that if one were to use the maximum likelihood principle, one would have to specify a likelihood function. This exercise would highlight the fact that "the coin is biased" is not a fully specified theory. However, this does not imply that only theories that are given as conditional distributions are sufficiently specified to satisfy the combination axiom.

[9] This is a variant of an example by Sujoy Mukerji.

reasonable consists of prediction problems in which some structure is given. Consider a simple regression problem where a variable x is used to predict another variable y. Does the method of ordinary least squares satisfy our axioms? The answer depends on the unit of analysis. If we consider the regression equation $y = \alpha + \beta x + \varepsilon$ and attempt to estimate the values of α and β given a sample $M = \{(x_i, y_i)\}_{i \leq n}$, the answer is in the affirmative. Consider, for instance, α. Let a, a' be two real numbers interpreted as estimates of α. Define $a \succsim_M a'$ if a has a higher value of the likelihood function given $\{(x_i, y_i)\}_{i \leq n}$ than does a'. This implies that $\succsim_M$ satisfies the combination axiom. Since the least squares estimator a is a maximum likelihood estimator of the parameter α (under the standard assumptions of regression analysis), choosing the estimate a is consistent with choosing a $\succsim_M$-maximizer.

Assume now that the units of analysis are the particular values of y_p for a new value of x_p. That is, rather than accepting the regression model $y = \alpha + \beta x + \varepsilon$ and asking what are the values of α and β, suppose that one is asked to predict (formulate $\succsim_M$) directly on potential values of y_p. The regression estimates a, b define a density function for y_p (a normal distribution centered around the value $a + bx_p$). This density function can be used to define $\succsim_M$, but these relations will generally not satisfy the combination axiom.

The reason is that the regression model is structured enough to allow some deductive reasoning. In ranking the plausibility of values of y for a given value of x, one makes two steps. First, one uses inductive reasoning to obtain estimates of the parameters a and b. Then, espousing a belief in the linear model, one uses these estimates to rank values of y by their plausibility. This second step involves deductive reasoning, exploiting the particular structure of the model. While the combination axiom is rather plausible for the first, inductive step, there is no reason for it to hold also for the entire inductive-deductive process.

To consider another example, assume that a coin is about to be tossed in an i.i.d. manner. The parameter of the coin is not known, but one knows probability rules that allow one to infer likelihood rankings of outcomes given any value of the unknown parameter. Again, when one engages in inference about the unknown parameter, one performs only inductive reasoning, and the combination axiom seems plausible. But when one is asked about particular outcomes, one uses inductive reasoning as well as deductive reasoning. In these cases, the combination axiom is too crude.[10]

[10] We have received several counterexamples to the combination axiom that are, in our view, of this nature. In particular, we would like to thank Bruno Jullien, Klaus Nehring, and Ariel Rubinstein.

In conclusion, there are classes of counterexamples to our axioms that result from under-specification of cases, of eventualities, or of memories. There are others that are more fundamental. Among these, two seem to deserve special attention. First, there are situations where second-order induction is involved, and the similarity function itself is learned. Indeed, our model deals with accumulated evidence but does not capture the emergence of new insights. Second, there are problems where some theoretical structure is assumed, and it can be used for deductive inferences. Our model captures some forms of inductive reasoning, but does not provide a full account of inferential processes involving a combination of inductive and deductive reasoning.

2.5 Other Interpretations

Decisions Theorem 1 can also have other interpretations. In particular, the objects to be ranked may be possible acts, with the interpretation of ranking as preferences. In this case, $v(x, c)$ denotes the support that case c lends to the choice of act x. The decision rule that results generalizes most of the decision rules of case-based decision theory (Gilboa and Schmeidler (2001)), as well as expected utility maximization, if beliefs are generated from cases in an additive way (see Gilboa and Schmeidler (2002)). Gilboa, Schmeidler, and Wakker (1999) apply this theorem, as well as an alternative approach, to axiomatize a theory of case-based decisions in which both the similarity function between problem-act pairs and the utility function of outcomes are derived from preferences. This model generalizes Gilboa and Schmeidler (1997), in which the utility function is assumed given and only the similarity function is derived from observed preferences.

Probabilities The main contribution of Gilboa and Schmeidler (2002) is to generalize the scope of prediction from eventualities to events. That is, in that paper we assume that the objects to be ranked belong to an algebra of subsets of a given set. Additional assumptions are imposed so that similarity values are additive with respect to the union of disjoint sets. Further, it is shown that ranking by empirical frequencies can also be axiomatically characterized in this set-up. Finally, tying the derivation of probabilities with expected utility maximization, one obtains a characterization of subjective expected utility maximization in face of uncertainty. As opposed to the behavioral axiomatic derivations of de Finetti (1937) and Savage (1954), which infer beliefs from decisions, this axiomatic derivation follows a presumed cognitive path leading from belief to decision.

2.6 Appendix: Proofs

Proof of Observation:

It is obvious that $\sim$ is reflexive and symmetric. To show that it is transitive, assume that $c \sim d$ and $d \sim e$ for distinct c, d, e. Let M be such that $c, e \notin M$. If $d \notin M$, then $\succsim_{M \cup \{c\}} = \succsim_{M \cup \{d\}}$ by $c \sim d$ and $\succsim_{M \cup \{d\}} = \succsim_{M \cup \{c\}}$ by $d \sim e$, and $\succsim_{M \cup \{c\}} = \succsim_{M \cup \{e\}}$ follows. If $d \in M$, define $N = M \backslash \{d\}$. Since $c, d \notin N \cup \{e\}$, $c \sim d$ implies $\succsim_{N \cup \{e\} \cup \{c\}} = \succsim_{N \cup \{e\} \cup \{d\}}$. Similarly, since $d, e \notin N \cup \{c\}$, $d \sim e$ implies $\succsim_{N \cup \{c\} \cup \{d\}} = \succsim_{N \cup \{c\} \cup \{e\}}$. It follows that $\succsim_{M \cup \{c\}} = \succsim_{N \cup \{c,d\}} = \succsim_{N \cup \{c,e\}} = \succsim_{N \cup \{d,e\}} = \succsim_{M \cup \{e\}}$. □

The Result is part of Theorem 1, and was stated only for expository purposes. We therefore prove only Theorem 1.

Proof of Theorem 1: The strategy of the proof is as follows. The notion of case equivalence allows us to reduce the discussion to vectors of non-negative integers. We define the set of *types* of cases to be the $\sim$-equivalence classes: $\mathbb{T} = \mathbb{C}/\sim$. Assume, for simplicity, that there are finitely many types and finitely many eventualities. Rather than referring to sets of specific cases (memories M), we focus on vectors of non-negative integers. Such a vector $I : \mathbb{T} \to \mathbb{Z}_+$ represents many equivalent memories by counting how many cases of each type are in each of these memories. Thus, instead of dealing with subsets of the set $\mathbb{C}$, most of the discussion will be conducted in the space $\mathbb{Z}_+^{\mathbb{T}}$. Next, using the combination axiom, we extend the family rankings $\{\succeq_I\}$ from $I \in \mathbb{Z}_+^{\mathbb{T}}$ to $I \in \mathbb{Q}_+^{\mathbb{T}}$.

Focusing on two eventualities, x and y, we divide the vectors $I \in \mathbb{Q}_+^{\mathbb{T}}$ to those that render x more likely than y, and to those that induce the opposite ranking. Completeness and combination are the key axioms that allow us to invoke a separating hyperplane theorem. With the aid of the Archimedean axiom, one can prove that the separating hyperplane precisely characterizes the memories for which x is (strongly or weakly) more likely than y.

If one has only two eventualities, the proof is basically complete. Most of the work is in showing that the hyperplanes, which were obtained for each *pair* of eventualities, can be represented by a single matrix. More concretely, the separation theorem applied to a pair x, y yields a vector v^{xy}, unique up to multiplication by a positive constant, such that x is at least as likely as y given memory I iff $v^{xy} \cdot I \geq 0$. One now wishes to find a vector v^x for each eventuality x such that v^{xy} is a positive multiple of $(v^x - v^y)$ (simultaneously for all x, y).

This can be done if and only if there is a selection of vectors $\{v^{xy}\}_{x,y}$ (where each is given only up to a multiplicative constant) such that $v^{xz} = v^{xy} + v^{yz}$ for every triple x, y, z. It turns out that, due to transitivity, this can be done for every triple x, y, z *separately*. The diversity axiom guarantees that this can also be done for sets of four eventualities, and the proof proceeds by induction.

The final two steps of the proof deal with extensions to infinitely many types and to infinitely many eventualities.

We finally turn to the formal proof. Let $\mathbb{T} = \mathbb{C}/\sim$ be the set of *types* of cases.[11] We prove the theorem in three steps. First we assume that there are finitely many types, that is, that $|\mathbb{T}| < \infty$. In this case the proof relies on an auxiliary result that is of interest in its own right. Since the proof of this theorem applies to an infinite set of eventualities X, we do not restrict the cardinality of X in this case. Step 2 proceeds to deal with the case in which $|\mathbb{T}|$ is unrestricted, but X is finite. Lastly, Step 3 deals with the general case in which both $|X|$ and $|\mathbb{T}|$ are unrestricted.

In all three steps, memories in $\mathbb{M}$ are represented by vectors of non-negative integers, counting how many cases of each type appear in memory. Formally, for every $T \subset \mathbb{T}$ define $\mathbb{J}_T = \mathbb{Z}_+^T = \{I \mid I : T \to \mathbb{Z}_+\}$ where $\mathbb{Z}_+$ stands for the non-negative integers. $I \in \mathbb{J}_T$ is interpreted as a counter vector, where $I(t)$ counts how many cases of type t appear in the memory represented by I. For $I \in \mathbb{J}_T$, if $\{t \mid I(t) > 0\}$ is finite, define $\succsim_I \subset X \times X$ as follows. Choose $M \in \mathbb{M}$ such that $M \subset \cup_{t \in T} t$ (recall that $t \subset \mathbb{C}$ is an equivalence class of cases) and $I(t) = \#(M \cap t)$ for all $t \in T$, and define $\succsim_I = \succsim_M$. Such a set M exists since, by the richness assumption, $|t| \geq \aleph_0$ for all $t \in \mathbb{T}$. For this reason, such a set M is not unique. However, if both $M_1, M_2 \in \mathbb{M}$ satisfy these properties, then $M_1 \sim M_2$ and $\succsim_{M_1} = \succsim_{M_2}$. Hence $\succsim_I$ is well-defined.

Moreover, this definition implies the following property, which will prove useful in the sequel: if $I \in \mathbb{J}_T$ and $I' \in \mathbb{J}_{T'}$ where $T \subset T'$, $I'(t) = I(t)$ for $t \in T$ and $I'(t) = 0$ for $t \in T' \backslash T$, then $\succsim_I = \succsim_{I'}$. Another obvious observation, to be used later, is that for every $M \in \mathbb{M}$ there exists a finite $T \subset \mathbb{T}$ and $I \in \mathbb{J}_T$ such that $M \subset \cup_{t \in T} t$ and $I(t) = \#(M \cap t)$ for all $t \in T$.

Step 1: The case $|\mathbb{T}| < \infty$.

Denote the set of all counter vectors by $\mathbb{J} = \mathbb{J}_T = Z_+^{\mathbb{T}}$. For $I \in \mathbb{J}$, define $\succsim_I \subset X \times X$ as above. We now re-state the main theorem for this case, in the language of counter vectors. In the following, algebraic operations on $\mathbb{J}$ are performed pointwise.

A1* Order: For every $I \in \mathbb{J}$, $\succsim_I$ is complete and transitive on X.

A2* Combination: For every $I, J \in \mathbb{J}$ and every $x, y \in X$, if $x \succsim_I y$ ($x \succ_I y$) and $x \succsim_J y$, then $x \succsim_{I+J} y$ ($x \succ_{I+J} y$).

A3* Archimedean Axiom: For every $I, J \in \mathbb{J}$ and every $x, y \in X$, if $x \succ_I y$, then there exists $l \in N$ such that $x \succ_{lI+J} y$.

[11] $\mathbb{C}/\sim$ is the set of equivalence classes of $\sim$.

Observe that in the presence of Axiom 2, Axiom 3 also implies that for every $I, J \in \mathbb{J}$ and every $x, y \in X$, if $x \succ_I y$, then there exists $l \in \mathbb{N}$ such that for all $k \geq l$, $x \succ_{kI+J} y$.

A4* Diversity: For every list (x, y, z, w) of distinct elements of X there exists $I \in \mathbb{J}$ such that $x \succ_I y \succ_I z \succ_I w$. If $|X| < 4$, then for any strict ordering of the elements of X there exists $I \in \mathbb{J}$ such that $\succ_I$ is that ordering.

Theorem 2: Let there be given X, $\mathbb{T}$, and $\{\succsim_I\}_{I \in \mathbb{J}}$ as above. Then the following two statements are equivalent:

(i) $\{\succsim_I\}_{I \in \mathbb{J}}$ satisfy A1*-A4*;

(ii) There is a diversified matrix $v : X \times \mathbb{T} \to \mathbb{R}$ such that:

$$\begin{cases} \text{for every } I \in \mathbb{J} \text{ and every } x, y \in X, \\ x \succsim_I y \quad \text{iff} \quad \sum_{t \in \mathbb{T}} I(t) v(x, t) \geq \sum_{t \in \mathbb{T}} I(t) v(y, t), \end{cases} \tag{3}$$

Furthermore, in this case the matrix v is unique in the following sense: v and u both satisfy (3) iff there are a scalar $\lambda > 0$ and a matrix $\beta : X \times \mathbb{T} \to \mathbb{R}$ with identical rows (i.e., with constant columns) such that $u = \lambda v + \beta$.

Theorem 2 is reminiscent of the main result in Gilboa and Schmeidler (1997). In that work, cases are assumed to involve numerical payoffs, and algebraic and topological axioms are formulated in the payoff space. Here, by contrast, cases are not assumed to have any structure, and the algebraic and topological structures are given by the number of repetitions. This fact introduces two main difficulties. First, the space of "contexts" for which preferences are defined is not a Euclidean space, but only integer points thereof. This requires some care with the application of separation theorems. Second, repetitions can only be non-negative. This fact introduces several complications, and, in particular, changes the algebraic implication of the diversity condition.

Before proceeding with the proof, we find it useful to present a condition that is equivalent to diversification of a matrix. We will use it both for the matrix $v : X \times \mathbb{T} \to \mathbb{R}$ of Theorem 2 and the matrix $v : X \times \mathbb{C} \to \mathbb{R}$ of Theorem 1. We therefore state it for an abstract set of columns:

Auxiliary Proposition: *Let Y be a set. Assume first $|X| \geq 4$. A matrix $v : X \times Y \to R$ is diversified iff for every list (x, y, z, w) of distinct elements of X, the convex hull of differences of the row-vectors $(v(x, \cdot) - v(y, \cdot))$, $(v(y, \cdot) - v(z, \cdot))$, and $(v(z, \cdot) - v(w, \cdot))$ does not intersect $\mathbb{R}^Y_-$. Similar equivalence holds for the case $|X| < 4$.*

Proof: We prove the auxiliary proposition for the case $|X| \geq 4$. The proof for $|X| < 4$ is similar. Assume first that a matrix v is diversified. Assume that the conclusion does not hold. Hence, there are distinct $x, y, z, w \in X$ and $\alpha, \beta, \gamma \geq 0$ with $\alpha + \beta + \gamma = 1$ such that

$$\alpha(v(x,\cdot) - v(y,\cdot)) + \beta(v(y,\cdot) - v(z,\cdot)) + \gamma(v(z,\cdot) - v(w,\cdot)) \leq 0.$$

If $\alpha > 0$, then

$$v(x,\cdot) \leq \frac{\alpha - \beta}{\alpha} v(y,\cdot) + \frac{\beta - \gamma}{\alpha} v(z,\cdot) + \frac{\gamma}{\alpha} v(w,\cdot)$$

which means that $v(x,\cdot)$ is dominated by an affine combination of $\{v(y,\cdot), v(z,\cdot), v(w,\cdot)\}$, in contradiction to the fact that v is diversified. If $\alpha = 0$, then, by a similar argument, if $\beta > 0$, then $v(y,\cdot)$ is dominated by an affine combination of $\{v(z,\cdot), v(w,\cdot)\}$. Finally, if $\alpha = \beta = 0$, then $v(z,\cdot)$ is dominated by $v(w,\cdot)$.

For the converse direction, assume that the convex hull of $\{(v(x,\cdot) - v(y,\cdot)), (v(y,\cdot) - v(z,\cdot)), (v(z,\cdot) - v(w,\cdot))\}$ (over all lists (x, y, z, w) of distinct elements in X) does not intersect $\mathbb{R}^Y_-$ but that, contrary to diversity of v, there are distinct $x, y, z, w \in X$ and $\lambda, \mu, \theta \in \mathbb{R}$ with $\lambda + \mu + \theta = 1$ such that

$$v(x,\cdot) \leq \lambda v(y,\cdot) + \mu v(z,\cdot) + \theta v(w,\cdot). \tag{4}$$

Since $\lambda + \mu + \theta = 1$, at least one of λ, μ, θ is non-negative. Assume, w.l.o.g., that $\theta \geq 0$. Hence $\lambda + \mu = 1 - \theta \leq 1$. This means that at least one of λ, μ cannot exceed 1. Assume, w.l.o.g., that $\lambda \leq 1$. Inequality (4) can be written as $v(x,\cdot) - \lambda v(y,\cdot) - \mu v(z,\cdot) - \theta v(w,\cdot) \leq 0$ or, equivalently, as

$$(v(x,\cdot) - v(y,\cdot)) + (1 - \lambda)(v(y,\cdot) - v(z,\cdot)) + (1 - \lambda - \mu)(v(z,\cdot) - v(w,\cdot)) \leq 0.$$

Since $1 - \lambda \geq 0$ and $1 - \lambda - \mu = \theta \geq 0$, dividing by the sum of the coefficients yields a contradiction to the convex hull condition. □

Proof of Theorem 2: We present the proof for the case $|X| \geq 4$. The proofs for the cases $|X| = 2$ and $|X| = 3$ will be described as by-products along the way.

Part 1: (i) implies (ii). We first note that the following homogeneity property holds:

Claim 2.1 *For every $I \in \mathbb{Z}^{\mathbb{T}}_+$ and every $k \in \mathbb{N}$, $\succsim_I = \succsim_{kI}$.*

Proof: Follows from consecutive application of the combination axiom. □

In view of this claim, we extend the definition of $\succsim_I$ to functions I whose values are non-negative rationals. Given $I \in \mathbb{Q}^{\mathbb{T}}_+$, let $k \in \mathbb{N}$ be such that $kI \in \mathbb{Z}^{\mathbb{T}}_+$ and define $\succsim_I = \succsim$. $\succsim_I$ is well-defined in view of Claim 1. By the definition and Claim 1 we also have:

Claim 2.2 (*Homogeneity*) *For every $I \in \mathbb{Q}^{\mathbb{T}}_+$ and every $q \in \mathbb{Q}$, $q > 0$: $\succsim_{qI} = \succsim_I$.*

Claim 2.2, A1*, and A2* imply:

Claim 2.3 *(The **order axiom**) For every $I \in \mathbb{Q}_+^{\mathbb{T}}$, $\succsim_I$ is complete and transitive on X, and (the **combination axiom**) for every $I, J \in \mathbb{Q}_+^{\mathbb{T}}$ and every $x, y \in X$ and $p, q \in \mathbb{Q}$, $p, q > 0$: if $x \succsim_I y$ ($x \succ_I y$) and $x \succsim_J y$, then $x \succsim_{pI+qJ} y$ ($x \succ_{pI+qJ} y$).*

Two special cases of the combination axiom are of interest: (i) $p = q = 1$, and (ii) $p + q = 1$. Claims 2 and 3, and the Archimedean axiom, A3*, imply the following version of the axiom for the $\mathbb{Q}_+^{\mathbb{T}}$ case:

Claim 2.4 *(The **Archimedean axiom**) For every $I, J \in \mathbb{Q}_+^{\mathbb{T}}$ and every $x, y \in X$, if $x \succ_I y$, then there exists $r \in [0, 1) \cap \mathbb{Q}$ such that $x \succ_{rI+(1-r)J} y$.*

It is easy to conclude from Claim 2.3 and 2.4 that for every $I, J \in \mathbb{Q}_+^{\mathbb{T}}$ and every $x, y \in X$, if $x \succ_I y$, then there exists $r \in [0, 1) \cap \mathbb{Q}$ such that $x \succ_{pI+(1-p)J} y$ for every $p \in (r, 1) \cap \mathbb{Q}$.

The following notation will be convenient for stating the first lemma. For every $x, y \in X$ let $A^{xy} \equiv \{I \in \mathbb{Q}_+^{\mathbb{T}} \mid x \succ_I y\}$ and $B^{xy} \equiv \{I \in \mathbb{Q}_+^{\mathbb{T}} \mid x \succsim_I y\}$.

Observe that by definition and A1*: $A^{xy} \subset B^{xy}$, $B^{xy} \cap A^{yx} = \emptyset$, and $B^{xy} \cup A^{yx} = \mathbb{Q}_+^{\mathbb{T}}$. The first main step in the proof of the theorem is:

Lemma 2.1 *For every distinct $x, y \in X$ there is a vector $v^{xy} \in \mathbb{R}^{\mathbb{T}}$ such that,*

(i) $B^{xy} = \{I \in Q_+^{\mathbb{T}} \mid v^{xy} \cdot I \geq 0\}$;

(ii) $A^{xy} = \{I \in Q_+^{\mathbb{T}} \mid v^{xy} \cdot I > 0\}$;

(iii) $B^{yx} = \{I \in Q_+^{\mathbb{T}} \mid v^{xy} \cdot I \leq 0\}$;

(iv) $A^{yx} = \{I \in Q_+^{\mathbb{T}} \mid v^{xy} \cdot I < 0\}$;

(v) Neither $v^{xy} \leq 0$ *nor* $v^{xy} \geq 0$;

(vi) $-v^{xy} = v^{yx}$.

Moreover, the vector v^{xy} satisfying (i)-(iv), is unique up to multiplication by a positive number.

The lemma states that we can associate with every pair of distinct eventualities $x, y \in X$ a separating hyperplane defined by $v^{xy} \cdot \xi = 0$ ($\xi \in \mathbb{R}^{\mathbb{T}}$), such that $x \succsim_I y$ iff I is in the half space defined by $v^{xy} \cdot I \geq 0$. Observe that if there are only two alternatives, Lemma 1 completes the proof of sufficiency: for instance, one may set $v^x = v^{xy}$ and $v^y = 0$. It then follows that $x \succsim_I y$ iff $v^{xy} \cdot I \geq 0$, i.e., iff $v^x \cdot I \geq v^y \cdot I$. More generally, we will show in the following lemmata that one can find a vector v^x for every alternative x, such that, for every $x, y \in X$, v^{xy} is a positive multiple of $(v^x - v^y)$.

Before starting the proof we introduce additional notation: let $\widehat{B}^{xy}$ and $\widehat{A}^{xy}$ denote the convex hulls (in $\mathbb{R}^{\mathbb{T}}$) of B^{xy} and A^{xy}, respectively. For a subset B of $\mathbb{R}^{\mathbb{T}}$ let $int(B)$ denote the set of interior points of B.

Proof of Lemma 2.1: We break the proof into several claims.

Claim 2.5 *For every distinct $x, y \in X$, $A^{xy} \cap int(\widehat{A}^{xy}) \neq \emptyset$.*

Proof: By the diversity axiom $A^{xy} \neq \emptyset$ for all $x, y \in X, x \neq y$. Let $I \in A^{xy} \cap \mathbb{Z}_+^{\mathbb{T}}$ and let $J \in \mathbb{Z}_+^{\mathbb{T}}$ with $J(t) > 1$ for all $t \in \mathbb{T}$. By the Archimedean axiom there is an $l \in \mathbb{N}$ such that $K = lI + J \in A^{xy}$. Let $(\xi_j)_{j=1}^{2^{|\mathbb{T}|}}$ be the $2^{|\mathbb{T}|}$ distinct vectors in $\mathbb{R}^{\mathbb{T}}$ with coordinates 1 and -1. For j, ($j = 1, ..., 2^{|\mathbb{T}|}$), define $\eta_j = K + \xi_j$. Obviously, $\eta_j \in \mathbb{Q}_+^{\mathbb{T}}$ for all j. By Claim 4 there is an $r_j \in [0, 1) \cap \mathbb{Q}$ such that $\varsigma_j = r_j K + (1 - r_j)\eta_j \in A^{xy}$ (for all j). Clearly, the convex hull of $\{ \varsigma_j \mid j = 1, ..., 2^{|\mathbb{T}|}\}$, which is included in $\widehat{A}^{xy}$, contains an open neighborhood of K. □

Claim 2.6 *For every distinct $x, y \in X$, $\widehat{B}^{yx} \cap int(\widehat{A}^{xy}) = \emptyset$.*

Proof: Suppose, by way of negation, that for some $\xi \in int(\widehat{A}^{xy})$ there are $(\eta_i)_{i=1}^k$ and $(\lambda_i)_{i=1}^k$, $k \in \mathbb{N}$ such that for all i, $\eta_i \in B^{yx}$, $\lambda_i \in [0, 1]$, $\Sigma_{i=1}^k \lambda_i = 1$, and $\xi = \Sigma_{i=1}^k \lambda_i \eta_i$. Since $\xi \in int(\widehat{A}^{xy})$, there is a ball of radius $\varepsilon > 0$ around ξ included in $\widehat{A}^{xy}$. Let $\delta = \varepsilon/(2\Sigma_{i=1}^k ||\eta_i||)$ and for each i let $q_i \in \mathbb{Q} \cap [0, 1]$ such that $|q_i - \lambda_i| < \delta$, and $\Sigma_{i=1}^k q_i = 1$. Hence, $\eta = \Sigma_{i=1}^k q_i \eta_i \in \mathbb{Q}_+^{\mathbb{T}}$ and $||\eta - \xi|| < \varepsilon$, which, in turn, implies $\eta \in \widehat{A}^{xy} \cap \mathbb{Q}_+^{\mathbb{T}}$. Since for all i: $\eta_i \in B^{yx}$, consecutive application of the combination axiom (Claim 3) yields $\eta = \Sigma_{i=1}^k q_i \eta_i \in B^{yx}$. On the other hand, η is a convex combination of points in $A^{xy} \subset \mathbb{Q}_+^{\mathbb{T}}$ and thus it has a representation with rational coefficients (because the rationals are an algebraic field). Applying Claims 3 consecutively as above, we conclude that $\eta \in A^{xy}$ – a contradiction. □

The main step in the proof of Lemma 2.1: The last two claims imply that (for all $x, y \in X, x \neq y$) $\widehat{B}^{xy}$ and $\widehat{A}^{yx}$ satisfy the conditions of a separating hyperplane theorem. (Namely, these are convex sets, where the interior of one of them is non-empty and does not intersect the other set.) So there is a vector $v^{xy} \neq 0$ and a number c so that

$$v^{xy} \cdot I \geq c \quad \text{for every } I \in \widehat{B}^{xy}$$
$$v^{xy} \cdot I \leq c \quad \text{for every } I \in \widehat{A}^{yx}\ .$$

Moreover,

$$v^{xy} \cdot I > c \quad \text{for every } I \in int(\widehat{B}^{xy})$$
$$v^{xy} \cdot I < c \quad \text{for every } I \in int(\widehat{A}^{yx})\ .$$

By homogeneity (Claim 2), $c = 0$. **Parts (i)-(iv) of the lemma** are restated as a claim and proved below.

Claim 2.7 *For all $x, y \in X, x \neq y$: $B^{xy} = \{I \in \mathbb{Q}_+^{\mathbb{T}} \mid v^{xy} \cdot I \geq 0\}$; $A^{xy} = \{I \in \mathbb{Q}_+^{\mathbb{T}} \mid v^{xy} \cdot I > 0\}$; $B^{yx} = \{I \in Q_+^{\mathbb{T}} \mid v^{xy} \cdot I \leq 0\}$; and $A^{yx} = \{I \in \mathbb{Q}_+^{\mathbb{T}} \mid v^{xy} \cdot I < 0\}$.*

Proof: (a) $B^{xy} \subset \{I \in \mathbb{Q}_+^{\mathbb{T}} \mid v^{xy} \cdot I \geq 0\}$ follows from the separation result and the fact that $z = 0$.

(b) $A^{xy} \subset \{I \in \mathbb{Q}_+^{\mathbb{T}} \mid v^{xy} \cdot I > 0\}$: assume that $x \succ_I y$, and, by way of negation, $v^{xy} \cdot I \leq 0$. Choose a $J \in A^{yx} \cap int(\widehat{A}^{yx})$. Such a J exists by Claim 5. Since $z = 0$, J satisfies $v^{xy} \cdot J < 0$. By Claim 4 there exists $r \in [0, 1)$ such that $rI + (1 - r)J \in A^{xy} \subset B^{xy}$. By (a), $v^{xy} \cdot (rI + (1 - r)J) \geq 0$. But $v^{xy} \cdot I \leq 0$ and $v^{xy} \cdot J < 0$, a contradiction. Therefore, $A^{xy} \subset \{I \in \mathbb{Q}_+^{\mathbb{T}} \mid v^{xy} \cdot I > 0\}$.

(c) $A^{yx} \subset \{I \in \mathbb{Q}_+^{\mathbb{T}} \mid v^{xy} \cdot I < 0\}$: assume that $y \succ_I x$ and, by way of negation, $v^{xy} \cdot I \geq 0$. By Claim 5 there is a $J \in A^{xy}$ with $J \in int(\widehat{A}^{xy}) \subset int(\widehat{B}^{xy})$. The inclusion $J \in int(\widehat{B}^{xy})$ implies $v^{xy} \cdot J > 0$. Using the Archimedean axiom, there is an $r \in [0, 1)$ such that $rI + (1 - r)J \in A^{yx}$. The separation theorem implies that $v^{xy} \cdot (rI + (1 - r)J) \leq 0$, which is impossible if $v^{xy} \cdot I \geq 0$ and $v^{xy} \cdot J > 0$. This contradiction proves that $A^{yx} \subset \{I \in \mathbb{Q}_+^{\mathbb{T}} \mid v^{xy} \cdot I < 0\}$.

(d) $B^{yx} \subset \{I \in Q_+^{\mathbb{T}} \mid v^{xy} \cdot I \leq 0\}$: assume that $y \succsim_I x$, and, by way of negation, $v^{xy} \cdot I > 0$. Let J satisfy $y \succ_J x$. By (c), $v^{xy} \cdot J < 0$. Define $r = (v^{xy} \cdot I)/(-v^{xy} \cdot J) > 0$. By homogeneity (Claim 2), $y \succ_{rJ} x$. By Claim 3, $I + rJ \in A^{yx}$. Hence, by (c), $v^{xy} \cdot (I + rJ) < 0$. However, direct computation yields $v^{xy} \cdot (I + rJ) = v^{xy} \cdot I + rv^{xy} \cdot J = 0$, a contradiction. It follows that $B^{yx} \subset \{I \in Q_+^{\mathbb{T}} \mid v^{xy} \cdot I \leq 0\}$.

(e) $B^{xy} \supset \{I \in \mathbb{Q}_+^{\mathbb{T}} \mid v^{xy} \cdot I \geq 0\}$: follows from completeness and (c).

(f) $A^{xy} \supset \{I \in \mathbb{Q}_+^{\mathbb{T}} \mid v^{xy} \cdot I > 0\}$: follows from completeness and (d).

(g) $A^{yx} \supset \{I \in \mathbb{Q}_+^{\mathbb{T}} \mid v^{xy} \cdot I < 0\}$: follows from completeness and (a).

(h) $B^{yx} \supset \{I \in \mathbb{Q}_+^{\mathbb{T}} \mid v^{xy} \cdot I \leq 0\}$: follows from completeness and (b). □

Completion of the proof of the Lemma.

Part (v) of the Lemma, i.e., $v^{xy} \notin \mathbb{R}_+^{\mathbb{T}} \cup \mathbb{R}_-^{\mathbb{T}}$ for $x \neq y$, follows from the facts that $A^{xy} \neq \varnothing$ and $A^{yx} \neq \varnothing$. Before proving part (vi), we prove **uniqueness**.

Assume that both v^{xy} and u^{xy} satisfy (i)-(iv). In this case, $u^{xy} \cdot \xi \leq 0$ implies $v^{xy} \cdot \xi \leq 0$ for all $\xi \in \mathbb{R}_+^{\mathbb{T}}$. (Otherwise, there exists $I \in \mathbb{Q}_+^{\mathbb{T}}$ with $u^{xy} \cdot I \leq 0$ but $v^{xy} \cdot I > 0$, contradicting the fact that both v^{xy} and u^{xy} satisfy (i)-(iv).) Similarly, $u^{xy} \cdot \xi \geq 0$ implies $v^{xy} \cdot \xi \geq 0$. Applying the same argument for v^{xy} and u^{xy}, we conclude that $\{\xi \in \mathbb{R}_+^{\mathbb{T}} \mid v^{xy} \cdot \xi = 0\} = \{\xi \in \mathbb{R}_+^{\mathbb{T}} \mid u^{xy} \cdot \xi = 0\}$. Moreover, since $int(\widehat{A}^{xy}) \neq \varnothing$ and $int(\widehat{A}^{yx}) \neq \varnothing$, it follows that $\{\xi \in \mathbb{R}_+^{\mathbb{T}} \mid v^{xy} \cdot \xi = 0\} \cap int(\mathbb{R}_+^{\mathbb{T}}) \neq \varnothing$. This implies that $\{\xi \in \mathbb{R}^{\mathbb{T}} \mid v^{xy} \cdot \xi = 0\} = \{\xi \in \mathbb{R}^{\mathbb{T}} \mid u^{xy} \cdot \xi = 0\}$, i.e., that v^{xy} and u^{xy} have the same null set and are therefore a multiple of each other. That is, there exists α such that $u^{xy} = \alpha v^{xy}$. Since both satisfy (i)-(iv), $\alpha > 0$.

Finally, we prove **part (vi)**. Observe that both v^{xy} and $-v^{yx}$ satisfy (i)-(iv) (stated for the ordered pair (x, y)). By the uniqueness result, $-v^{xy} = \alpha v^{yx}$ for some positive number α. At this stage we redefine the vectors $\{v^{xy}\}_{x,y \in X}$ from the separation result as follows: for every unordered pair $\{x, y\} \subset X$ one of the two ordered pairs, say (y, x), is arbitrary chosen and then v^{xy} is rescaled such that $v^{xy} = -v^{yx}$. (If X is uncountable, the axiom of choice has to be used.) □

Lemma 2.2 *For every three distinct eventualities, $x, y, z \in X$, and the corresponding vectors v^{xy}, v^{yz}, v^{xz} from Lemma 1, there are unique $\alpha, \beta > 0$ such that:*

$$\alpha v^{xy} + \beta v^{yz} = v^{xz}.$$

The key argument in the proof of Lemma 2.2 is that, if v^{xz} is not a linear combination of v^{xy} and v^{yz}, one may find a vector I for which $\succ_I$ is cyclical.

If there are only three alternatives $x, y, z \in X$, Lemma 2 allows us to complete the proof as follows: choose an arbitrary vector v^{xz} that separates between x and z. Then choose the multiples of v^{xy} and of v^{yz} defined by the lemma. Proceed to define $v^x = v^{xz}$, $v^y = \beta v^{yz}$, and $v^z = 0$. By construction, $(v^x - v^z)$ is (equal and therefore) proportional to v^{xz}, hence $x \succsim_I z$ iff $v^x \cdot I \geq v^z \cdot I$. Also, $(v^y - v^z)$ is proportional to v^{yz} and it follows that $y \succsim_I z$ iff $v^y \cdot I \geq v^z \cdot I$. The point is, however, that, by Lemma 2, we obtain the same result for the last pair: $(v^x - v^y) = (v^{xz} - \beta v^{yz}) = \alpha v^{xy}$ and $x \succsim_I y$ iff $v^x \cdot I \geq v^y \cdot I$ follows.

Proof of Lemma 2:

First note that for every three distinct eventualities, $x, y, z \in X$, if v^{xy} and v^{yz} are colinear, then for all I either $x \succ_I y \Leftrightarrow y \succ_I z$ or $x \succ_I y \Leftrightarrow z \succ_I y$. Both implications contradict diversity. Therefore any two vectors in $\{v^{xy}, v^{yz}, v^{xz}\}$ are linearly independent. This immediately implies the uniqueness claim of the lemma. Next we introduce

Claim 2.8 *For every distinct $x, y, z \in X$, and every $\lambda, \mu \in \mathbb{R}$, if $\lambda v^{xy} + \mu v^{yz} \leq 0$, then $\lambda = \mu = 0$.*

Proof: Observe that Lemma 1(v) implies that if one of the numbers λ, and μ is zero, so is the other. Next, suppose, per absurdum, that $\lambda\mu \neq 0$,and consider $\lambda v^{xy} \leq \mu v^{zy}$. If, say, $\lambda, \mu > 0$, then $v^{xy} \cdot I \geq 0$ necessitates $v^{zy} \cdot I \geq 0$. Hence there is no I for which $x \succ_I y \succ_I z$, in contradiction to the diversity axiom. Similarly, $\lambda > 0 > \mu$ precludes $x \succ_I z \succ_I y$; $\mu > 0 > \lambda$ precludes $y \succ_I x \succ_I z$; and $\lambda, \mu < 0$ implies that for no $I \in \mathbb{Q}_+^{\mathbb{T}}$ is it the case that $z \succ_I y \succ_I x$. Hence the diversity axioms holds only if $\lambda = \mu = 0$. □

We now turn to the main part of the proof. Suppose that v^{xy}, v^{yz}, and v^{zx} are column vectors and consider the $|\mathbb{T}| \times 3$ matrix (v^{xy}, v^{yz}, v^{zx}) as a 2-person 0-sum game. If its value is positive, then there is an $\xi \in \Delta(\mathbb{T})$ such that $v^{xy} \cdot \xi > 0$, $v^{yz} \cdot \xi > 0$, and $v^{zx} \cdot \xi > 0$. Hence there is an $I \in \mathbb{Q}_+^{\mathbb{T}} \cap \Delta(\mathbb{T})$ that satisfies the same inequalities. This, in turn, implies that $x \succ_I y$, $y \succ_I z$, and $z \succ_I x$—a contradiction.

Therefore the value of the game is zero or negative. In this case there are $\lambda, \mu, \zeta \geq 0$, such that $\lambda v^{xy} + \mu v^{yz} + \zeta v^{zx} \leq 0$ and $\lambda + \mu + \zeta = 1$. The claim above implies that if one of the numbers λ, μ and ζ is zero, so are the other two. Thus $\lambda, \mu, \zeta > 0$. We therefore conclude that there are $\alpha = \lambda/\zeta > 0$ and $\beta = \mu/\zeta > 0$ such that

$$\alpha v^{xy} + \beta v^{yz} \leq v^{xz} \tag{5}$$

Applying the same reasoning to the triple z, y, and x, we conclude that there are $\gamma, \delta > 0$ such that

$$\gamma v^{zy} + \delta v^{yx} \leq v^{zx}. \tag{6}$$

Summation yields

$$(\alpha - \delta)v^{xy} + (\beta - \gamma)v^{yz} \leq 0. \tag{7}$$

Claim 8 applied to inequality (7) implies $\alpha = \delta$ and $\beta = \gamma$. Hence inequality (6) may be rewritten as $\alpha v^{xy} + \beta v^{yz} \leq v^{xz}$, which together with (5) yields the desired representation. □

Lemma 2 shows that, if there are more than three alternatives, the likelihood ranking of every triple of alternatives can be represented as in the theorem. The question that remains is whether these separate representations (for different triples) can be "patched" together in a consistent way.

Lemma 2.3 *There are vectors $\{v^{xy}\}_{x,y\in X, x\neq y}$, as in Lemma 1, such that for any three distinct acts, $x, y, z \in X$, the Jacobi identity $v^{xy} + v^{yz} = v^{xz}$ holds.*

Proof: The proof is by induction, which is transfinite if X is uncountably infinite. The main idea of the proof is the following. Assume that one has rescaled the vectors v^{xy} for all alternatives x, y in some subset of acts $A \subset X$, and one now wishes to add another act to this subset, $w \notin A$. Choose $x \in A$ and consider the vectors v^{xw}, v^{yw} for $x, y \in A$. By Lemma 2, there are unique positive coefficients α, β such that $v^{xy} = \alpha v^{xw} + \beta v^{wy}$. One would like to show that the coefficient $\alpha = \alpha_y$ does not depend on the choice of $y \in A$. We will show that, if α_y did depend on y, one would find that there are $x, y, z \in A$ such that the vectors v^{xw}, v^{yw}, v^{zw} are linearly dependent, and this would contradict the diversity axiom.

Claim 2.9 *Let $A \subset X$, $|A| \geq 3$, $w \in X \backslash A$. Suppose that there are vectors $\{v^{xy}\}_{x,y\in A, x\neq y}$, as in Lemma 1, and for any three distinct acts, $x, y, z \in X$, $v^{xy} + v^{yz} = v^{xz}$ holds. Then there are vectors $\{v^{xy}\}_{x,y\in A\cup\{w\}, x\neq y}$, as in Lemma 1, and for any three distinct acts, $x, y, z \in X$, $v^{xy} + v^{yz} = v^{xz}$ holds.*

Proof: Choose distinct $x, y, z \in A$. Let $\hat{v}^{xw}, \hat{v}^{yw}$, and $\hat{v}^{zw}$ be the vectors provided by Lemma 1 when applied to the pairs (x, w), (y, w), and (z, w), respectively. Consider the triple $\{x, y, w\}$. By Lemma 2 there are unique coefficients $\lambda(\{x, w\}, y), \lambda(\{y, w\}, x) > 0$ such that

$$v^{xy} = \lambda(\{x,w\},y)\hat{v}^{xw} + \lambda(\{y,w\},x)\hat{v}^{wy} \tag{8}$$

Applying the same reasoning to the triple $\{x,z,w\}$, we find that there are unique coefficients $\lambda(\{x,w\},z), \lambda(\{z,w\},x) > 0$ such that

$$v^{xz} = \lambda(\{x,w\},z)\hat{v}^{xw} + \lambda(\{z,w\},x)\hat{v}^{wz}.$$

or

$$v^{zx} = \lambda(\{x,w\},z)\hat{v}^{wx} + \lambda(\{z,w\},x)\hat{v}^{zw}. \tag{9}$$

We wish to show that $\lambda(\{x,w\},y) = \lambda(\{x,w\},z)$. To see this, we consider also the triple $\{y,z,w\}$ and conclude that there are unique coefficients $\lambda(\{y,w\},z), \lambda(\{z,w\},y) > 0$ such that

$$v^{yz} = \lambda(\{y,w\},z)\hat{v}^{yw} + \lambda(\{z,w\},y)\hat{v}^{wz}. \tag{10}$$

Since $x,y,z \in A$, we have

$$v^{xy} + v^{yz} + v^{zx} = 0$$

and it follows that the summation of the right-hand sides of (8), (9), and (10) also vanishes:

$$[\lambda(\{x,w\},y) - \lambda(\{x,w\},z)]\hat{v}^{xw} + [\lambda(\{y,w\},z) - \lambda(\{y,w\},x)]\hat{v}^{yw}$$
$$+ [\lambda(\{z,w\},x) - \lambda(\{z,w\},y)]\hat{v}^{zw} = 0.$$

If some of the coefficients above are not zero, the vectors $\{\hat{v}^{xw}, \hat{v}^{yw}, \hat{v}^{zw}\}$ are linearly dependent, and this contradicts the diversity axiom. For instance, if $\hat{v}^{xw}$ is a non-negative linear combination of $\hat{v}^{yw}$ and $\hat{v}^{zw}$, for no I will it be the case that $y \succ_I z \succ_I w \succ_I x$.

We therefore obtain $\lambda(\{x,w\},y) = \lambda(\{x,w\},z)$ for every $y,z \in A \backslash \{x\}$. Hence for every $x \in A$ there exists a unique $\lambda(\{x,w\}) > 0$ such that, for every distinct $x,y \in A$ $v^{xy} = \lambda(\{x,w\})\hat{v}^{xw} + \lambda(\{y,w\})\hat{v}^{wy}$. Defining $v^{xw} = \lambda(\{x,w\})\hat{v}^{xw}$ completes the proof of the claim. □

To complete the proof of the lemma, we apply the claim consecutively. In case X is not countable, the induction is transfinite (and assumes that X can be well ordered). □

Note that Lemma 3, unlike Lemma 2, guarantees the possibility to rescale *simultaneously* all the v^{xy}-s from Lemma 1 such that the Jacobi identity will hold on X.

We now complete the proof that (i) implies (ii). Choose an arbitrary act, say, g in X. Define $v^g = 0$, and for any other alternative, x, define $v^x = v^{xg}$, where the v^{xg}-s are from Lemma 3.

Given $I \in \mathbb{Q}_+^{\mathbb{T}}$ and $x, y \in X$ we have:

$$x \succsim_I y \Leftrightarrow v^{xy} \cdot I \geq 0 \Leftrightarrow (v^{xg} + v^{gy}) \cdot I \geq 0 \Leftrightarrow$$
$$(v^{xg} - v^{yg}) \cdot I \geq 0 \Leftrightarrow v^x \cdot I - v^y \cdot I \geq 0 \Leftrightarrow v^x \cdot I \geq v^y \cdot I$$

The first implication follows from Lemma 1(i), the second from the Jacobi identity of Lemma 3, the third from Lemma 1(vi), and the fourth from the definition of the v^x-s. Hence, (3) of the theorem has been proved.

It remains to be shown that the vectors defined above are such that $conv(\{v^x - v^y, v^y - v^z, v^z - v^w\}) \cap \mathbb{R}_-^{\mathbb{T}} = \emptyset$. Indeed, in Lemma 1(v) we have shown that $v^x - v^y \notin \mathbb{R}_-^{\mathbb{T}}$. To see this one only uses the diversity axiom for the pair $\{x, y\}$. Lemma 2 has shown, among other things, that a non-zero linear combination of $v^x - v^y$ and $v^y - v^z$ cannot be in $\mathbb{R}_-^{\mathbb{T}}$, using the diversity axiom for triples. Linear independence of all three vectors was established in Lemma 3. However, the full implication of the diversity condition will be clarified by the following lemma. Being a complete characterization, we will also use it in proving the converse implication, namely, that part (ii) of the theorem implies part (i). The proof of the lemma below depends on Lemma 1. It therefore holds under the assumptions that for any distinct $x, y \in X$ there is an I such that $x \succ_I y$.

Lemma 2.4 *For every list (x, y, z, w) of distinct elements of X, there exists $I \in \mathbb{J}$ such that*

$$x \succ_I y \succ_I z \succ_I w \quad \textit{iff} \quad conv(\{v^{xy}, v^{yz}, v^{zw}\}) \cap \mathbb{R}_-^{\mathbb{T}} = \emptyset\,.$$

Proof: There exists $I \in \mathbb{J}$ such that $x \succ_I y \succ_I z \succ_I w$ iff there exists $I \in \mathbb{J}$ such that $v^{xy} \cdot I, v^{yz} \cdot I, v^{zw} \cdot I > 0$. This is true iff there exists a probability vector $p \in \Delta(\mathbb{T})$ such that $v^{xy} \cdot p, v^{yz} \cdot p, v^{zw} \cdot p > 0$.

Suppose that v^{xy}, v^{yz}, and v^{zw} are column vectors and consider the $|\mathbb{T}| \times 3$ matrix (v^{xy}, v^{yz}, v^{zw}) as a 2-person 0-sum game. The argument above implies that there exists $I \in \mathbb{J}$ such that $x \succ_I y \succ_I z \succ_I w$ iff the maximin in this game is positive. This is equivalent to the minimax being positive, which means that for every mixed strategy of player 2 there exists $t \in \mathbb{T}$ that guarantees player 1 a positive payoff. In other words, there exists $I \in \mathbb{J}$ such that $x \succ_I y \succ_I z \succ_I w$ iff for every convex combination of $\{v^{xy}, v^{yz}, v^{zw}\}$ at least one entry is positive, i.e., $conv(\{v^{xy}, v^{yz}, v^{zw}\}) \cap \mathbb{R}_-^{\mathbb{T}} = \emptyset$. □

This completes the proof that (i) implies (ii). □

Part 2: (ii) implies (i)

It is straightforward to verify that if $\{\succsim_I\}_{i \in \mathbb{Q}_+^{\mathbb{T}}}$ are representable by $\{v^x\}_{x \in X}$ as in (3), they have to satisfy Axioms 1-3. To show that Axiom 4 holds, we quote Lemma 4 of the previous part. □

Part 3: Uniqueness

It is obvious that if $u^x = \alpha v^x + \beta$ for some scalar $\alpha > 0$, a vector $\beta \in \mathbb{R}^{\mathbb{T}}$, and all $x \in X$, then part (ii) of the theorem holds with the matrix u replacing v.

Suppose that $\{v^x\}_{x\in X}$ and $\{u^x\}_{x\in X}$ both satisfy (3), and we wish to show that there are a scalar $\alpha > 0$ and a vector $\beta \in \mathbb{R}^{\mathbb{T}}$ such that for all $x \in X$, $u^x = \alpha v^x + \beta$. Recall that, for $x \neq y$, $v^x \neq \lambda v^y$ and $u^x \neq \lambda u^y$ for all $0 \neq \lambda \in \mathbb{R}$ by A4.

Choose $x \neq g$ ($x, g \in X$, g satisfies $v^g = 0$). From the uniqueness part of Lemma 1 there exists a unique $\alpha > 0$ such that $(u^x - u^g) = \alpha(v^x - v^g) = \alpha v^x$. Define $\beta = u^g$.

We now wish to show that, for any $y \in X$, $u^y = \alpha v^y + \beta$. It holds for $y = g$ and $y = x$, hence assume that $x \neq y \neq g$. Again, from the uniqueness part of Lemma 1 there are unique $\gamma, \delta > 0$ such that $(u^y - u^x) = \gamma(v^y - v^x)$ and $(u^g - u^y) = \delta(v^g - v^y)$. Summing up these two with $(u^x - u^g) = \alpha(v^x - v^g)$, we get

$$0 = \alpha(v^x - v^g) + \gamma(v^y - v^x) + \delta(v^g - v^y) = \alpha v^x + \gamma(v^y - v^x) - \delta v^y.$$

Thus $(\alpha - \gamma)v^x + (\gamma - \delta)v^y = 0$.

Since $v^x \neq v^g = 0$, $v^y \neq v^g = 0$, and $v^x \neq \lambda v^y$ if $0 \neq \lambda \in \mathbb{R}$, we get $\alpha = \gamma = \delta$. Plugging $\alpha = \gamma$ into $(u^y - u^x) = \gamma(v^y - v^x)$ proves that $u^y = \alpha v^y + \beta$. □

This completes the proof of Theorem 2. □□

We now turn to complete the proof of Step 1. First we prove that (i) implies (ii). Assume that $\{\succcurlyeq_M\}_M$ satisfy A1-A4. It follows that $\{\succcurlyeq_I\}_I$ satisfy A1*-A4*. Therefore, there is a representation of $\{\succcurlyeq_I\}_I$ by a matrix $v : X \times \mathbb{T} \to \mathbb{R}$ as in (3) of Theorem 2. We abuse notation and extend v to specific cases. Formally, we define $v : X \times \mathbb{C} \to \mathbb{R}$ as follows. For $x \in X$ and $c \in \mathbb{C}$, define $v(x, c) = v(x, t)$ for $t \in \mathbb{T} \equiv \mathbb{C}/\sim$ such that $c \in t$. With this definition, (2) of Theorem 1 holds. Obviously, $c \sim d$ implies $v(\cdot, c) = v(\cdot, d)$. The converse also holds: if $v(\cdot, c) = v(\cdot, d)$, (2) implies that $c \sim d$. Finally, observe that, for every distinct four eventualities $x, y, z, w \in X$, the vectors $v(x, \cdot), v(y, \cdot), v(z, \cdot), v(w, \cdot) \in \mathbb{R}^{\mathbb{C}}$ are obtained from the corresponding vectors in $\mathbb{R}^{\mathbb{T}}$ by replication of columns. Since $v : X \times \mathbb{T} \to \mathbb{R}$ is diversified, we also get that $v : X \times \mathbb{C} \to \mathbb{R}$ is diversified.

We now turn to prove that (ii) implies (i). Assume that a diversified matrix $v : X \times \mathbb{C} \to \mathbb{R}$, respecting case equivalence, is given. One may then define $v : X \times \mathbb{T} \to \mathbb{R}$ by $v(x, t) = v(x, c)$ for $t \in \mathbb{T} = \mathbb{C}/\sim$ such that $c \in t$, which is unambiguous because $v(\cdot, c) = v(\cdot, d)$ whenever $c \sim d$. Obviously, (3) of Theorem 2 follows from (2) of Theorem 1, and $v : X \times \mathbb{T} \to \mathbb{R}$ is diversified as well. Defining $\{\succcurlyeq_I\}_I$ by the matrix $v : X \times \mathbb{T} \to \mathbb{R}$ and (3), we find that $\{\succcurlyeq_I\}_I$ satisfy A1*-A4*. Also, $\succcurlyeq_M = \succcurlyeq_{I_M}$ for every $M \in \mathbb{M}$. Hence $\{\succcurlyeq_M\}_M$ satisfy A1-A4.

To see that uniqueness holds, assume that $v, u : X \times \mathbb{C} \to \mathbb{R}$ both satisfy (2) of Theorem 1, and respect case equivalence. Define $v, u : X \times \mathbb{T} \to \mathbb{R}$ as above. The uniqueness result in Theorem 2 yields the desired result. □□

Step 2: The case of arbitrary $|\mathbb{T}|$ and finite $|X|$.

We first prove that (i) implies (ii). Observe that a representation as in (ii) is guaranteed for every finite $T \subset \mathbb{T}$, provided that T is rich enough to satisfy the diversity axiom A4. We therefore restrict attention to such sets T, and show that the representations obtained for each of them can be "patched" together.

For every ordered list $(x, y, z, w) \in X$, choose $M \in \mathbb{M}$ such that $x \succ_M y \succ_M z \succ_M w$. Such an M exists by A4. Let M_0 be the union of all sets M so obtained. Since X is finite, so is M_0, i.e., $M_0 \in \mathbb{M}$. Let T_0 be the set of types (equivalence classes) of cases in M_0. Choose $g \in X$. Apply Theorem 2 to obtain a representation of $\{\succcurlyeq_I\}_{I \in \mathbb{J}_{T_0}}$ by $v_{T_0} : X \times T_0$ and (3) for all $I \in \mathbb{J}_{T_0} \equiv \mathbb{Z}_+^{T_0}$, such that $v_{T_0}(g, \cdot) = 0$. For every finite $T \subset \mathbb{T}$ such that $T_0 \subset T$, apply Theorem 2 again to obtain a representation of $\{\succcurlyeq_I\}_{I \in \mathbb{J}_T}$ by $v_T : X \times T$ and (3) for all $I \in \mathbb{J}_T \equiv \mathbb{Z}_+^T$, such that $v_T(g, \cdot) = 0$ and such that v_T extends v_{T_0}. v_T is uniquely defined by these conditions. Moreover, if $T \subset T_1 \cap T_2$, $T_0 \subset T$, and T_1 and T_2 are finite, then the restriction of v_{T_1} and of v_{T_2} to T coincide. The union of $\{v_T\}_{|T| < \infty}$ defines $v : X \times \mathbb{T} \to \mathbb{R}$ satisfying (3) for all $I \in \mathbb{J}_T$ for some finite $T \subset \mathbb{T}$. Defining v on $X \times \mathbb{C}$ as above yields a function that satisfies (2) of Theorem 1 and that respects case equivalence.

We now turn to prove that (ii) implies (i). Given a representation via a matrix $v : X \times \mathbb{C} \to \mathbb{R}$ as in (2), it follows that $\{\succcurlyeq_M\}_M$ satisfy A1 and A2. A3 also holds since v respects case equivalence. It remains to show that the above, for a diversified v, imply A4. Assume not. Then there are distinct $(x, y, z, w) \in X$ such that for no finite memory M is it the case that $x \succ_M y \succ_M z \succ_M w$. We wish to show that this condition contradicts the fact that v is diversified.

By diversification of v we know that

$$conv\{(v(x,\cdot) - v(y,\cdot)), (v(y,\cdot) - v(z,\cdot)), (v(z,\cdot) - v(w,\cdot))\} \cap \mathbb{R}_-^{\mathbb{C}} = \varnothing.$$

This implies that, for every vector (α, β, γ) in the two-dimensional simplex Δ^2, it is not the case that

$$\alpha(v(x,\cdot) - v(y,\cdot)) + \beta(v(y,\cdot) - v(z,\cdot)) + \gamma(v(z,\cdot) - v(w,\cdot)) \leq 0.$$

In other words, for every $(\alpha, \beta, \gamma) \in \Delta^2$ there exists a case $c \in \mathbb{C}$ such that

$$\alpha(v(x,c) - v(y,c)) + \beta(v(y,c) - v(z,c)) + \gamma(v(z,c) - v(w,c)) > 0.$$

Thus

$$\{(\alpha, \beta, \gamma) \in \Delta^2 | \alpha(v(x,c) - v(y,c)) + \beta(v(y,c) - v(z,c)) + \gamma(v(z,c) - v(w,c)) > 0\}_{c \in \mathbb{C}}$$

is an open cover of Δ^2 in the relative topology. But Δ^2 is compact in this topology. Hence it has an open sub-cover. But this implies that there is a finite memory $M \in \mathbb{M}$ such that, restricting v to $X \times M$,

$$conv\{(v(x,\cdot) - v(y,\cdot)), (v(y,\cdot) - v(z,\cdot)), (v(z,\cdot) - v(w,\cdot))\} \cap \mathbb{R}^M_- = \varnothing.$$

Let T be the set of types of cases appearing in M. Define $v : X \times T \to \mathbb{R}$ as above. It also follows that

$$conv\{(v(x,\cdot) - v(y,\cdot)), (v(y,\cdot) - v(z,\cdot)), (v(z,\cdot) - v(w,\cdot))\} \cap \mathbb{R}^T_- = \varnothing.$$

By Theorem 2 this implies that there exists $I \in \mathbb{J}_T$ for which $x \succ_I y \succ_I z \succ_I w$. Let M' be a set of cases such that $I(t) = \#(M' \cap t)$, and $M' \subset \cup_{t \in T} t$. It follows that $x \succ_{M'} y \succ_{M'} z \succ_{M'} w$, a contradiction.

Finally, uniqueness follows from the uniqueness result in Step 1. □□

Step 3: The case of infinite X, $\mathbb{T}$.

We first prove that (i) implies (ii). Choose $e, f, g, h \in X$. For $A_0 = \{e, f, g, h\}$ there exists a diversified function $v_{A_0} : A_0 \times \mathbb{C} \to \mathbb{R}$ satisfying (2) and respecting case equivalence, as well as $v_{A_0}(e,\cdot) = 0$. Moreover, all such functions differ only by a multiplicative positive constant. Fix such a function $\widehat{v}_{A_0}$. For every finite set $A \subset X$ such that $A_0 \subset A$, there exists a diversified function $v_A : A \times \mathbb{C} \to \mathbb{R}$ satisfying (2) and respecting case equivalence. Moreover, there exists a unique v_A that extends $\widehat{v}_{A_0}$. Let us denote it by $\widehat{v}_A$. We now define $v : X \times \mathbb{C} \to \mathbb{R}$. Given $x \in X$, let A be a finite set such that $A_0 \cup \{x\} \subset A$. Define $v(x,\cdot) = \widehat{v}_A(x,\cdot)$. This definition is unambiguous, since, for every two finite sets A_1 and A_2 such that $A_0 \cup \{x\} \subset A_1, A_2$, we have $\widehat{v}_{A_1}(x,\cdot) = \widehat{v}_{A_1 \cup A_2}(x,\cdot) = \widehat{v}_{A_2}(x,\cdot)$. To see that v satisfies (2), choose $x, y \in X$ and consider $A = A_0 \cup \{x, y\}$. Since $v(x,\cdot) = \widehat{v}_A(x,\cdot)$, $v(y,\cdot) = \widehat{v}_A(y,\cdot)$ and $\widehat{v}_A$ satisfies (2) on A, v satisfies (2) on X. Next consider respecting case equivalence, namely, that $v(\cdot, c) = v(\cdot, d)$ iff $c \sim d$. The "if" part follows from the fact that, if $c \sim d$, then for every finite A, $\widehat{v}_A(\cdot, c) = \widehat{v}_A(\cdot, d)$. As for the "only if" part, it follows from the representation by (2) as in Step 1. Finally, to see that v is diversified, let there be given x, y, z, w and choose $A = A_0 \cup \{x, y, z, w\}$. Since $\widehat{v}_A$ is diversified, the desired conclusion follows.

The that (ii) implies (i) is follows from the corresponding proof in Step 2, because each of the axioms A1-A4 involves only finitely many eventualities. Finally, uniqueness is proven as in Step 1. □□□

Proof of Proposition – Insufficiency of A1–3:

To see that without the diversity axiom representability is not guaranteed, let $X = [0, 1]^2$ and let $\succsim_L$ be the lexicographic order on X.[12] Define, for every

[12] A1–3 do not suffice for the existence of a representation as in (2) even if X is finite. See Gilboa and Schmeidler (1997) for an example with $|X| = 4$, which can be easily adapted to the present set-up.

non-empty $M \in \mathbb{M}$, $\succsim_M = \succsim_L$, and $\succsim_\emptyset = X \times X$. It is easy to see that $\{\succsim_M\}_{M \in \mathbb{M}}$ satisfy A1–3. However, there cannot be a representation as in (2) since for any non-empty M, $\succsim_M$ is not representable by a real-valued function. □

Proof of Remark:

Consider an example in which $\{\succsim_M\}_M$ rank eventualities by relative frequencies, with a tie-breaking rule that is reflected by small additions to the value of v. These small additions, however, vary from case to case and their sum converges. Specifically, let $X = \{1, 2, 3, 4\}$. Define $\mathbb{T} = \{1, 2, 3, 4\}$. $\mathbb{T}$ will indeed end up to be the set of types of cases, as will become clear once we define $\{\succsim_M\}_M$. For the time being we will abuse the term and will refer to elements of $\mathbb{T}$ as "types". Let the set of cases be $\mathbb{C} \equiv T \times N$. We now turn to define $v : X \times \mathbb{C} \to \mathbb{R}$. For $x \in X$, $t \in \mathbb{T}$, and $i \in \mathbb{N}$, if $x \neq t$, $v(x, (t, i)) = 0$. Otherwise (i.e., if $x = t$), if $x \in \{1, 2, 3\}$, then $v(x, (t, i)) = 1$. Finally, $v(4, (4, i)) = 1 + \frac{1}{2^i}$ for $i \in \mathbb{N}$. Define $\{\succsim_M\}_M$ by v via (2).

We claim that two cases $(t, i), (s, j) \in \mathbb{T} \times \mathbb{N}$ are equivalent $((t, i) \sim (s, j))$ iff $t = s$. It is easy to see that if $t \neq s$, then (t, i) and (s, j) are not equivalent. (For instance, $t \succ_{\{(t,i)\}} s$ but $s \succ_{\{(s,j)\}} t$.) Moreover, if $t = s \in \{1, 2, 3\}$, then $v(\cdot, (t, i)) = v(\cdot, (s, j))$. By (2), $(t, i) \sim (s, j)$. It remains to show that, for all $i, j \in \mathbb{N}$, $(4, i) \sim (4, j)$ despite the fact that $v(\cdot, (4, i)) \neq v(\cdot, (4, j))$.

Observe, first, that $\{\succsim_M\}_M$ agree with relative frequency rankings. Specifically, consider a memory $M \in \mathbb{M}$. Let $I_M \in \mathbb{Z}_+^4$ be defined by $I_M(t) = \#\{ i \in \mathbb{N} \mid (t, i) \in M \}$ for $t \in \{1, 2, 3, 4\}$. For any $s, t \in \{1, 2, 3, 4\}$, if $I_M(t) > I_M(s)$, it follows that $t \succ_M s$. Also, if $I_M(t) = I_M(s)$ and $s, t < 4$, then $t \approx_M s$. Finally, if, for $t \in \{1, 2, 3\}$, $I_M(t) = I_M(4)$, then $4 \succ_M t$.

Let there be given $M \in \mathbb{M}$ such that $(4, i), (4, j) \notin M$. The memories $M \cup \{(4, i)\}$ and $M \cup \{(4, j)\}$ agree on relative frequencies of the types, that is, $I_{M \cup \{(4,i)\}} = I_{M \cup \{(4,j)\}}$. Hence $\succsim_{M \cup \{(4,i)\}} = \succsim_{M \cup \{(4,j)\}}$ and $(4, i) \sim (4, j)$ follows.

Thus v satisfies (2) but does not respect case equivalence.[13] □

2.7 References

Akaike, H. (1954), "An Approximation to the Density Function", *Annals of the Institute of Statistical Mathematics*, **6**: 127–32.

Cover, T. and P. Hart (1967), "Nearest Neighbor Pattern Classification", IEEE *Transactions on Information Theory*, **13**: 21–7.

[13] Observe that the relations $\{\succsim_M\}_M$ satisfy A1 and A2 (as they do whenever they are defined by some v via (2)), as well as A4, but not A3. Indeed, such an example cannot be generated if A3 holds as well. Specifically, one can prove the following result: if $\{\succsim_M\}_M$ are defined by v via (2), and satisfy A3 and A4, then $v(x, c) - v(y, c) = v(x, d) - v(y, d)$ whenever $c \sim d$. If, for instance, $v(e, \cdot) \equiv 0$ for some $e \in X$, then v respects case equivalence.

de Finetti, B. (1937), "La Prevision: Ses Lois Logiques, Ses Sources Subjectives", *Annales de l'Institute Henri Poincare*, **7**: 1–68.

de Groot, M. H. (1975), *Probability and Statistics*. Reading, MA: Addison-Wesley Publishing Co.

Devroye, L., L. Gyorfi, and G. Lugosi (1996), *A Probabilistic Theory of Pattern Recognition*. New York: Springer-Verlag.

Fix, E. and J. Hodges (1951), "Discriminatory Analysis. Nonparametric Discrimination: Consistency Properties". Technical Report 4, Project Number 21-49-004, USAF School of Aviation Medicine, Randolph Field, TX.

Fix, E. and J. Hodges (1952), "Discriminatory Analysis: Small Sample Performance". Technical Report 21-49-004, USAF School of Aviation Medicine, Randolph Field, TX.

Forsyth, R., and R. Rada (1986), *Machine Learning: Applications in Expert Systems and Information Retrieval*. New York: John Wiley and Sons.

Gilboa, I. and D. Schmeidler (1995), "Case-Based Decision Theory", *Quarterly Journal of Economics*, **110**: 605–39.

Gilboa, I. and D. Schmeidler (1997), "Act Similarity in Case-Based Decision Theory", *Economic Theory*, **9**: 47–61.

Gilboa, I. and D. Schmeidler (2002), "A Cognitive Foundation of Probability", *Mathematics of Operations Research*, **27**: 68–81.

Gilboa, I. and D. Schmeidler (2001), *A Theory of Case-Based Decisions*. Cambridge: Cambridge University Press.

Gilboa, I., D. Schmeidler, and P. P. Wakker (1999), "Utility in Case-Based Decision Theory", Foerder Institute for Economic Research Working Paper No. 31–99.

Hacking, I. (1975), *The Emergence of Probability*. Cambridge: Cambridge University Press.

Hume, D. (1748), *Enquiry into the Human Understanding*. Oxford: Clarendon Press.

Myerson, R. B. (1995), "Axiomatic Derivation of Scoring Rules Without the Ordering Assumption", *Social Choice and Welfare*, **12**: 59–74.

von Neumann, J. and O. Morgenstern (1944), *Theory of Games and Economic Behavior*. Princeton, NJ: Princeton University Press.

Parzen, E. (1962), "On the Estimation of a Probability Density Function and the Mode", *Annals of Mathematical Statistics*, **33**: 1065–76.

Ramsey, F. P. (1931), "Truth and Probability", *The Foundation of Mathematics and Other Logical Essays*. New York: Harcourt, Brace and Co.

Riesbeck, C. K. and R. C. Schank (1989), *Inside Case-Based Reasoning*. Hillsdale, NJ: Lawrence Erlbaum Associates, Inc.

Rosenblatt, M. (1956), "Remarks on Some Nonparametric Estimates of a Density Function", *Annals of Mathematical Statistics*, **27**: 832 7.

Royall, R. (1966), *A Class of Nonparametric Estimators of a Smooth Regression Function*. Ph.D. Thesis, Stanford University, Stanford, CA.

Savage, L. J. (1954), *The Foundations of Statistics*. New York: John Wiley and Sons.

Schank, R. C. (1986), *Explanation Patterns: Understanding Mechanically and Creatively*. Hillsdale, NJ: Lawrence Erlbaum Associates.

Scott, D. W. (1992), *Multivariate Density Estimation: Theory, Practice, and Visualization*. New York: John Wiley and Sons.

Silverman, B. W. (1986), *Density Estimation for Statistics and Data Analysis*. London and New York: Chapman and Hall.

Stone, C. (1977), "Consistent Nonparametric Regression", *Annals of Statistics*, **5**: 689–705.

Young, H. P. (1975), "Social Choice Scoring Functions", *SIAM Journal of Applied Mathematics*, **28**: 824–38.

3

Subjectivity in Inductive Inference

3.1 Introduction

3.1.1 *Inductive Inference*

Inductive inference is the art of selecting theories based on observations. It is at the heart of scientific and statistical research, as well as much of everyday reasoning. The economist who engages in model selection to explain data, the investor who seeks trends in the behavior of financial markets, and the executive who plans her next marketing campaign all share the same question: Given what I've seen, which rule (or "theory" or "model") should I use to predict future observations?

A first fundamental principle is that one should only consider theories that have *not* been refuted by the data. But how should we choose among the theories that best match the data?

People typically bring subjective criteria to bear in making this choice, tending to select theories that seem a priori reasonable, intuitive, simple, elegant, familiar, or that satisfy a variety of other considerations. Why does such subjective reasoning persist? Would it not be better to base model selection on objective criteria alone? Admittedly, perfectly objective inference is impossible: even the purest of classical statisticians must exercise their judgment when deciding which variables to include in a model, which significance level to choose, and so forth. But shouldn't we strive to be as objective as possible?

This chapter addresses these questions. We explain how and why subjective criteria are essential to effective reasoning. We conclude that inference cannot effectively be based on objective arguments alone—simply observing that one theory fits the data better than another is not sufficient to prefer the former to the latter. Instead, one must also argue that the candidate theory fares well in terms of consistently applied subjective auxiliary criteria.

3.1.2 *Objectivity and Subjectivity*

We consider an agent who faces a sequence of prediction problems. In each period, she observes an input and must predict the value of an output. To make her prediction, the agent selects a theory, which specifies a distribution over possible predictions, given the history of past inputs and outputs.

The agent's choice of a theory in each period is made according to a preference relation over theories. We are interested in the degree of objectivity of such criteria, as defined by the degree to which they depend on data, that is, on the history of past inputs and outputs. We say that the agent's preference over theories is *(purely) objective* if it depends only on the conditional probabilities of past observations given theories. For example, if theories are ranked according to the likelihood function, the agent's preferences are objective. However, one may choose to maximize other functions of the conditional probabilities, such as the minimal probability assigned by a theory to the observations encountered, and the resulting preference will also be objective according to our definition.

We say that the agent's preference over theories is *(purely) subjective* if it is independent of the data. Subjective criteria for ranking theories include a preference for simplicity and a preference for intuitive explanations. A Bayesian approach that assigns prior probabilities to theories also defines a subjective criterion. When a Bayesian prior is updated in response to accumulating observations, it defines a criterion that is partly subjective and partly objective.

One might think of other distinctions between objective and subjective. Our notion of objectivity does not specify which function is applied to conditional probabilities, and it thus leaves room for the agent's subjective discretion. On the other hand, one may attempt to find some objectivity in history-independent criteria, such as in agreement on the concept of simplicity, or optimality of a prior belief. However, for our purposes, objectivity is defined by dependence on conditional probabilities alone, and subjectivity is defined by independence of history.

To consider an example, suppose that the agent observes the sequence $1, 2, 4, 8$ and is asked to predict the next observation. Clearly, the deterministic theory that predicts the observation $f(n) = 2^{n-1}$ at period n fits the data perfectly well, and predicts that the number 16 will come up next. However, the theory

$$g(n) = -\frac{1}{3}n^4 + \frac{7}{2}n^3 - \frac{73}{6}n^2 + 18n - 8,$$

also provides a perfect match to the first four observations, but predicts the number 7. We would say that, based on objective criteria alone, one cannot distinguish between f and g. Should one prefer f to g based on the relative simplicity of the former, we would refer to this as applying a subjective criterion, because the judgment that f is simpler than g can be made before any data were observed, and does not change with additional observations. Putting these criteria together, the choice of the simplest theory that matches the data will be considered a combination of a subjective and an objective criterion.

3.1.3 *Results*

Our model of inductive inference leads to three conclusions:

- There is no reason to view subjective aspects of inductive inference as shortcomings that push us away from a goal of being as objective as possible. Instead, effective induction requires subjectivity. Inductive inference based on objective criteria alone is bound to fail, while incorporating subjective criteria alongside objective ones can lead to successful learning. Indeed, effective learning requires a willingness to sacrifice goodness-of-fit in return for enhanced subjective appeal.
- Not all subjective criteria are created equal—a subjective criterion will necessarily be effective if and only if it discriminates between theories sufficiently finely, in a sense we make precise below. Within this class, however, the content of the subjective criterion is much less important. A wide variety of criteria can lead to effective learning.
- Induction will be effective if goodness-of-fit and subjective considerations are balanced so as to produce some stability in the theories used to predict future observations.

We begin in Section 3.3 with a simple deterministic model that conveys the basic point. Supplementing (objective) likelihood considerations with the consistent application of a subjective ranking of theories dominates relying on objective criteria alone. This result rests on a simple enumeration argument: the subjective reasoner will eliminate incorrect theories until she gets to the correct one, thereafter predicting the environment with precision. In contrast, an agent who seeks only to maximize likelihood may never settle on the correct theory, being ultimately doomed to predict no better than chance.

Section 3.4 extends the results to more realistic settings in which the world about which the agent reasons is random rather than deterministic. Our conclusion that the agent cannot simply rely on goodness-of-fit comparisons is strengthened in this environment. It is an optimal strategy for the agent to regularly reject theories that provide *superior* fits in favor of less successful but subjectively more appealing ones, for much the same reasons that statisticians prefer simpler models and scientists prefer more parsimonious theories in order to avoid the dangers of overfitting their data. To ensure this subjective strategy is successful, however, it must be coupled with a preference for stability. The agent will thus embrace a theory promising enhanced explanatory power only if it is sufficiently subjectively appealing *and* has provided a sufficiently good fit for a sufficiently long time.

Section 3.5 discusses extensions and qualifications of our analysis.

This chapter complements a vast body of literature in statistics and machine learning that deals with statistical learning.[1] In contrast to this literature, we are interested in optimal learning without assuming that there is an underlying probability law from which the learner can sample in an independent-and-identically-distributed manner. Instead, our main concern is the learning of a pattern that has been selected once and for all at the beginning of time. For example, while statistical learning might be concerned with the prediction of the weather on a given day, assuming that it follows an i.i.d. distribution, our main concern would be in determining whether global warming is underway. We are thus interested in a learning problem that is non-trivial even for deterministic processes.

3.2 The Model

We consider a repeated prediction problem. In each period $0, 1, \dots,$ an agent is called upon to predict an observation from the set $\{0, 1\}$. The agent receives a stage payoff of 1 for a correct prediction and 0 for an incorrect one. The agent's objective is to maximize the long-run average of her expected stage payoffs.[2]

The observations are produced by a data generating process, which is a function from histories into current observations. The agent's prediction problem would be trivial if she knew the data generating process. We assume she does not, giving rise to a decision problem under uncertainty, where the states of the world correspond to the possible data generating processes.

The agent makes her prediction with the help of theories. A theory, like the data generating process, is a function from all conceivable histories to predictions. The agent has a history-dependent preference relation over theories. In each period, she uses this preference relation to select a theory, which we

[1] For example, the Vapnik-Chervonenkis (1971) theory, recently applied to decision theory by Al-Najjar (2008), deals with the rate at which one can simultaneously learn the probabilities of multiple events.

[2] An obvious alternative would be to consider the discounted sum of expected payoffs. We can obtain approximate versions of our results under this payoff criterion, provided that the agent is sufficiently patient.

interpret as her preferred explanation for the history she has observed, and which she then uses to make her prediction. This chapter studies the basic problem facing the agent, which is to choose the preference relation over theories that will induce her to make payoff-maximizing predictions.

3.2.1 *Observations*

At the beginning of each period $n \in \{0, 1, \ldots\}$, the agent observes a profile of variables $x_n = (x_n^1, \ldots, x_n^m) \in \{0, 1\}^m \equiv X$. The agent then predicts the value of another variable, $y_n \in \{0, 1\}$, to be revealed at the end of period n. We fix a sequence $\{x_n\}_{n \geq 0}$ and conduct the discussion relative to this sequence, without specifying the process that generated it.[3] Indeed, one could simplify the notation by eliminating the x_n from the model altogether, but we find them helpful for interpretations.

A history of length $n \geq 0$ is a sequence $h_n = \left((x_0, y_0), \ldots, (x_{n-1}, y_{n-1}), x_n\right)$. The set of all histories of length n is denoted by $H_n = (X \times \{0, 1\})^n \times X$. The set of all histories is $H = \cup_{n \geq 0} H_n$, with h denoting an element of H.

3.2.2 *The Data Generating Process*

A *data generating process* is a function $d : H \to [0, 1]$, with $d(h_n)$ being the probability that $y_n = 1$ given history h_n. We let D be the set of possible data generating processes, and hence $D \subset [0, 1]^H$. We will often be interested in problems in which the set of possible data generating processes is a strict subset of $[0, 1]^H$. For example, we will initially consider the set $\{d \in [0, 1]^H \mid d(h) \in \{0, 1\} \ \forall h \in H\} \equiv D_0$ of all deterministic data generating processes.

In the course of our discussion, we will consider several possibilities for the set D. In particular, we will be especially interested in cases in which D is a subset of the set of data generating processes considered possible by the agent, or (equivalently, in our view) that the agent is capable of conceiving or understanding. We do this not because we are convinced the agent can understand anything that might occur in Nature, but because learning will be a hopeless task if the data generating process lies outside the set considered possible by the agent. Since our argument is that objective criteria may not suffice for learning, we focus on a setting in which learning is possible. It is useful for future reference to collect the notation for the various sets of data generating processes in Figure 1.

[3] None of our results depends on the characteristics of this data generating process or on realizations of the data having particular properties. In a more general model, some of these variables might be determined by the agent, who might decide to perform experiments and test various theories. Our focus in this chapter is on learning without experimentation.

D Set of data generating processes ($\subset [0,1]^H$).
D_0 Set of deterministic data generating processes (i.e., with outputs $\{0,1\}$).
D_0^T Set of Turing machines with inputs H and outputs $\{0,1\}$.
D_0^H Set of Turing machines in D_0^T that halt for all $h \in H$.
D_0^B Set of Turing machines in D_0^T with bounded halting time.
D_ε Set of data generating processes with outputs $\{\varepsilon, 1-\varepsilon\}$.

Figure 1. Data Generating Processes. In each case, "Set of Turing machines... " should be read "set of data generating process that can be implemented by a Turing machine..."

3.2.3 *Predictions*

The agent uses theories to make her predictions. A theory is a function $t : H \to [0,1]$, and hence is simply a candidate data generating function. Which theory the agent uses depends on the history she has observed. This history may tell her that some theories are obviously inapplicable, while suggesting that others are relatively likely to generate correct predictions.

The basic characteristic of an agent is a collection of relations $\{\succsim_h \subset D \times D;\ h \in H\} \equiv \succsim$ that captures the link between histories and theories. Having reached period n and observed history h_n, the agent uses $\succsim_{h_n}$ to select a theory t_{h_n} from the set D.[4] The agent then uses the theory t_{h_n} to predict the period-n value y_n given history h_n. If $t_{h_n}(h_n) > 0.5$, the agent predicts $y_n = 1$. She predicts $y_n = 0$ if $t_{h_n}(h_n) < 0.5$, and predicts 0 and 1 with equal probability if $t_{h_n}(h_n) = 0.5$.

We assume that, for every h, $\succsim_h$ is complete and transitive, and that it has maximal elements. We define

$$B_{\succsim_h} = \left\{ t \in D \,|\, t \succsim_h t' \quad \forall t' \in D \right\}$$

to be the set of "best" theories in the eyes of the agent (characterized by $\succsim_h$) faced with history h.

Our interest thus centers on the relation $\succsim$. Which specifications of $\succsim$ will allow the agent to earn high payoffs?

[4] Assuming that the set of data generating processes D is also the set of theories to which the agent appeals when making predictions gives rise to a relatively favorable environment for prediction. It rules out cases in which the agent cannot conceive of some possible data generating processes (e.g. the agent chooses from a subset of D), in which case effective prediction might well be a priori impossible. Since most of our results are obtained for each possible data generating process in D, no loss of generality is implied by assuming that this set is at least as large as the set considered by the agent. Sections 3.5.1 and 3.5.2 examine the implications of allowing the agent's set of possible theories to differ from the set D of possible data generating processes.

3.2.4 *Payoffs*

Given a history h_n, data generating process d and theory t_{h_n}, the probability that the next (period-n) prediction is correct is

$$\pi(d, t_{h_n}, h_n) = d(h_n)\mathbf{1}_{t_{h_n}(h_n)>.5} + \left(1 - d(h_n)\right)\mathbf{1}_{t_{h_n}(h_n)<.5} + \frac{1}{2}\mathbf{1}_{t_{h_n}(h_n)=.5}.$$

Intuitively, given a data generating process d and a set of theory-selection relations $\succsim$, we would like to take the long-term payoff to the agent to be the limit of the average expected value of these payoffs, or

$$\lim_{T\to\infty} \mathcal{E}\left\{\frac{1}{T}\sum_{n=0}^{T-1} \pi(d, t_{h_n}, h_n)\right\}, \tag{1}$$

where the expectation $\mathcal{E}$ captures the randomness over the histories generated by d and the randomness in selecting theories under $\succsim$. However, this limit need not exist. Let $\Lambda : [0, 1]^\infty \to [0, 1]$ be a Banach limit defined on the set of infinite sequence of numbers in $[0, 1]$. Then we let the agent's payoff $\Pi(d, \succsim)$, when facing data generating process d and using relation $\succsim$ to choose theories, be given by the Banach limit of the resulting sequence of expected values from (1). The key property of Banach limits we need is that

$$\liminf_{T\to\infty} \mathcal{E}\left\{\frac{1}{T}\sum_{n=0}^{T-1} \pi(d, t_{h_n}, h_n)\right\} \leq \Pi(d, \succsim) \leq \limsup_{T\to\infty} \mathcal{E}\left\{\frac{1}{T}\sum_{n=0}^{T-1} \pi(d, t_{h_n}, h_n)\right\},$$

and any payoff criterion with this property would suffice for our results.

3.2.5 *The Likelihood Relation*

The most common objective criterion for theory selection is the *likelihood relation*, ranking theories according to their fit to the data.[5] Formally, define the likelihood of theory t given history h_n,

$$L(t, h_n) = \Pi_{j=0}^{n-1}[t(h_j)y_j + (1 - t(h_j))(1 - y_j)].$$

Then the likelihood relation $\succsim^L$ ranks theories after any history h by their likelihood:

$$\forall h \in H, \quad t \succsim^L_h t' \quad \Longleftrightarrow \quad L(t, h) \geq L(t', h).$$

[5] We focus throughout on the likelihood relation, but analogous results and proofs hold for any objective relation. In particular, no matter what objective relation is used to cull theories, a sufficiently rich set of data generating processes will include some survivors predicting a 0 as the next observation and other survivors predicting a 1. At this point, the objective relation will have exhausted its implications, dooming the agent to random choice.

The likelihood relation thus calls for agents to base their inferences on their data, and on no other criterion.

In the simplest case, when only deterministic theories are considered, $\succsim_h^L$ boils down to two equivalence classes. All theories that perfectly fit the data are equivalent, having $L(t, h) = 1$, and they are all preferred to all theories that have been refuted by the data, where the latter are also equivalent to each other and satisfy $L(t, h) = 0$.

3.3 Deterministic Data Processes: Subjectivity in Inductive Inference

This section uses an elementary deterministic model to show how subjective criteria can be useful in inductive inference. The key restriction in the model is contained in the following assumption, which puts some structure on the data generating processes. Its first two parts require the set of data generating processes be simple enough to be learned, and the final part requires it be rich enough to describe any possible finite sequence of observations. The latter is intended to rule out trivial cases in which a finite set of observations suffices to single out a unique theory, i.e., cases where the problem of induction does not arise.

Assumption 3.1

[3.1.1] $D \subset D_0$, *the set of deterministic data generating processes.*

[3.1.2] D *is countable.*

[3.1.3] *For every history* $h \in H$ *there exists* $d \in D$ *such that* $L(d, h) = 1$.

Given Assumption 3.1.1, the remaining requirements are satisfied if (for example) D is the set D_0^H of all Turing machines generating functions $d \in D_0$ (i.e. D_0^H is the set of Turing machines that accept elements of the set H as inputs, halt, and produce outputs from the set $\{0, 1\}$). The countability restriction will be discussed and relaxed in Section 3.5.1 below.

3.3.1 *Applying the Likelihood Relation*

We now consider the performance of an agent who consistently applies the likelihood relation $\succsim^L$ as a guide to making predictions, but applies no other criteria.

First, note that the agent's choice of theory when using an arbitrary relation $\succsim$ and following history h is unambiguous if $B_{\succsim_h}$ is a singleton, but this may often fail to be the case. What does the agent do if there are a number of theories in $B_{\succsim_h}$? We assume that the agent treats the various best theories symmetrically, in the sense that she makes a choice that wherever possible exhibits no bias for theories that predict 0 versus theories that predict 1 in the next observation.

To make this assumption precise, notice that if D is the set D_0^T (of all Turing machines generating functions $d \in D_0$) or D_0^H (of all Turing machines that do so and halt), then for any history of observations h, and for every data generating process d in D consistent with h, there is another data generating process in D that is also consistent with h but whose subsequent datum will be precisely the opposite of d, generating a 0 whenever d produces a 1 and vice versa. As a result, the sets $\left\{t \in B_{\succsim_h} \mid t(h) = 0\right\}$ and $\left\{t \in B_{\succsim_h} \mid t(h) = 1\right\}$ will not only be non-empty but will be symmetric in their treatment of the next observation. The obvious implementation of our unbiased-choice provision is then:[6]

Assumption 3.2 *The agent chooses a theory from $B_{\succsim_h}$ according to a measure $\mu_{B_{\succsim_h}}$ on $B_{\succsim_h}$ satisfying*

$$\mu_{B_{\succsim_h}}\left(\left\{t \in B_{\succsim_h} \mid t(h) < 0.5\right\}\right) = \mu_{B_{\succsim_h}}\left(\left\{t \in B_{\succsim_h} \mid t(h) > 0.5\right\}\right)$$

whenever

$$\left\{t \in B_{\succsim_h} \mid t(h) < 0.5\right\}, \left\{t \in B_{\succsim_h} \mid t(h) > 0.5\right\} \neq \varnothing.$$

We then have:

Proposition 3.1 *Let Assumptions 3.1 and 3.2 hold. Then $\Pi(d, \succsim^L) = \frac{1}{2}$.*

The proof, contained in Section 3.6, is built on the following observations. There are always many theories consistent with whatever data the agent has observed. In particular, after every history, the set of unfalsified theories available to the agent contains theories that predict a 0 as well as theories that predict a 1, and leave the agent with no means of choosing between the two sets of theories. The agent's choice is thus random, ensuring a long-run payoff of 1/2. Without some means of eliminating theories, the agent can thus never predict better than chance. Unfortunately, the data alone provide no possibilities for such elimination.

[6] A less demanding version of Assumption 3.2 would assume only that $\mu_{B_{\succsim_h}}\left(\left\{t \in B_{\succsim_h} \mid t(h) < 0.5\right\}\right)$ and $\mu_{B_{\succsim_h}}\left(\left\{t \in B_{\succsim_h} \mid t(h) > 0.5\right\}\right)$ are both positive when both sets are nonempty. Assumption 3.2 is used in Propositions 3.1, 3.4, 3.5, and 3.9. In each case, the role of Assumption 3.2 is to place a bound on the performance of the likelihood relation. The virtue of Assumption 3.2 is that it makes this bound particularly simple to state and establish. We could establish analogous but more cumbersome results with the weaker version. The likelihood ratio might then generate a payoff larger than 1/2 for some data generating processes, but only at the cost of generating smaller payoffs for other data generating processes, and the subjective relation would continue to dominate the likelihood relation.

3.3.2 *The Subjective Relation*

We now consider an agent who brings subjective criteria to bear in choosing between theories. To define such a theory-selection procedure, we begin with a subjective order $\succcurlyeq^S \subset D \times D$.[7] Observe that it is defined a priori, independently of history. We require $\succcurlyeq^S$ to be complete and transitive. In addition, we say that $\succcurlyeq^S$ is a *discriminating* subjective order if

$$\#\left\{t' \in D \mid t' \succcurlyeq^S t\right\} < \infty \qquad \forall t \in D. \tag{2}$$

Condition (2) has two important implications. Most obviously, it ensures that the subjective order's indifference classes are not too large. The problem with the likelihood relation is that it leaves the agent with too many indifferences, in the sense that the agent will be stuck choosing among too many theories that fit the data. The subjective order will help select between such indifferent theories, but will be effective only if it does a good enough job of breaking indifferences. In the absence of condition (2), for example, the definition of a subjective order would be consistent with the trivial order $\succcurlyeq^S = D \times D$, according to which no theory is ranked ahead of another, giving the agent absolutely no help in choosing between theories. More generally, (2) rules out cases in which the subjective order is permissive enough to allow for infinitely many strategies to be grouped in a single indifference class. However, (2) does much more than simply limit indifference classes, as we make clear in Section 3.3.3.

One natural way to ensure that (2) holds is to enumerate D and set $t_i \succ^S t_{i+1}$ for every $i \geq 1$. Our condition is less demanding, and allows for non-singleton equivalence classes of the order $\sim^S$, but not for infinite ones. Nonetheless, under the assumption that D is countable, discriminating subjective orders are closely related to enumerations of D. Specifically, for every discriminating order $\succcurlyeq^S$ there exists an enumeration $D = \{t_1, t_2, \ldots\}$ such that $t_i \succcurlyeq^S t_{i+1}$, with strict preference $\succ^S$ occurring for infinitely many i's. Alternatively, $\succcurlyeq^S$ is a discriminating subjective order if and only if it can be represented by a function $C : D \to \mathbb{N}$ such that[8]

$$t \succcurlyeq^S t' \quad \Longleftrightarrow \quad C(t) \leq C(t') \tag{3}$$

[7] In an effort to keep things straight, we use $\succsim$ to denote a relation by which the agent chooses theories, and $\succcurlyeq$ to denote a subjective order over theories. We similarly associate the label "relation" with the former and "order" with the latter (though they have the same properties, i.e. each is complete and transitive).

[8] While there are obviously many different enumerations of D, and hence many functions C with their induced orders $\succcurlyeq^S$, they cannot be too different in the following sense. Let C_1 and C_2 be two such functions. Then, for every k there exists $l = l(k)$ such that $C_1(t) > l$ implies $C_2(t) > k$. That is, a theory that has a sufficiently high index according to C_1 will also have a high index according to C_2.

and

$$|C^{-1}(k)| < \infty \qquad \forall k \in \mathbb{N}. \tag{4}$$

Given a subjective order $\succcurlyeq^S$, we define the associated subjective relation $\succsim^{LS}$ for choosing theories as follows:

$$\forall h \in H, \quad t \succsim_h^{LS} t' \iff \begin{cases} \{t \succ_h^L t'\} \\ or\ \{t \sim_h^L t' \ and \ t \succcurlyeq^S t'\} \end{cases}. \tag{5}$$

The relation $\succsim^{LS}$ thus uses the subjective order $\succcurlyeq^S$ to choose among those theories with the highest likelihood. The likelihood and subjective relations $\succsim^L$ and $\succsim^{LS}$ agree in that they only choose theories with maximal likelihoods, with the likelihood relation being indifferent over such theories and the subjective relation providing the criterion for making this choice.

A discriminating subjective order may still frequently render the agent indifferent over many theories. The following result does not depend upon how these indifferences are broken, and hence requires no counterpart of Assumption 3.2.

Proposition 3.2 *Let Assumption 3.1 hold. For every discriminating subjective order $\succcurlyeq^S$ and every $d \in D$, $\Pi(d, \succsim^{LS}) = 1$. Hence, for a discriminating subjective order $\succcurlyeq^S$, the induced subjective relation $\succsim^{LS}$ strictly dominates the likelihood relation $\succsim^L$.*

The agent begins the prediction process with no data, and accordingly chooses from the first indifference class in her subjective order. This indifference class may not be a singleton, and she may shift among the theories in the class as data accumulate, even if none are falsified. However, the only event that will push her outside this indifference class is for each of its elements to be falsified by the data. Moreover, this first indifference class is finite. If it contains the actual data generating process, the agent will never be pushed out of this class, and will eventually be limited to a collection of theories that are observationally equivalent to the data generating process, ensuring correct predictions. Alternatively, if this indifference class contains neither the actual data generating process nor any observationally equivalent process, the agent will eventually be pushed into her second indifference class. Here, we can repeat the same reasoning, continuing until the agent settles on a theory that makes correct predictions.

3.3.3 *Which Subjective Relations Work?*

EXPLOITATION AND EXPLORATION

What makes the subjective relation work, and what stymies the likelihood relation? The subjective relation allows effective prediction because it embodies the principles of "exploitation and exploration". The agent exploits theories that have worked by sticking with them, while effectively exploring new theories when necessary. The persistent appeal to the agents' subjective order, whatever the order might be, ensures that a theory that fits the data is not abandoned, while the enumeration provided by the order ensures that the agent will "try out" all theories (as long as a perfect fit has not been found). The likelihood relation's lack of the first characteristic dooms its adherents to randomness.

TWO EXAMPLES

The assumption that the subjective order is discriminating plays a role in ensuring both exploration and exploitation. We illustrate with two examples.

Example 1: Consider a subjective order that ranks any theory predicting an initial 0 in a single indifference class that comes ahead of all others, and then enumerates the remaining theories and (strictly) ranks them accordingly. Suppose the actual data generating process produces a 0 in the first period. Then the agent will never be pushed beyond her first indifference class. In addition, the subjective relation provides no guidance as to how the agent should choose from this topmost indifference class, leaving the agent in the same random-choice predicament as does the likelihood relation. In this case, the subjective order does not ensure adequate exploitation. The most obvious purpose of (2), noted just after its introduction, is to preclude such cases. ∎

Example 2: Suppose the subjective order is based on a lexicographic accounting of 1s. Theory t is ranked ahead of t' if t predicts a 1 in the first period and t' a 0. If they make the same first-period prediction, then t is ranked ahead of t' if t predicts a 1 in the second period and t' a 0. If they make the same predictions in the first two periods, then t is ranked ahead of t' if t predicts a 1 in the third period and t' a 0, and so on. No two theories are indifferent under this order, so that exploiting a theory corresponding to the actual data generating process, once one has reached it, is assured. Suppose, however, the data generating process produces a perpetual string of 0s. The theory corresponding to this outcome ranks below every other possible theory. The agent will never reach this theory, and indeed will predict a 1 in every period, earning a payoff of 0 that makes random choice look inspired. In this case, it is exploration that is lacking. The second key aspect of (2) is to preclude such possibilities. For every possible theory, there are only finitely many preferred theories under $\succsim^S$, ensuring that exploration guided by $\succsim^S$ will eventually hit upon the data generating process (or something observationally equivalent), at which point this theory will be effectively exploited. ■

AN INERTIAL LIKELIHOOD RELATION

Suppose we build more effective exploitation into the likelihood relation by assuming that agents do not abandon a theory until receiving evidence of its falsity. In particular, the proof of Proposition 3.1 shows that an agent guided by the likelihood relation falters because every period there is a multitude of theories with perfect likelihood scores, including the truth and a host of imposters. The agent's arbitrary choice from this set implies that even if she hits upon the truth, she soon abandons it in favor of another seemingly equivalent theory. Will it not suffice to assume that the agent sticks to something that has worked in the past?

The phenomenon of inertia, or a preference for a status quo, is familiar from casual observations as well as from psychological studies. Kuhn (1996) argued that scientists tend to cling to old theories rather than adopt those theories that fit the data best. More recently, we see traces of inertia in the status-quo preference used in behavioral economics. Indeed, we might think of inertia as another subjective consideration used to supplement the likelihood relation.

To see if inertia suffices for effective learning, we define the *inertial* relation as that selecting the theory chosen in the previous period if the latter maximizes the likelihood function, and otherwise choosing as does the likelihood relation. Formally, define $\succsim^{LI}$ as follows for all $n > 1$,

$$\forall h \in H, \qquad t \succsim_h^{LI} t' \iff \begin{cases} \{L(t,h) > L(t',h)\} \\ or \;\; \{L(t,h) = L(t',h) \;\; and \;\; t = t_{n-1}\} \\ or \;\; \{L(t,h) = L(t',h) \;\; and \;\; t, t' \neq t_{n-1}\} \end{cases},$$

with $t \sim_{h_0}^{LI} t'$ for all t, t', so that in the absence of any evidence, all theories are equally likely.

The following example shows that inertia alone does not suffice to ensure effective learning.

Example 3: Let D consist of the following set of deterministic theories:

$$D = \left\{ y \in \{0,1\}^{\mathbb{N}} \mid \exists n \geq 0, \;\; y(k) = 0 \; \forall k \geq n \right\}.$$

The possible data generating processes are thus all those that generate only 0 from some point on. For example, the theories may be describing the availability of a random resource, which is known to be depletable, but whose date of ultimate exhaustion is uncertain.

The agent chooses theories from a subset of D. Given history h_n, let $\{t^{h_n,n+k}\}_{k=0}^{\infty}$ be a collection of theories, with the theory $t^{h_n,n+k}$ given by

$$t^{h_n,n+k}(h_n h_l) = \begin{cases} 1 \text{ if } l = k \\ 0 \text{ otherwise.} \end{cases} \tag{6}$$

Theory $t^{h_n,n+k}$ thus predicts that history h_n will be followed by k periods in which 0 is observed, followed by a 1, and then followed by 0 forever.

Having observed history h_n, the agent's selection rule over theories is given by

$$\mu_{B_{\succsim^{LI}_{h_n}}}\left(t^{h_n,n+k}\right) = \frac{1}{2^{k+1}} \qquad k = 0, \ldots. \tag{7}$$

Hence, given any history h_n, the agent attaches positive probability only to continuations that feature a single observation of 1 (and otherwise all 0's), with probability $1/2^{k+1}$ attached to the theory that generates its observation of a 1 in period $n+k$. Under this selection rule, theories predicting a 0 on the next step are equally likely as theories predicting a 1, in accordance with (3.2).

Suppose the data generating process is such that $y_n = 0$ for all n, and consider $\succsim^{LI}_{h_n}$ for a history h_n consisting of n 0s. Given (6)–(7), $\succsim^{LI}_{h_n}$ will choose a theory that predicts a sequence of 0s, until being falsified when the theory predicts its lone 1. The probability that the agent chooses a theory lasting k periods before being falsified is $1/2^{k+1}$. Upon having a theory falsified, the agent must choose a new theory, putting the agent in a position identical to that of the initial period and giving payoff equal to the agent's initial payoff. The agent's payoff is thus given by $\Pi(y_0, \succsim^{LI}) = \frac{1}{2}$.[9] ■

The difficulty in this example is that the selection rule over the various sets $B_{\succsim^{LI}_{h_n}}$ invariably ignores the correct theory. Exploitation is assured, but exploration is not. Proposition (3.3) shows that inertia can be valuable, in effect serving as a safeguard against the excessive fickleness of random choice, if we also take steps to ensure effective exploration.

[9] To calculate this payoff, let v_k^t be the expected average payoff in the next $t \geq 1$ periods, given that the predictor's current theory has been correct in the last $k \geq 0$ periods (but not in the $(k+1)$-st if there was one). Then

$$\begin{aligned} v_k^t &= \frac{1}{2}\left(\frac{1}{t}\cdot 0 + \frac{t-1}{t}v_0^{t-1}\right) + \frac{1}{2}\left(\frac{1}{t}1 + \frac{t-1}{t}v_{k+1}^{t-1}\right) \\ &= \frac{1}{t}\cdot\frac{1}{2} + \frac{t-1}{t}\cdot\left(\frac{1}{2}v_0^{t-1} + \frac{1}{2}v_{k+1}^{t-1}\right) \end{aligned}$$

but we also have $v_k^1 = \frac{1}{2}$ for all k and hence $v_k^t = \frac{1}{2}$ for all k, t, hence

$$\Pi(y_0, \succsim^{LI}) = \lim_{t\to\infty} v_0^t = \frac{1}{2}.$$

Assumption 3.3 *There exists a strictly positive measure λ on the countable set D such that for any $h \in H$, $\mu_{B_{\succsim_h}}$ equals λ conditioned on $B_{\succsim_h}$.*

Under Assumption 3.3, the agent choosing a theory attaches positive probability to every unfalsified theory in D. This ensures that the agent cannot assuredly avoid selecting the data generating process, as in Example 3.

Proposition 3.3 *Under Assumptions 3.1 and 3.3, for all $d \in D$, $\Pi(d, \succsim_h^{LI}) = 1$.*

Behind this result lies the observation that, under Assumption 3.3, the theory selection process is guaranteed to select the correct theory, d, at least once. Once d has been chosen, inertia ensures that it will not be abandoned, and hence the optimal payoff is obtained.

Observe that, in terms of our definitions, the inertial likelihood relation $\succsim^{LI}$ is not purely objective. Specifically, assume that one is given the conditional probabilities of each possible observation given each theory, for every prefix of a history h. This information does not suffice to determine the selection of the relation $\succsim^{LI}$: this relation gives priority to the theory that has been chosen in the past, and this past selection is not deterministically implied by the data. Thus, we regard Proposition 3.3 as consistent with the message of this chapter. Under Assumption 3.3, $\succsim^{LI}$ leads to effective learning, but the inertial tendency is a subjective consideration.

BAYESIAN

If the set of conceivable data generating processes is countable (cf. Assumption 3.1) and the agent has a strictly positive Bayesian prior over this set, then the relation "has at least as high a prior as" can be viewed as a subjective order—it is a weak order that is monotonically decreasing along an enumeration of the theories, with finite equivalence classes. In other words, a Bayesian prior defines a subjective order. Conversely, one may use a subjective relation to define a Bayesian prior: theories ranked higher under the subjective order are considered more likely.

There is a continuum of priors that are consistent with a given subjective order. These priors are all equivalent in our model, because we suggest that the agent choose a most-likely theory to generate the next prediction. By contrast, the Bayesian approach constructs an expected prediction, using all possible theories. Either formulation gives a limiting payoff of 1.

3.4 Random Data Generating Processes: Likelihood Tradeoffs

The assumption that the data generating process is deterministic (i.e. that $d(h) \in \{0, 1\}$ for all h) is unrealistic. Worse still, it beclouds the interesting trade-off between likelihood and subjective considerations in the choice of theories. So far, the choice of theories was made among the theories that fit the data perfectly, and thus subjective idiosyncracies involved no cost. But when random data generating processes are introduced, subjective considerations are no longer a free good, but impose a price in terms of likelihood. Should the agent be willing to give up a better fit for a subjectively more appealing theory, and if so, to what extent?

3.4.1 *Uniform Errors*

To get some insight into this problem, we begin with a minimal modification of our benchmark model. Define, for $\varepsilon \in (0, 1/2)$,

$$D_\varepsilon = \{d \in [0,1]^H \,|\, d(h) \in \{\varepsilon, 1-\varepsilon\} \; \forall h \in H\}.$$

Thus, D_ε can be thought of as the deterministic data generating processes, D_0, with an error probability of ε added to the output.

The likelihood function, for a theory $t \in D_\varepsilon$ and a history $h \in H_n$, is

$$L(t, h_n) = \Pi_{j=0}^{n-1}(t(h_j)y_j + (1 - t(h_j))(1 - y_j)).$$

In the presence of randomness, the likelihood function will inevitably converge to zero for any theory: its largest possible value in period n is $(1-\varepsilon)^n$, since the best any theory can do is attach probability $1-\varepsilon$ in each period to the outcome that happened to be realized in that period. This convergence makes the likelihood an awkward standard for comparing theories. It is more convenient to consider the average of the logarithm of the likelihood function,

$$\begin{aligned} l(t, h_n) &= \frac{1}{n}\log(L(t, h_n)) \\ &= \frac{1}{n}\sum_{j=0}^{n-1}\log\left[t(h_j)y_j + (1 - t(h_j))(1 - y_j)\right], \end{aligned} \tag{8}$$

which does not converge to zero. We hereafter use "likelihood" to denote the average log likelihood, given by (8).

Let us say that a theory is "correct" in period t if it predicts a 1 with probability $1-\varepsilon$ and a 1 occurs, or if it predicts a 0 with probability $1-\varepsilon$ and a 0 occurs. It is helpful to define the function

$$\theta(p) = p\log(1-\varepsilon) + (1-p)\log\varepsilon.$$

Then $\theta(p)$ is the (average log) likelihood of a theory that has been correct proportion p of the time.

$\log(1-\varepsilon)$	$=$	$\theta(1)$	Maximum possible limiting value.
$(1-\varepsilon)\log(1-\varepsilon)+\varepsilon\log\varepsilon$	$=$	$\theta(1-\varepsilon)$	Value achieved by the data generating process.
$\frac{1}{2}\log(1-\varepsilon)+\frac{1}{2}\log\varepsilon$	$=$	$\theta(\frac{1}{2})$	Value achieved by random choice.

Figure 2. Key values of the limiting average-log-likelihood function (8).

A theory that is correct in every period would give likelihood $\theta(1)$. This is the highest possible likelihood. The theory that corresponds to the data generating process gives a limiting likelihood of $\theta(1-\varepsilon)$, and an agent who always uses the data generating process to predict would achieve payoff $1-\varepsilon$.[10] Predicting randomly would give likelihood $\theta\left(\frac{1}{2}\right)$ and payoff $\frac{1}{2}$. Figure 2 summarizes these observations.

The counterpart of Assumption 3.1 is now:

Assumption 3.4

[3.4.1] $D \subset D_\varepsilon$.

[3.4.2] *D is countable.*

[3.4.3] *For every history $h \in H$ there exists $d \in D$ such that $l(d,h) = \theta(1)$.*

Assumption 3.4.3 indicates that for any finite stream of data, there is a theory that would have been correct in every period. Ex post, one can rationalize anything.

3.4.2 *Tolerance in Learning*

The agent could once again adopt a relation over theories that first restricts attention to likelihood-maximizing theories, such as the likelihood relation $\succsim^L$ of Section 3.2.5 or the subjective relation $\succsim^{LS}$ of Section 3.3.2. In the random environment, this ensures that the agent will eventually *exclude* the data generating process as a possible theory. In each period, the realization may differ from the true theory's prediction with probability ε. Hence, the true theory will eventually almost surely have a likelihood value lower than $\theta(1)$, whereas there will always be other theories with a likelihood value of $\theta(1)$. That is, insisting on maximum-likelihood theories will lead to constant theory hopping.

This suggests that the agent's learning might be more effective if it incorporates some tolerance for inaccuracy. For any $\gamma \in [0,1]$, we say that a theory t is a "γ-best fit" to the data after history h if

$$l(t,h) \geq \theta(\gamma).$$

[10] For large n, the likelihood will be approximately$(1-\varepsilon)^{(1-\varepsilon)n}\varepsilon^{\varepsilon n}$ and the average log likelihood $l(d,h)$ will converge to $\theta(1-\varepsilon)$.

The counterpart of the likelihood relation is then

$$\forall h \in H, \quad t \succsim_h^{L,\gamma} t' \quad \Longleftrightarrow \quad L^\gamma(t,h) \geq L^\gamma(t',h)$$

where

$$L^\gamma(t,h) = \min\{L(t,h), \theta(\gamma)\}.$$

When working with D_0, the likelihood relation $\succsim^L$ separated theories into two classes, those that predicted perfectly and those that did not. The key characteristic of the relation $\succsim_h^{L,\gamma}$ is that it allows us to group the theories achieving a likelihood of at least $\theta(\gamma)$ into a single equivalence class.

What would be a good value of γ? One suspects that we should set $\gamma < 1 - \varepsilon$, since any value $\gamma > 1 - \varepsilon$ will eventually surely exclude the true data generating process. However, simply relaxing the likelihood threshold to $\gamma < 1 - \varepsilon$ does not suffice if one insists on using the likelihood criterion alone to choose theories. The true theory will not be ruled out, but there is no guarantee that it be selected. An argument analogous to that establishing Proposition 3.1 immediately provides the (omitted) proof of:

Proposition 3.4 *Let Assumptions 3.2 and 3.4 hold. Then* $\Pi(d, \succsim^{L,\gamma}) = \frac{1}{2}$.

Intuitively, whatever the value of γ, the agent has a wealth of theories with likelihoods exceeding $\theta(\gamma)$ from which to choose. In the absence of another selection criterion, the agent is doomed to random prediction.

Once the agent is willing to pay the price of less than maximum likelihood, she can afford to use an additional subjective criterion in a meaningful way. Define

$$\forall h \in H, \quad t \succsim_h^{LS,\gamma} t' \Longleftrightarrow \begin{cases} \{t \succ_h^{L,\gamma} t'\} \\ or\ \{t \sim_h^{L,\gamma} t' \ and \ t \succsim^S t'\} \end{cases}.$$

The agent thus uses the subjective order to choose among the γ-best fits.

Under the subjective relation, setting $\gamma > 1 - \varepsilon$ again implies that the agent will discard the data generating process as a possible theory and subsequently hop between imposters. The implications of this switching between strategies are now not completely obvious. The agent uses here subjective criteria to choose among the γ-best-fit theories. While the correct theory is not among them, it is not clear how well their predictions are correlated with the true data generating process. The following assumption ensures that the top-rated theories in the subjective order are rich enough to contain theories that predict 0 and theories that predict 1.

Assumption 3.5 *For a subjective order $\succsim^{LS,\gamma}$ with $\gamma > 1 - \varepsilon$ and sufficiently large n,* $\left\{t \in B_{\succsim_h^{LS,\gamma}} \mid t(h) = 1 - \varepsilon\right\}$ *and* $\left\{t \in B_{\succsim_h^{LS,\gamma}} \mid t(h_n) = \varepsilon\right\}$ *are nonempty.*

It is not obvious that the subjective relation should have this property. If, for example, we observe the pattern 00000, it may not be that one of the theories ranked highest by the subjective order will predict 1. However, when n is large, the actual data generating process has surely been discarded by the order $\succsim_h^{LS,\gamma}$ and any theory amassing a likelihood above γ is surely a fluke. As a result, it is not clear what a priori information, if any, should be brought to bear, in which case Assumption 3.5 may be reasonable. The (omitted) proof of the following is then immediate:

Proposition 3.5 *Let Assumptions 3.2, 3.4.1–3.4.2 and 3.5 hold. Let $\gamma > 1 - \varepsilon$. Then $\Pi(d, \succsim^{LS,\gamma}) = \frac{1}{2}$.*

The key point is that setting $\gamma > 1 - \varepsilon$ forces the agent to abandon any theory that sufficiently often predicts as does the true theory, in the process placing constraints on the payoff of which the agent can be assured. Assumption 3.5 makes these constraints precise, dooming the agent to random choice.

3.4.3 *Stability in Learning*

One virtue of a subjective order in a deterministic environment is that it prevents the agent from abandoning perfectly good theories. Setting $\gamma < 1 - \varepsilon$ ensures that the data generating process will at least eventually be among the γ-best fits considered by the agent. This alone, however, does not ensure effective learning. Selecting the subjectively best of the γ-best fits leaves open the possibility that the agent may switch back and forth between theories, where, at each period, one of the theories provides a γ-best fit, but fails to predict correctly. This is possible if the subjective order selects theories that tend to be wrong precisely when they are used for prediction, but "catch up" in terms of the likelihood during periods in which they are not used for prediction. To see that this learner's nightmare might come true, consider the following.

Example 4 Fix $\gamma < (1 - \varepsilon)$ and let d be the data generating process. To simplify the presentation, but without losing any generality, assume that d predicts 1 in each period (with probability $1 - \varepsilon$).

We construct k theories, denoted by $t_1, \ldots, t_k$, which will be ranked at the top of the subjective order: $t_1 \succ^S t_2 \succ^S \ldots \succ^S t_k$ and $t_k \succ^S t'$ for all $t' \notin \{t_1, \ldots, t_k\}$. The essential feature of these theories is that any theory whose likelihood falls short of γ predicts 1 (thereby improving its likelihood). If some theories exhibit a likelihood above γ, the one that ranks highest (under $\succ^S$) predicts 0, and the others predict 1.[11]

In each period, at least $k-1$ of the theories $(t_1, \ldots, t_k)$ will produce a prediction matching that of d, and—if and only if some reach the appropriate likelihood threshold—one of these theories will dissent. Let ε_n be the proportion of realized 0's up to time n. The collective number of correct predictions among the k theories $(t_1, \ldots, t_k)$ in history h_n will thus be at least

$$[(1-\varepsilon_n)(k-1)]n,$$

where ε_n gets arbitrarily close to ε with arbitrarily large probability as n gets large. Hence, a lower bound on the number of correct predictions, among the k theories $(t_1, \ldots, t_k)$ over periods $0, \ldots, n-1$ is given by

$$[(1-\varepsilon-\delta)(k-1)]n$$

for some $\delta > 0$. We can choose n^* sufficiently large that

$$\delta < \frac{(1-\varepsilon)-\gamma}{2}$$

and then k sufficiently large that, for all $n > n^*$,

$$\left[\left(1-\varepsilon-\frac{(1-\varepsilon)-\gamma}{2}\right)(k-1)\right]n > k\gamma n, \tag{9}$$

or

$$\frac{k-1}{k}\left(\frac{1-\varepsilon+\gamma}{2}\right) > \gamma.$$

(Since $1-\varepsilon > \gamma$, such a k exists.) From (9), we see that the theories $(t_1, \ldots, t_k)$ must have collectively amassed at least $k\gamma n$ correct predictions for any $n > n^*$, ensuring that at least one of them must have at least γn correct predictions, and hence a likelihood of at least $\theta(\gamma)$. As a result, one of these theories will be used for prediction in every period $n > n^*$, and by definition predicts that

[11] We can formally describe the theories by an algorithm. For $n = 0$, $t_i(h_0) = 1$ for all $i \le k$. For $n > 0$, given history h_n, every t_i $(i \le k)$ computes the predictions of all t_j $(j \le k,\ j = i$ included) for all sub-histories h_m of h_n (for all $m < n$). By induction, this is a computable task. Next, each t_i computes $l(t_j, h_n)$ for all $j \le k$. If none of them has a likelihood $l(t_j, h_n) \ge \gamma$, t_i predicts 1. Otherwise, t_i finds the best (under $\succ^S$) of the theories in $\{t_1, \ldots, t_k\}$ with $l(t_j, h_n) \ge \gamma$. If it is itself, it predicts 0; otherwise, it predicts 1. Observe that each theory $\{t_1, \ldots, t_k\}$ basically performs the same algorithm, which simulates the calculations of all previous periods, and halts by induction. The difference between the predictions of the different theories in $\{t_1, \ldots, t_k\}$ arises only out of the very last step of the algorithm, in case some of them obtain a likelihood value above the threshold.

outcome which appears with probability ε under the data generating process d. Hence, the agent's payoff converges to ε. ■

It is not important for this example that the theories $(t_1, \ldots, t_k)$ occupy the top k places in the subjective order $\succ^S$. We need only that other theories ranked ahead of any of $(t_1, \ldots, t_k)$ be sufficiently different from d as to have likelihoods that eventually fall (and remain) below those of $(t_1, \ldots, t_k)$.

The key to addressing this difficulty is to rely on theories that have been *consistently* successful at explaining the data, rather than theories that boast a great likelihood only at the present moment. Formally, let there be given $\gamma \leq 1 - \varepsilon$ and $k \geq 1$. For a theory t and history $h \in H_n$, $n \geq k$, define

$$\Gamma_{\gamma,k}(t) = \sum_{j=k}^{n} \delta_j,$$

where

$$\delta_j = \begin{cases} 1 \ \mathit{if} \ \ l\big(t, h_j\big) \geq \theta(\gamma) \\ 0 \ \mathit{if} \ \ l(t, h_j) < \theta(\gamma) \end{cases}$$

(where h_j is the j-th prefix of h). Next, define the relations $\succsim_h^{LS,\gamma k}$ for $h \in H$ as follows:

$$t \succsim_h^{LS,\gamma k} t' \iff \begin{cases} \quad [\Gamma_{\gamma,k}(t) > \Gamma_{\gamma,k}(t')] \\ \mathit{or}\ [\Gamma_{\gamma,k}(t) = \Gamma_{\gamma,k}(t') \quad \mathit{and} \quad t \succsim^S t']. \end{cases}$$

Thus, a maximizer of $\succsim_h^{LS,\gamma k}$ has to be a theory that has obtained an average log-likelihood of at least $\theta(\gamma)$ as often as possible over the past consecutive $n - k + 1$ periods. In particular, if there are several theories that obtained this likelihood threshold in each of the past $n - k + 1$ periods, the maximizer has to be one that is ranked topmost by the subjective order. If no theory has done as well as $\theta(\gamma)$ for $n - k + 1$ periods (perhaps because $k > n$), $\succsim_h^{LS,\gamma k}$ selects the subjectively-best-ranked among those that have achieved at least $\theta(\gamma)$ for at least $(n - k)$ periods out of the past $(n - k + 1)$ periods. If no theory has done as well as $\theta(\gamma)$ for $n - k$ out of the past $n - k + 1$ periods, $\succsim_h^{LS,\gamma k}$ selects the subjectively-best-ranked among those that have achieved at least $\theta(\gamma)$ for at least $(n - k - 1)$ periods out of the past $(n - k + 1)$ periods, and so forth.

Clearly, the choice of the parameters γ and k allows a wide range of relations $\left(\succsim_h^{LS,\gamma k}\right)$. What should be the values of γ and k and how are they determined?[12] In particular, different values of ε will call for different values of γ and k.

[12] Notice that it makes no sense to insist on stability if one sets $\gamma > 1 - \varepsilon$, since we know that no theory can long sustain a likelihood above $1 - \varepsilon$.

3.4.4 *Optimal Tolerance*

Suppose first that γ and k are selected a priori, either as a deliberate choice on the part of the agent or as the result of an evolutionary process that favors effective values of the tolerance for accuracy γ and the taste for stability k, at the expense of ineffective values. How much inaccuracy should the reasoner be willing to tolerate? The critical value $1-\varepsilon$ builds sufficient tolerance for inaccuracy into the agent's choices as to ensure effective learning:

Proposition 3.6 *Under Assumption 3.4, for every discriminating subjective order* $\succcurlyeq^S$ *and for every* $d \in D$, $\Pi(d, \succsim^{LS,\gamma k}) \to (1-\varepsilon)$ *as* $\gamma \nearrow 1-\varepsilon$ *and* $k \to \infty$.

We thus find that, in the presence of randomness, augmenting the subjective order with a preference for stability again enhances the agent's payoff. The argument is quite similar to that of Proposition 3.2. There are only finitely many theories ranked ahead of the true data generating process d under the discriminating subjective relation. Setting $\gamma < 1-\varepsilon$ ensures that likelihood considerations do not exclude d, while pushing γ quite close to $1-\varepsilon$ ensures that theories whose predictions are quite close to those of d but nonetheless different are eventually excluded. Finally, as k becomes large, the chances that one of the theories ranked ahead of d by the subjective order can have predicted as well as d over any string of k periods becomes negligible. This ensures that the agent will eventually use a theory other than d to make predictions only in extraordinarily rare circumstances, giving the result.

We view this result as intuitive. We tend to trust experts who have *always* provided good explanations more than experts who have *sometimes* provided good explanations. Even if two experts, or theories, reach the same level of goodness of fit at present, a better history may well be a reason to prefer one over the other.

Observe that one cannot do away with the subjective order and rely on stability alone. In the absence of the subjective order, for every history h_n there exists a theory t_n such that $l(t_n, h_j) = \theta(1)$ for *every* $j \leq n$. Such a theory would maximize the likelihood function for each prefix of the history h_n, and would therefore be chosen for prediction. Thus the preference for stability alone does not provide a safeguard against overfitting the data by choosing a theory post-hoc.

3.4.5 *Endogenously Determined Tolerance*

Proposition 3.6 suggests that for effective decision making, the optimal tolerance level γ must be large, but not too large. Can we expect the agent to simply be endowed with the optimal level of tolerance? Such serendipity is not necessary. The agent's decisions provide the information required to ascertain an effective value of the tolerance level γ.

Proposition 3.7 *Let Assumption 3.4 hold. For every discriminating subjective order* $\succcurlyeq^S$ *there exists a relation* $\succsim^{S*}$*, independent of* ε*, such that*

(i) for every $d \in D$*, we have* $\Pi(d, \succsim^{S*}) = 1 - \varepsilon$

and

(ii) for every $\varepsilon \in (0, 1/2)$ *and* $d \in D$*, almost surely (with respect to the measure over histories induced by d), there exist sequences* $\gamma_n \to 1 - \varepsilon$ *and* $k_n \to \infty$ *such that for any* $t, t' \in D$*,*

$$t \succsim_{h_n}^{S*} t' \quad \Longleftrightarrow \quad t \succcurlyeq_{h_n}^{LS,\gamma_n k_n} t'.$$

The idea behind this result is that the agent can adjust her level of γ in light of her experience. An agent who sets a level of γ too high will soon find herself switching frequently between theories. This switching can serve as a signal to the agent that she needs to reduce γ. The relation $\succsim^{S*}$ essentially adjusts γ in response to such signals until finding the boundary at which higher values of γ lead to volatile theory choices. As the data accumulate, this boundary level will (almost surely) approach $1 - \varepsilon$. At each step of the process, the relation exploits the boundary level of γ much as would an agent who sets the boundary value a priori and implements $\succsim^{LS,\gamma k}$.

The agent who implements $\succsim^{S*}$ engages not only in learning but also in meta-learning. This agent selects theories that provide a γ-best fit and that fare well under the subjective order, but at the same time, she observes her own learning process and learns from this process itself. Specifically, the agent looks at the choices she would have made for various levels of γ and asks, "What can I learn from the fact that for some levels of γ my learning process would have continued indefinitely, whereas for others I would have settled on a specific theory?" The fact that a certain level of γ does not let the agent converge on a given theory is taken to be an indication that this level is too high.

3.4.6 *More General Error Specifications*

The arguments behind Propositions 3.6 and 3.7 make it clear that nothing depends on the fixed error rate ε. Let D_* be the set of data generating processes with the property that, for every outcome h, there exists a pair $(\underline{\rho}, \overline{\rho}) \in [0, 1/2) \times (1/2, 1]$, such that

$$\lim_{T\to\infty} \frac{1}{T_+(h(n))} \sum_{n=1}^{T-1} d_+(h_n) = \overline{\rho}$$

$$\lim_{T\to\infty} \frac{1}{T_-(h(n))} \sum_{n=1}^{T-1} d_-(h_n) = \underline{\rho},$$

where $d_+(h_n)$ equals $d(h_n)$ if the latter exceeds 1/2 and is zero otherwise, $d_-(h_n)$ is analogous for values of $d(h_n)$ less than 1/2, $T_+(h(n))$ is the number of times theory d has produced a prediction exceeding 1/2 on the history h_n, and $T_-((n))$ is analogous for predictions less than 1/2. We are thus assuming that the average error rate in the data generating process, when predicting either 1 or 0, converges (though not necessarily to the same limits). If this is not the case, there is no hope for the agent to identify the appropriate error rates for effective learning. Then arguments analogous to those giving Proposition 3.7 allow us to establish that for every discriminating subjective order $\succcurlyeq^S$, there exists a strategy $\succsim^{S*}$ such that the agent's limiting payoff in periods in which a 1 is predicted approaches $\overline{\rho}$ and the agent's limiting payoff in periods in which a 0 is predicted approaches $\underline{\rho}$.

3.4.7 *Smooth Trade-Offs*

Our central result is that effective learning couples concerns about a theory's likelihood with an auxiliary subjective criterion. Studies of model selection in statistics and in machine learning often similarly suggest a trade-off between likelihood and simplicity. Simplicity takes the place of our subjective order in these criteria, while our lexicographic criterion is typically replaced by a smooth objective function.

The general form of these measures is

$$\log L(t) - \alpha C(t), \tag{10}$$

where $C(t)$ is a "complexity function" (i.e. a function $C : D \to \mathbb{N}$ satisfying (4)) and α a constant determining the relative weights placed on the likelihood and on the complexity of the theory.[13] Gilboa and Schmeidler (2008) offer an axiomatization of this criterion.

We cannot apply (10), designed to evaluate theories given a fixed set of data, directly to our setting. As we have noted, the likelihood $L(t)$ inevitably declines to zero and hence its log decreases without bound as observations accumulate. This ensures that complexity considerations or any other

[13] For example, the Akaike Information Criterion (Akaike 1974) is given by

$$\log(L(t)) - 2k,$$

where $L(t)$ is the likelihood function of theory t and k is the number of parameters used in model t. Related to Kolmogorov's complexity measure (Kolmogorov (1968; 1998), Chaitin (1966), Solomonoff (1964)), the Minimal Message Length criterion (Rissanen (1978), Wallace and Boulton (1968)) suggests

$$\log(L(t)) - MDL(t),$$

where the $MDL(t)$ is the minimum description length of the theory t. (See also Wallace (2005) and Wallace and Dowe (1999).)

subjective considerations would eventually play no role in the analysis. We accordingly examine

$$l(t,h) - \alpha C(t), \tag{11}$$

ensuring that likelihood and complexity considerations remain on a common footing.[14]

We can draw a connection between smooth measures such as (11) and our lexicographic criterion. Fix a complexity function $C(t)$ and parameter α, and let $\succsim^{\alpha}$ be the resulting order over theories induced by (11). How does $\succsim^{\alpha}$ compare to $\succsim^{LS}$, where the latter is based on the subjective order over theories defined by (5), corresponding to the complexity function induced by $C(t)$ via (3)?

To simplify the discussion, let us restrict attention to a set of data generating processes $D_{\varepsilon}^{C} \subset D_{\varepsilon}$ with the property that for any $d, d' \in D_{\varepsilon}^{C}$, the average log likelihood ratio $l(d', h_n)$ converges with probability one, when the data generating process is d. If we did not do this, $\succsim^{\alpha}$ could fall prey to instability of the type presented in Example 4, and would have to be supplemented by the type of stability criterion presented in Section 3.4.3 to be effective. Doing so would be straightforward, but would clutter the argument.

Proposition 3.8 *Let $D \subset D_{\varepsilon}^{C}$ be countable. Then*

$$\lim_{\alpha \to 0} \Pi(d, \succsim^{\alpha}) = 1 - \varepsilon.$$

For a fixed α, the criterion $L(t) - \alpha C(t)$ restricts attention to a finite subset of D_{ε}^{C} as possible maximizers of $L(t) - \alpha C(t)$, since a theory that is too complex can never amass a likelihood value large enough to exceed the value $L(t) - \alpha C(t)$ attained by the simplest theory. Among this finite set, no theory can consistently achieve a likelihood above $1 - \varepsilon$. If α is too large, this finite set will exclude the data generating process itself, and all of the eligible theories may well fall short of likelihood $1 - \varepsilon$. Smaller values of α will not exclude the data generating process a priori, but may still lead to the selection of a simpler theory and an attendant likelihood loss. As α gets arbitrarily small, we can be assured that the data generating process is encompassed in the set of eligible theories and that very little likelihood is sacrificed in the interests of simplicity, leading to a payoff approaching $1 - \varepsilon$.

Notice, however, that $\Pi(d, \succsim^{0}) = \Pi(d, \succsim^{L})$, and hence $\Pi(d, \succsim^{0})$ equals 1/2 (given Assumptions 3.2 and 3.4.3). In addition, we cannot say a priori how small α must be in order to ensure that $\Pi(d, \succsim^{\alpha})$ is close to $1 - \varepsilon$. We thus

[14] In so doing, we move close to criteria such as the Schwarz Information Criterion (also known as the Bayesian Information Criterion (Schwarz (1978))), which retains the additive trade-off but uses a complexity measure that depends on the number of observations.

need to make α arbitrarily close to zero, without actually equalling zero. This is just what our lexicographic criterion does. We can accordingly view the lexicographic criterion as the limiting case of the smooth criteria that have been offered in the literature.

3.5 Discussion

This section explores several aspects of our model and results. To keep the discussion simple, we present formal results in Sections 3.5.1–3.5.2 for the case of a deterministic data generating process.

3.5.1 *Countability*

We have assumed the set of data generating processes D is countable. The countability of D may seem quite restrictive. Indeed, most statistical models allow continuous parameters, and thereby seemingly refer to uncountable families of processes. However, our inclination is to be persuaded by Church's thesis—if the agent can make a particular set of predictions, then there must be a Turing machine generating these predictions (Hopcraft and Ullman 1979; Chapter 7), and hence the set of conceivable data generating processes can reasonably be taken to be countable.[15]

But this limitation on the agent's cognitive abilities need not be shared by the set of possible data generating processes. To make this distinction, let D be the set of possible data generating processes, and T the set of theories of which the agent can conceive. We may then have a set D that is an (uncountable) superset of T. How will the agent fare then? Worse still, what if the data generating process is malevolent, using a (noncomputable) strategy that predicts the agent's (computable) predictions in order to then generate unpredicted observations? To investigate this possibility, we retain the assumption that $T \subset D_0$ is countable, but allow $D \subset D_0$ to be a superset of T.

The standard way for the agent to protect himself against a malevolent data generating process is to randomize. Specifically, for a discriminating

[15] Alternatively, one may arrive at countability via a more lenient model, in which a Turing machine (or, equivalently, a PASCAL program) can also perform algebraic operations on arbitrary real-valued variables, where the actual computations of these operations are performed by an "oracle" that is not part of the machine's computation. A stricter interpretation of computability, which does not resort to "oracles,"would restrict attention to statistical models in which all parameters are computable numbers. A number $x \in \mathbb{R}$ is *computable* if there exists a Turing machine M that, given the description of any rational $\varepsilon > 0$, performs a computation that halts, and writes a number $M(\varepsilon) \in \mathbb{Q}$ such that $|M(\varepsilon) - x| < \varepsilon$. All rational numbers are computable, but so is any irrational number that can be described by a well-defined algorithm, including algebraic irrational numbers (such as $\sqrt{2}$), e, and π.

subjective order $\succcurlyeq^S$ and for $\varepsilon > 0$, let the relation $\succsim^{LS,\varepsilon}$ be defined by augmenting $\succsim^{LS}$ with a "safety net". If the average payoff at history h_n is lower than $0.5 - \varepsilon/\log n$, then $\succsim^{LS,\varepsilon}_{h_n} = T \times T$. Otherwise, $\succsim^{LS,\varepsilon}_{h_n} = \succsim^{LS}_{h_n}$.

Proposition 3.9 *Let $T \subset D_0$ be countable. Let Assumption 3.2 hold and let T satisfy Assumptions 3.1.1 and 3.1.3 (while allowing $D \subset D_0$ to be a superset of T). Then $\succsim^{LS,\varepsilon}$ weakly dominates $\succsim^L$ for every discriminating subjective relation $\succcurlyeq^S$, with $\succsim^{LS,\varepsilon}$ performing strictly better for data generating processes $d \in T$.*

We can think of the relation $\succsim^{LS,\varepsilon}$ as mimicking the relation $\succsim^{LS}$ as long as "all goes well". All will go well, and the use of the discriminating subjective order $\succcurlyeq^S$ will then ensure a payoff approaching unity, whenever the data generating process is drawn from T. This will also be the case for many data generating processes drawn from outside the set T. The signal that things are not going well is an average payoff that dips below $1/2$. In this event, the agent resorts to randomizing equally over predicting 0 and predicting 1. This ensures a payoff of $1/2$, which is at least as large as that garnered by the likelihood relation. The agent thus effectively learns when learning is possible, and otherwise does not do worse than if no subjective considerations entered the prediction process.

3.5.2 *Computability*

We have justified the assumption that the set of conceivable theories is countable by appealing to computability arguments, in the form of an assumption that the agent can only implement predictions generated by a Turing machine. Continuing in this spirit, we now take computability issues more seriously. Let us first restrict the data generating process to the set D_0^H of deterministic data generating processes implementable by Turing machines that halt after every input $h \in H$.

In contrast, we now allow the agent to consider the set D_0^T of all Turing machines, even those that do not always halt. It is a relatively easy task for the agent to enumerate all Turing machines, but it is not an easy task to check which of them do indeed define a data generating process.[16] A model that respects the agents' computability constraints must then allow the set T to include *pseudo theories*: all machines that can be written in a certain language (and therefore appear to define a data generating process), even if they may not halt for all histories. Clearly, this additional freedom cannot help the agent: if, at a given history h, the agent chooses a machine that does not halt for that history, she will never be able to make a prediction

[16] One could simulate the computation of any given machine given input h, but there is no way to distinguish between computations that take a long time and computations that never end.

(in which case we take her payoff to be 0). However, "helping" the agent by assuming that $T \subset D_0^H$ would be unreasonable, as it would be tantamount to magically endowing the agent with the ability to solve the celebrated halting problem.[17]

We also restrict the agent to relations $\succsim$ that are computable, in the sense that for every $h \in H$, the choice made by the relation $\succsim_h$ from the set $B_{\succsim_h} \subset D_0^T$ could itself be implemented by a Turing machine that inevitably halts. This restriction is a binding constraint for some data generating processes:

Proposition 3.10 *For every computable relation $\succsim \subset D_0^T \times D_0^T$, there exists a data generating process $d \in D_0^H$ such that $\Pi(d, \succsim) \leq 0.5$.*

Proposition 3.10 imposes a bound on what can be guaranteed by a computable strategy, in the sense that any such strategy must fare no better than chance against *some* data generating processes. The proof consists of observing that if the agent's strategy is computable, then one may always construct a malevolent strategy d that mimics the agent's computation and chooses an observation that refutes it.

The malevolent strategy d used to prove Proposition 3.10 is quite far from most statistical models. In particular, it is counterintuitive to imagine the world simulating the agent's reasoning, not to mention refuting the resulting belief period after period. Will a more neutral model of the data generating process allow a possibility result? One way to obtain a more realistic set of data generating processes is to limit their computations. Specifically, let D_0^B be the set of data generating processes that are implementable by Turing machines that halt within a bounded number of steps. That is, for $d \in D_0^B$ there exists a Turing machine $M(d)$ and an integer $K(d)$ such that, for every history h_n and attendant prediction y_n, the computation of $M(d)$ on h_n halts within $K(d)$ steps, producing y_n.

The agent is restricted to have a (discriminating) subjective order that is represented by a computable function $C : D_0^T \to \mathbb{N}$, so that

$$C(t) \leq C(t') \qquad \Longleftrightarrow \qquad t \succcurlyeq^S t'.$$

Thus, because C is computable, the agent can compute $\succcurlyeq^S$.

The following result adapts subjective-based rankings to the computable set-up.

[17] Formally speaking, the objects of choice for the agent are not theories but descriptions thereof. A rigorous treatment of this problem would call for the definition of a formal language and of a means of describing programs in that language. Some descriptions give rise to well-defined theories (i.e. that halt for every history), whereas others would not. In such a model, every theory would have infinitely many equivalent descriptions. Thus, the function that maps descriptions to theories is not defined for all descriptions and is not one-to-one.

Proposition 3.11 *For every computable subjective order* $\succcurlyeq^S \subset D_0^T \times D_0^T$, *there exists a computable relation* $\succsim$ *with each* $\succsim_h \subset D_0^T \times D_0^T$ *such that*

(3.11.1) $\Pi(d, \succsim) = 1$ *for every* $d \in D_0^B$;

(3.11.2) for every $d, d' \in D_0^B$ *there exists* N *such that, for every* $n \geq N$ *and every* $h \in H_n$ *for which* $L(d, h) = L(d', h)$,

$$d \succ_h^S d' \Rightarrow d \succ_h d'.$$

Proposition 3.11 ensures the existence of a computable strategy yielding optimal payoffs, as well as its asymptotic agreement with the (strict part of) the given subjective ordering $\succcurlyeq^S$ over D_0^T.[18] The relation $\succsim$ cannot follow $\succsim^{LS}$ precisely, but it does so for long enough histories. In other words, it is possible that for a short history the relation $\succsim$ will not reflect the subjective ranking $\succcurlyeq^S$, but in the long run, any two theories that are equally accurate will be ranked according to $\succcurlyeq^S$.

Observe that most deterministic statistical models encountered in the social sciences are in D_0^B. The deterministic version of models such as linear regression, non-linear regression, as well as many models in machine learning, can be described by an algorithmic rule whose computation time does not depend on the input. A notable exception are time series in economics, where the model describes the dependence of y_n on $\{y_i\}_{i<n}$, and thus the length of the computation increases with the length of history, n.

3.5.3 *Simplicity*

There are many sources of subjective bias that distinguish among theories. We are especially intrigued by the possibility that a preference for simplicity may play a role in subjective evaluations. A preference for simplicity is among the most universal criteria for theory selection—people tend to prefer simpler explanations and simpler theories to more complex ones.[19]

The notion of simplicity raises several fundamental questions: What does it mean to say that "theory t is simpler than theory t'?" To what extent can such an ordering be viewed as objective? Where does the ordering come from in the first place? These questions have been the subject of an immense literature (e.g. Sober (1975)). Importantly, ever since Goodman

[18] In a context focusing on computability, it would be natural to think of $d \succcurlyeq^S d'$ if the Kolmogorov complexity of d is lower than that of d', i.e., if d has a shorter minimal description length than d'. This still leaves some freedom in defining $\succcurlyeq^S$. For instance, one may choose a description in a given programming language, such as PASCAL, as opposed to Turing machines, and one may take the description of constant values into account in the measurement of the description length, or decide to ignore them, and so on.

[19] This preference for simplicity has been championed on normative grounds (most famously by William of Occam (see Russell, 1946)) and has long been offered as a descriptive model of human reasoning (e.g. Wittgenstein 1922).

(1954) presented the "grue-bleen" paradox, it has been evident that the notion of simplicity is language-dependent and that it eludes obvious definition. Indeed, Kolmogorov's operationalization of the notion of simplicity (Kolmogorov (1965), Chaitin 1966) clarifies that using different languages as primitives can lead to different simplicity orderings (though there are some limitations on the divergence of different orderings if the relevant languages can be translated to each other (see Solomonoff (1964))). We hope that the framework provided in this chapter may be used to investigate the role of simplicity in inductive inference.

3.6 Appendix: Proofs

3.6.1 *Proof of Proposition 3.1*

Assumption 3.1.3 ensures that, for every history h_n there are theories $t \in D$ consistent with h_n, that is, theories satisfying $L(t, h_n) = 1$. Consider the set of such theories,

$$B_{\succsim_h^L} = \{ d \mid L(d, h) = 1 \}.$$

For any finite continuation of h_n there is a theory $t \in B_{\succsim_h^L}$ that is consistent with this continuation. In particular, this is true for the history h_{n+1} generated from h_n and $y_n = 0$ (coupled with x_{n+1}) as well as for the history h'_{n+1} generated from h_n and $y_n = 1$ (coupled with x_{n+1}). Assumption 3.2 then ensures that the order $\succsim^L$ is equally likely to select a theory predicting $y_n = 0$ as it is to select a theory $y_n = 1$. Thus, the probability of making a correct prediction is 1/2, and hence $\pi(d, h_n, t_n) = 0.5$, regardless of the true process d. This establishes

$$\Pi(d, \succsim_h^L) = 0.5.$$

■

3.6.2 *Proof of Proposition 3.2*

Fix $d \in D$. Since $\succcurlyeq^S$ is discriminating, there are finitely many theories in $S(d) \equiv \{t \in D \mid t \succcurlyeq^S d\}$, i.e., that are ranked ahead of or indifferent to d by the subjective order $\succcurlyeq^S$. Choose some $t \in S(d)$ and suppose that t and d are not observationally equivalent, meaning that they do not generate identical outcomes $((x_0, y_0), \ldots, (x_n, y_n), \ldots)$. Then at some period n theory t will be refuted, i.e. the data generating process will produce a history $h_n = ((x_0, y_0), \ldots, (x_{n-1}, y_{n-1}), x_n)$ for which $L(t, h_n) = 0$ and hence $d \succ_h^{LS} t$. Applying this argument to the finitely many theories in $S(d)$, there must exist a finite time n' by which either theory d is chosen by $\succsim_{h_{n'}}^{LS}$ or some element

$t \in S(d)$ is chosen by $\succsim^{LS}_{h_{n'}}$ that is observationally equivalent to d. Thereafter, $\pi(d, t_n, h_n) = 1$ holds. This yields $\Pi(d, \succsim^{LS}) = 1$. We conclude that, for every relation $\succsim^S$ derived from a discriminating subjective order $\succcurlyeq^S$, and for every data generating process d, the limit payoff under $\succsim^{LS}$ is 1, while it is only 0.5 under $\succsim^L$. Hence, $\succsim^{LS}$ strictly dominates $\succsim^L$. ∎

3.6.3 *Proof of Proposition 3.3*

Consider an agent characterized by $\succsim^{LI}$ and a data generating process d. If $\Pi(d, \succsim^{LI}) < 1$, it must be that infinitely often, $\pi(d, t_j, h_j) = 0$. Hence, the agent infinitely often chooses a new theory but never chooses d. By Assumption 3.3, the probability that the agent chooses a new theory n times without choosing d is at most $(1 - \lambda(d))^n$. Since $\lim_{n\to\infty}(1 - \lambda(d))^n = 0$, the probability that $\Pi(d, \succsim^{LI}) < 1$ is zero, and hence the expected value of $\Pi(d, \succsim^{LI})$ is unity. ∎

3.6.4 *Proof of Proposition 3.6*

Fix a data generating process d. Assume that γ satisfies $\theta(\gamma) = \theta(1 - \varepsilon) - \delta$ for $\delta > 0$. For any $\eta > 0$, there exists k such that, with probability $1 - \eta$ at least, for all $n \geq k$,

$$l(d, h_n) > \left[(1 - \varepsilon)\log(1 - \varepsilon) + \varepsilon \log \varepsilon\right] - \delta = \theta(1 - \varepsilon) - \delta = \theta(\gamma).$$

Thus, from period k on, it is likely that the correct theory d is among the γ-maximizers of $l(\cdot, h_n)$. If d is the maximizer of $\succsim^{LS,\gamma k}$ used for prediction, a payoff of $(1 - \varepsilon)$ is guaranteed. We wish to show that, if another theory is used for prediction, it cannot be much worse than d itself.

Let us condition on the probability $1 - \eta$ event that for every $n > k$, $l(d, h_n) > \theta(\gamma)$. If a theory $t \neq d$ is used for prediction at period $n \geq k$, then it must be the case that (i) t is a γ-best fit for all periods $j = k, \ldots, n$; and (ii) $t \succcurlyeq^S d$. Hence, for each period $n > k$, there are only a finite number of theories satisfying conditions (i) and (ii), of which the highest-ranked by the subjective order will be chosen. Moreover, the set of such theories is decreasing in n (since a theory whose likelihood ratio drops below γ is subsequently disqualified). Eventually, a period n' will be reached such that some theory t (possibly d) satisfying (i) and (ii) will be used in all subsequent periods. Let $n > n'$, and let α be the proportion of times, up to n, that t made the correct prediction. Then, since t is a γ-best fit at n, we have

$$\begin{aligned} l(t, h) &= \alpha \log(1 - \varepsilon) + (1 - \alpha)\log \varepsilon \\ &= \alpha\left[\log(1 - \varepsilon) - \log \varepsilon\right] + \log \varepsilon \\ &= \alpha \log \frac{1 - \varepsilon}{\varepsilon} + \log \varepsilon \end{aligned}$$

$$
\begin{aligned}
&\geq \theta(\gamma) \\
&= \theta(1-\varepsilon) - \delta \\
&= (1-\varepsilon)\log(1-\varepsilon) + \varepsilon \log \varepsilon - \delta \\
&= (1-\varepsilon)\left[\log(1-\varepsilon) - \log \varepsilon\right] + \log \varepsilon - \delta \\
&= (1-\varepsilon)\log \frac{1-\varepsilon}{\varepsilon} + \log \varepsilon - \delta.
\end{aligned}
$$

This gives

$$
\alpha \log \frac{1-\varepsilon}{\varepsilon} + \log \varepsilon \geq (1-\varepsilon)\log \frac{1-\varepsilon}{\varepsilon} + \log \varepsilon - \delta
$$

or

$$
\left[\alpha - (1-\varepsilon)\right] \log \frac{1-\varepsilon}{\varepsilon} \geq -\delta
$$

that is,

$$
\alpha \geq (1-\varepsilon) - \frac{\delta}{\log \frac{1-\varepsilon}{\varepsilon}}.
$$

Intuitively, the payoff obtained by predicting according to t cannot be much lower than $(1-\varepsilon)$. Taking into account the probability of convergence by time k we get

$$
\Pi(d, \succsim^{LS,\gamma k}) \geq (1-\eta)\left[(1-\varepsilon) - \frac{\delta}{\log \frac{1-\varepsilon}{\varepsilon}}\right],
$$

which converges to $(1-\eta)(1-\varepsilon)$ as $\delta \searrow 0$. Finally, increasing k results in decreasing η to any desired degree, and the result follows. ■

3.6.5 *Proof of Proposition 3.7*

The basic idea is have the agent simulate the choices of theories that would have corresponded to $\succsim^{LS,\gamma k}$ for different values of γ and of k. For values of γ larger than $1-\varepsilon$, the agent will find that the maximizers of $\succsim^{LS,\gamma k}$ keep changing, indicating that γ is too high. For values of γ that are lower than $1-\varepsilon$, the agent will find many theories that get selected asymptotically, an indication that γ might be too low. By refining the search for γ, while simultaneously gathering more observations, the reasoner will approach $1-\varepsilon$ and make predictions according to the correct theory.

We make these ideas precise in the form of a reasoning algorithm that is simple, but makes no claims to efficiency. At stage n the reasoner considers as possibilities for γ all values in

$$\Gamma_n = \left\{ \frac{r}{2^n} \mid r = 0, 1, \ldots, 2^n \right\}.$$

Given n, define $k = \llcorner n/2 \lrcorner$. For each $\gamma \in \Gamma_n$, and for each $m = k, \ldots, n$, the reasoner finds all the maximizers of $\succsim_{h_m}^{LS,\gamma k}$ (to make this an algorithm, we need to assume that an oracle can perform this task). Denote the set of maximizers for each γ by $M(m, k, \gamma)$. This is a finite set, due to the agent's preference for simplicity. Then, for each γ, define

$$M^*(n, \gamma) = \cap_{k \le m \le n} M(m, k, \gamma).$$

Thus, $M^*(n, \gamma)$ contains precisely those theories that have been among the "γ-best" theories for the past $n/2$ periods.

If $M^*(n, \gamma) = \varnothing$ for all $\gamma \in \Gamma_n$, define $\succsim_{h_n}^{S*} = D \times D$. In this case all theories are equivalent in terms of $\succsim_{h_n}^{S*}$, and the reasoner's choice will be arbitrary.

If, however, $M^*(n, \gamma) \neq \varnothing$ for some $\gamma \in \Gamma_n$, let γ_n be the maximal such value in Γ_n, and define

$$t \succsim_{h_n}^{S*} t' \quad \Longleftrightarrow \quad \begin{cases} \quad t \in M^*(n, \gamma_n) & \textit{and} \quad t' \notin M^*(n, \gamma_n) \\ \textit{or} \quad t, t' \in M^*(n, \gamma_n) & \textit{and} \quad t \succcurlyeq^S t' \\ \textit{or} \quad t, t' \notin M^*(n, \gamma_n). \end{cases}$$

That is, the $\succcurlyeq^S$-most-prefered theories in $M^*(n, \gamma_n)$ are considered to be the "best" theories and one of them will be used for prediction.

To see that the definition of $\succsim^{S*}$ satisfies the desired properties, observe that, by the proof of Proposition 3.6, if $\gamma > 1 - \varepsilon$, $M^*(n, \gamma) = \varnothing$ for large n. For $\gamma < 1 - \varepsilon$, $d \in M^*(n, \gamma)$ for large n. As $n \to \infty$, the minimal γ for which $M^*(n, \gamma) \neq \varnothing$ converges to $1 - \varepsilon$, and d is among the maximizers of $\succsim^{S*}$. We then repeat the argument of Proposition 3.6, by which any theory $t \neq d$ such that $t \in M^*(n, \gamma)$ obtains a payoff that converges to $(1 - \varepsilon)$ as $\gamma \nearrow 1 - \varepsilon$. ■

3.6.6 *Proof of Proposition 3.8*

Fix a complexity function $C(t)$, a value $\alpha > 0$, and a data generating process d^*. Let $\hat{d} \in \arg\min_{d \in D_\varepsilon^C} C(d)$. Then no theory d for which $\theta(1) - \alpha C(d) < \theta(\varepsilon) - \alpha C(\hat{d})$ will ever be chosen by the relation $\succsim^\alpha$, no matter what the history. The agent's choice of theory in each period will thus be drawn from the finite set $D_\varepsilon^C(\alpha) \equiv \{d \in D_\varepsilon^C : \theta(1) - \alpha C(d) < \theta(\varepsilon) - \alpha C(\hat{d})\}$.

For sufficiently small α, the data generating process d^* is contained in $D_\varepsilon^C(\alpha)$. In addition, with probability 1, the limit $\lim_{n \to \infty} l(d, h_n)$ exists for all $d \in D_\varepsilon^C(\alpha)$. Since this set is finite, with probability 1, the agent's choice of theory becomes constant across periods, being the maximizer over $D_\varepsilon^C(\alpha)$ of

$$\lim_{n \to \infty} l(d, h_n) - \alpha C(d).$$

But since $d^* \in D_\varepsilon^C(\alpha)$ for small α, the agent's payoff is bounded below by

$$\lim_{n\to\infty} l(d,h_n) - \alpha C(d) = \theta(1-\varepsilon) - \alpha C(d^*).$$

Taking α to zero then gives the result. ■

3.6.7 *Proof of Proposition 3.9*

The relation $T \times T$ guarantees a random choice (by Assumption 3.1.3), and hence this relation ensures an expected payoff of 0.5 at each period in which it is played. Thus, if $\succsim^{LS,\varepsilon} = T \times T$ for a long enough period, the average payoff converges to 0.5 with probability 1. Moreover, it does so at a rate proportional to $n^{-1/2}$. It follows that, with probability 1, the sustained application of relation $T \times T$ leads to a period n at which the average payoff surpasses the threshold $0.5 - \varepsilon/\log n$, at which point $\succsim^{LS,\varepsilon}$ switches to $\succsim^{LS}$.

Suppose $d \in T$. Since $\succsim^{LS,\varepsilon} = \succsim^{LS}$ infinitely often, $\succsim^{LS,\varepsilon}$ will eventually select d or a theory equivalent to d. Predictions will subsequently be perfect, ensuring that $\succsim^{LS,\varepsilon}$ will not revert to $T \times T$ and that $\Pi(d, \succsim^{LS,\varepsilon}) = 1$.

If $d \notin T$, the lowest the average payoff at history h_n can drop without ensuring $\succsim^{LS,\varepsilon} = T \times T$ is $0.5 - \varepsilon/\log n - 1/n$ (obtained by coupling a history of length $n-1$ in which the payoff is precisely $0.5 - \varepsilon/\log(n-1)$ with one more incorrect observation). Hence $\Pi(d, \succsim^{LS,\varepsilon}) \geq 0.5$. Combining the two, we thus find that $\Pi(d, \succsim^{LS,\varepsilon}) \geq \Pi(d, \succsim^{L})$ for all $d \in D$, with strict equality for every $d \in T$. ■

3.6.8 *Proof of Proposition 3.10*

Let $\succsim$ be computable. Then there is a Turing machine τ that implements $\succsim$ by, for any history h, computing a maximizer of $\succsim$ from the set D^H. Let d simulate the machine τ, for any history h, finding the maximizer t_h that the agent will use for prediction, and then generating prediction 1 if $t_h(h) \leq 0.5$ and 0 if $t_h(h) > 0.5$. A deterministic t will result in a payoff of 0. The maximal payoff for the agent at each period is 0.5, obtained by the random prediction $t_h(h) = 0.5$. ■

3.6.9 *Proof of Proposition 3.11*

The basic idea is to construct the relation $\succsim$ by combining the underlying subjective order $\succcurlyeq^S$ with the time complexity of the machine.

Let $D_0^T = \{t_1, t_2, \ldots\}$ be the class of all Turing machines, including those that always halt and those that do not halt for certain inputs $h \in H$. There is no difficulty in writing a machine that generates D_0^T, or, equivalently, that can accept $i \geq 1$ as an input and, after a finite number of steps, provide the description of t_i.

Assume we are given a history h and we wish to select a theory that has high likelihood and that halts for h. When considering a machine t, we thus need to determine whether it fits the data, namely whether $L(t, h_n) = 1$ (taking $L(t, h_n) = 0$ if the machine fails to halt for any prefix of h_n), and we need to compute its prediction for y_n, or $t(h_n)$, taking into account the possibility that it may not halt when making this prediction. That is, we need to know the result of $n+1$ computations of t_i (one to verify that the theory fits the observation generated in each of the preceding n periods, and one to generate the current prediction), each of which may not halt.

Let $C : D \to \mathbb{N}$ be a computable complexity function for the underlying subjective order $\succcurlyeq^S$, so that

$$C(t) \leq C(t') \qquad \Longleftrightarrow \qquad t \succcurlyeq^S t'.$$

Define $c : D \times H \to \mathbb{N} \cup \{\infty\}$ to be the length of computation, that is, $c(t, h) \in \{1, 2, \ldots, \infty\}$ is the number of steps that t takes to compute where h is its input. Next define a function $C^* : D \times H \to \mathbb{R}_+ \cup \{\infty\}$ by

$$C^*(t, h) = C(t) + \frac{1}{n^2} \sum_{j=0}^{n} c(t, h_j)$$

where $t \in D$, $h \in H_n$ and h_j is the j-th prefix of h. Using this function, we define our candidate relation over theories:

$$t' \succsim_h t \qquad \Longleftrightarrow \qquad \begin{cases} L(t', h) > L(t, h) \\ \text{or } [L(t', h) = L(t, h) \text{ and } C^*(t', h) \leq C^*(t, h)] \end{cases}.$$

We argue that it is a computable task to find a maximizer of $\succsim_h$ from among those machines that halt on history h, and that this maximizer will have likelihood one. First observe that for every h there exists a machine t such that $L(t, h_n) = 1$ and $C^*(t, h_n) < \infty$. To see this, it suffices to consider a machine t that generates history h_n irrespective of the data. For any history longer than n, the machine can generate 0. This takes a computation time $c(t, h) = O(n)$. By construction, $t \in D_0^B$. Since this machine appears somewhere in the enumeration corresponding to $\succcurlyeq^S$, we have $C(t) < \infty$ and hence $C^*(t, h) < \infty$.

Given $C^*(t, h)$, there are finitely many machines t' with $C(t') \leq C^*(t, h)$, and therefore only finitely many machines that can beat t according to $\succsim$. Each of these has to be simulated only a bounded number of steps, $C^*(t, h)$, to see if, indeed, it gives $L(t', h_n) = 1$ and a lower value for $C^*(t', h)$.

Note that for all $d \in D_0^B$, $c(t, h_n) \leq K(d)$ and

$$\frac{1}{n^2}\sum_{j=0}^{n} c(t, h_j) \leq \frac{1}{n^2} nK(d) \to 0$$

hence,

$$C^*(t, h) \to C(t).$$

Now consider $d, d' \in D_0^B$ with $d \succ^S d'$ and hence $C(d) \leq C(d')$. Then for all sufficiently large n, $C^*(d, h_n) < C^*(d', h_n)$, and hence $L(d, h_n) = L(d', h_n) \Rightarrow d \succ_h d'$. This establishes (3.11.2).

We now turn to (3.11.1), namely that $\Pi(\succsim, d) = 1$ for every $d \in D_0^B$. For $t' \succsim_h d$ to hold, we must have $L(t', h) = 1$ and $C(t') \leq C(d)$. An argument analogous to that of the proof of Proposition 3.2 ensures that at some point, d or a theory equivalent to it is found, and from that point on only such theories (predicting $d(h)$ for every h) can be maximizers of $\succsim$. Hence the agent makes perfect predictions and obtains $\Pi(\succsim, d) = 1$. ■

3.7 References

Akaike, H. (1974), “A new look at the statistical model identification”, *IEEE Transactions on Automatic Control*, **19**(6): 716–23.

Al-Najjar, N. I. (2008), Decision makers as statisticians. Technical report, Northwestern University.

Chaitin, G. J. (1966), “On the length of programs for computing binary sequences”, *Journal of the Association for Computing Machinery*, **13**(4): 547–69.

Gilboa, I. and D. Schmeidler (2008), Likelihood and simplicity: An axiomatic approach. Mimeo, Tel Aviv University.

Goodman, N. (1954), Fact, Fiction and Forecast. Harvard University Press: Cambridge, Massachusetts.

Hopcraft, J. E. and J. D. Ullman, (1979), *Introduction to Automata Theory, Languages and Computation*. Addison Wesley: Reading, Mass.

Kolmogorov, A. N. (1965), “Three approaches to the quantitative definition of information”, *Probability and Information Transmission*, **2**(1): 4–7.

Kolmogorov, A. N. (1998, originally 1963), “On tables of random numbers”, *Theoretical Computer Science*, **207**(6): 387–95.

Kuhn, T. S. (1996), *The Structure of Scientific Revolutions*. University of Chicago Press: Chicago.

Rissanen, J. (1978), “Modelling by shortest data description”, *Automatica*, **14**(5): 465–71.

Russell, B. (2004. Originally 1946), *History of Western Philosophy*. Routledge: London.

Schwarz, G. (1978). “Estimating the dimension of a model”, *Annals of Statistics*, **6**(2): 461–4.

Sober, E. (1975), *Simplicity*. Clarendon Press: Oxford.

Solomonoff, R. (1964), "A formal theory of inductive inference I,II", *Information control*, **7**(1,2): 1–22, 224–54.

Vapnik, V. N. (1998), *Statistical Learning Theory*. Wiley: New York.

Vapnik, V. N. and A. Y. Chervonenkis, (1971), "On the uniform convergence of relative frequencies of events to their probabilities", *Theory of Probability and its Applications*, **16**: 264–80.

Wallace, C. S. (2005), *Statistical and Inductive Inference by Minimum Message Length*. Springer: New York.

Wallace, C. S. and D. M. Boulton, (1968), "An information measure of classification", *The Computer Journal*, **13**: 185–94.

Wallace, C. S. and D. L. Dowe, (1999), "Minimal message length and Kolmogorov complexity", *The Computer Journal*, **42**: 270–83.

Wittgenstein, L. (1922), *Tractatus Logico-Philosophicus*. Routledge and Kegan Paul: London.

4

Dynamics of Inductive Inference in a Unified Framework

4.1 Introduction

Economic theory typically assumes that agents reason about uncertainty in a Bayesian way: they formulate prior probabilities over a state space and update them in response to new information according to Bayes's rule. This model is powerful, but does not always reflect the way that people think about uncertainty. In particular, when completely unexpected outcomes occur, people question their probabilistic models, relying on alternative reasoning techniques until perhaps developing a new probabilistic model.

For example, the New York Stock Exchange was closed for five days following the September 11, 2001 terrorist attacks on the United States. On the following Sunday, September 16, a leading economist was asked to predict the behavior of the Dow Jones Industrial Average on Monday. He did not respond by reasoning that "I used to attach (the quite small) probability ε to such attacks, and now I need only update this probability, and then apply my usual model of the stock market". Instead, there was a sense that the probabilistic model he would have used under normal circumstances was inappropriate for the present situation, and that he had to start from basics in reasoning about the future. He responded by invoking analogies to past cases in which the United States had been surprised by attack, most notably Pearl Harbor. (As it turned out, his prediction was quite accurate.)

Similarly, following the collapse of Lehman Brothers in September 2008, the head of a major investment firm confronted clients anxious to sell their assets, even assets that had already lost 90 per cent of their value. Again, the analyst did not apply Bayes's rule to a prior that had taken into account a possible failure of Lehman Brothers. Instead, he argued that something totally unexpected had happened, and that "obviously, the models do not work". The analyst convinced his clients to hold such assets, invoking the simple rule that "an asset that has lost 90 per cent of its value cannot lose much more". (His clients were convinced, and subsequently appreciated the advice.)

In both examples, one could, post-hoc, construct a prior probability distribution that allows the experts' reasoning to follow from Bayesian updating. However, such a description would say very little about the actual reasoning process of the agents involved, and (more importantly) would not be of much help in predicting their reasoning in the future. In this chapter, our interest is in modeling the agents' actual reasoning processes, in the hope of better understanding when these processes generate probabilistic beliefs, which beliefs are likely to be formed by the agents, and how the agent might form beliefs when driven away from familiar probabilistic models. To do so, we need a model that can simultaneously describe probabilistic and non-probabilistic reasoning, as well as the dynamics by which weights shift between modes of reasoning.

We take it for granted that when statistical analysis is possible, rational agents will perform such analysis correctly. In contrast, our interest is in the way economists model agents who face problems that do not naturally lend themselves to statistical analysis. Predicting financial crises, economic growth, the outcome of elections, or the eruptions of wars and revolutions, are examples where it is difficult to define iid random variables and, more generally, where the assumptions of statistical models do not seem to be good approximations.

To set the context for our model, consider an agent who each year is called upon to predict the price of oil over the subsequent year. To keep this illustrating example simple, suppose the agent need only predict whether the average price will be higher or lower than the previous year's price. We can imagine the agent working for a hedge fund that is interested in whether it should bet for or against an increasing price.

To support her decision, the agent's research staff regularly compiles a list of data potentially relevant to the price of oil, as well as data identifying past values of the relevant variables and past oil prices. For our example, let us assume that the data include just two variables: a measure of the change in the demand for oil and a measure of the change in the severity of conflict in the Middle East. Each is assumed to take two values, indicating whether there has been an increase or decrease. Each year the agent receives the current changes in demand and in conflict, examines the data from previous years, and then predicts whether the price will increase or decrease. How do and how should agents reason about such problems?

Our model captures three types of reasoning.[1] The most common in economic modeling is *Bayesian*. The agent first formulates the set of possible states of the world, where a state identifies the strength of demand, the measure of conflict, and the price of oil, in each year over the course of her horizon. The agent then formulates a prior probability distribution over this state space. This prior distribution will reflect models and theories of the market for oil that the agent finds helpful, her analysis of past data and past outcomes in this market, and any other prior information she has at her command. Once this prior has been formulated, the agent's predictions are a relatively straightforward matter of applying Bayes's rule, as new observations allow her to rule out some states and condition her probability distribution on the surviving states.

An alternative mode of reasoning is *case-based*. The agent considers past observations and predicts the outcome that appeared more often in those past cases that are considered similar. For example, predicting that following the September 11 attacks, the DJIA would change in a similar way to its change following Pearl Harbor would be considered case-based reasoning. If all past observations are considered equally similar, the case-based prediction is simply the mode, that is, the outcome that is most frequent in the database. If the agent uses a similarity function that puts all its weight on the most recent outcome, her prediction will simply be that outcome.[2] If the agent views the current state of conflict in the Middle East as a repetition of affairs in 1991 or in 2003, the agent will predict that there will soon be a war and an increase in the price of oil.

Finally, *rule-based* reasoning calls for the agent to base her predictions on regularities that she believes characterize the market for oil. For example, the agent may adopt a rule that any increase in the level of demand leads to an increase in the price of oil. Based on this and her expectation that the Chinese economy will continue to grow, the agent might reasonably predict that the price is about to rise.

The boundaries between the three modes of reasoning are not always sharp. Our focus is on the Bayesian approach. By "Bayesian reasoning" we refer to the common approach in economic theory, according to which *all* reasoning is Bayesian. *Any* source of uncertainty is modeled in the state space, and all reasoning about uncertainty takes the form of updating a prior probability via Bayes's rule.

This chapter presents (in Sections 4.2–4.3) a framework that unifies these three modes of reasoning (and potentially others), allowing us to view them

[1] In personal conversation, a hedge fund principal indicated that his fund used all three methods of reasoning introduced in this section in predicting the likelihood of mortgage defaults.

[2] Indeed, Alquist and Kilian (2010) find that the best prediction of the future price of oil is the current price.

as special cases of a general learning process. The agent attaches weights to conjectures. Each conjecture is a set of states of the world, capturing a way of thinking about how outcomes in the world will develop. The associated weights capture the relative influence that the agent attaches to the various conjectures. To generate a prediction, the agent sums the weight of all nontrivial conjectures consistent with each possible outcome, and then ranks outcomes according to their associated total weights. In the special case where each conjecture consists of a single state of the world, our framework is the standard Bayesian model, and the learning algorithm is equivalent to Bayesian updating. Employing other conjectures, which include more than a single state each, we can capture other modes of reasoning, as illustrated by simple examples of case-based and of rule-based reasoning.

Our model could be used to address either positive or normative questions. In this chapter we focus on positive ones, describing how the reasoning process of an agent evolves as observations are gathered. Within the class of such questions, our model could be used to capture a variety of psychological biases and errors, but the focus of this chapter is on the reasoning of an agent who makes no obvious errors in her reasoning. Such an agent may well be surprised by circumstances that she has deemed unlikely, that is, by "black swans," but will never be surprised by a careful analysis of her own reasoning. The optimality of this reasoning process is a normative question, which we do not address here.

Our main results concern the dynamics of the weight put on Bayesian vs. non-Bayesian reasoning. In Section 4.4.1 we suggest conditions under which Bayesian reasoning will give way to other modes of reasoning, and alternative conditions under which the opposite conclusion holds. Section 4.4.3 briefly discusses how probabilistic reasoning may emerge periodically, with other modes of reasoning used between the regimes of different probabilistic models. Section 4.5 concludes.

4.2 The Framework

4.2.1 *The Environment*

At each period $t \in \{0, 1, \ldots\}$ there is a *characteristic* $x_t \in X$ and an *outcome* $y_t \in Y$. The sets X and Y are assumed to be finite and non-empty, with Y containing at least two possible outcomes.[3]

In predicting the price of oil, the characteristic x_t might identify the type of political regime and the state of political unrest in various oil-producing countries, describe the extent of armed conflict in the Middle East, indicate

[3] The extension to infinite sets X and Y can be carried out with no major difficulties.

whether new nuclear power plants have come on line or existing ones been disabled by accidents, describe the economic conditions of the major oil importers, summarize climate conditions, and so on. In our simplified example, Y has only two elements, $\{0,1\}$, and each $x = (x^1, x^2) \in X$ has two components, each also taking values in $\{0,1\}$, with a 1 in each case indicating an increase in the relevant variable.

We make no assumptions about independence or conditional independence of the variables across periods. In fact, for most of our analysis we do not assume any probability on the state space, so that independence of the variables cannot even be defined. The model can be augmented by assumptions about the underlying probability measure that drives the process, allowing one to state results about learning the "true" state of the world. While some of our examples below are of this nature, the general framework is silent on the actual data generating process.

A *state of the world* ω identifies the characteristic and outcome that appear in each period t, i.e. $\omega : \{0,1,\ldots\} \to X \times Y$. We let $(\omega_X(t), \omega_Y(t))$ denote the element of $X \times Y$ appearing in period t given state ω, and let

$$\Omega = (X \times Y)^\infty$$

denote the set of states of the world. In our example, a state identifies the sign of changes in the strength of demand, the level of conflict, and the price of oil in each period.

A period-t history

$$h_t = (\omega_X(0), \omega_Y(0), \ldots, \omega_X(t-1), \omega_Y(t-1), \omega_X(t))$$

identifies the characteristics (e.g. changes in the levels of demand and of conflict) and outcomes (e.g. changes in the price of oil) that have appeared in periods 0 through $t-1$, as well as the period-t characteristic, given state ω. We let H_t denote all possible histories at period t. For a particular history h_t we define the corresponding event

$$[h_t] = \{\omega \in \Omega \mid (\omega(0), \ldots, \omega(t-1), \omega_X(t)) = h_t\}$$

consisting of all states that are compatible with the history h_t. In other words, $[h_t]$ is the set of states whose period-t history matches h_t, with different states in this set corresponding to different possible future developments. We define, for $h_t \in H_t$ and $Y' \subset Y$, the event

$$[h_t, Y'] = \{\omega \in [h_t] \mid \omega_Y(t) \in Y'\}$$

consisting of all states that are compatible with the history h_t and with a period-t outcome in the set Y'.

In each period t the agent observes a history h_t and makes a prediction about the period-t outcome, $\omega_Y(t) \in Y$. A *prediction* is a ranking of subsets in Y given h_t. Hence, for $h_t \in H_t$ there is a binary relation $\succsim_{h_t} \subset 2^Y \times 2^Y$ that ranks subsets of outcomes according to their plausibility.

4.2.2 *Predictions*

Predictions are made with the help of conjectures. Each conjecture is a subset $A \subset \Omega$. A conjecture can represent a specific scenario, that is, a single state of the world, in which case $A = \{\omega\}$. However, conjectures can contain more than one state, and thereby capture rules and analogies. In general, any reasoning aid one may employ in predicting y_t can be described by the set of states that are compatible with it.

In principle, a conjecture could be *any* subset of Ω, but the set of all subsets of Ω is rather large and unwieldy. Nothing is lost by taking the set of conjectures to be the σ-algebra $\mathcal{A}$ generated by the events $\{[h_t]\}_{t \geq 0, h_t \in H_t}$.[4]

To make predictions in period t, the agent first identifies, for any subset of outcomes $Y' \subset Y$, the set of conjectures that have not been refuted by the history h_t and that predict an outcome in Y'. A conjecture $A \in \mathcal{A}$ has not been refuted by history h_t if $A \cap [h_t] \neq \varnothing$. The set of conjectures that have not been refuted by history h_t *and* predict an outcome in Y' is[5]

$$\mathcal{A}(h_t, Y') = \{A \in \mathcal{A} \mid \varnothing \neq A \cap [h_t] \subset [h_t, Y']\}. \quad (1)$$

The agent evaluates the relative likelihoods of outcomes Y' and Y'', at history h_t, by comparing the sets $\mathcal{A}(h_t, Y')$ and $\mathcal{A}(h_t, Y'')$. The agent makes this comparison by using a *credence function* φ_{h_t}. Formally, φ_{h_t} is a finite, non-zero σ-additive measure on a sigma-algebra $\mathcal{E} \subset 2^{\mathcal{A}}$ to be defined shortly.[6] We interpret $\varphi_{h_t}(\mathcal{A}(h_t, Y'))$ as the weight the agent attaches to conjectures consistent with the outcomes Y', and $\varphi_{h_t}(\mathcal{A}(h_t, Y''))$ as the weight the agent attaches to conjectures consistent with the outcomes Y''.[7]

To make predictions, the agent ranks Y' as "at least as likely as" Y'', denoted $Y' \succsim_{h_t} Y''$, iff

$$\varphi_{h_t}(\mathcal{A}(h_t, Y')) \geq \varphi_{h_t}(\mathcal{A}(h_t, Y'')). \quad (2)$$

[4] Note that this is the same σ-algebra generated by $\{[h_t, Y']\}_{t \geq 0, h_t \in H_t, Y' \subset Y}$ and that it contains all singletons, i.e., $\{\omega\} \in \mathcal{A}$ for every $\omega \in \Omega$.

[5] Observe that the conjectures $\varnothing$ and Ω are never included in $\mathcal{A}(h_t, Y')$ for any $Y' \subsetneq Y$. The impossible conjecture $\varnothing$ is not compatible with any history h_t, whereas the certain conjecture Ω is tautological at every history h_t.

[6] There is no loss of generality in taking φ_{h_t} to be a probability measure, but it economizes on notation to refrain from imposing this normalization. For example, we thereby avoid the need to constantly make special provision for cases in which denominators are zero.

[7] The weighting function φ_{h_t} is equivalent to a belief function in the Dempster-Shafer theory of evidence (Dempster (1967), Shafer (1976)). See Appendix B for a brief introduction.

In Appendix B we provide a characterization of binary ("at least as likely as") relations over subsets of Y that can be represented by belief functions, as $\succsim_{h_t}$ is by represented φ_{h_t} in (2).

Intuitively, one may think of each conjecture A as an expert, who argues that the state of the world has to be in the event A. The weight $\varphi_{h_t}(\{A\})$ is a measure of the expert's reliability in the eyes of the agent. The agent listens to the forecasts of all experts and, when comparing two possible predictions Y' and Y'', chooses the prediction that commands higher total support from the experts. When an expert is proven wrong, he is asked to leave the room and his future forecasts are ignored. For example, upon reaching a history h_t at which the input $\omega_X(t)$ indicates that the demand for oil has declined, perhaps because of a worldwide recession, the oil analyst from Section 4.1 will discard all conjectures pertaining to the price of oil in conditions of currently expanding demand. The set of surviving conjectures $\mathcal{A}(h_t)$ may include a conjecture consistent with a decrease in the price of oil (perhaps because the recession has reduced demand) as well as a conjecture consistent with an increase in the price of oil (perhaps because the price increased during a previous recession that the analyst remembers vividly).

To complete this definition, we need to specify the σ-algebra $\mathcal{E} \subset 2^{\mathcal{A}}$ over which the measures φ_{h_t} are defined.[8] For convenience, the domain of the function φ_{h_t} will be the same σ-algebra $\mathcal{E}$ for each history h_t, even though only a subset of conjectures, namely $\cup_{Y' \subsetneq Y} \mathcal{A}(h_t, Y')$, is relevant for prediction at h_t, and the definition of φ_{h_t} outside this set is irrelevant.

First, for each conjecture $A \in \mathcal{A}$, it will be useful to be able to refer to its weight of credence as $\varphi_{h_t}(\{A\})$, which requires that $\{A\}$ be a measurable set. Let $\mathcal{E}_0$ be the σ-algebra generated by all such sets. Next, since predictions will be made by comparing the φ_{h_t} values of subsets of the type $\mathcal{A}(h_t, Y')$, we need to make sure that these are measurable. Let $\mathcal{E}_1$ be the σ-algebra generated by all such sets. Finally, the set of singletons contained in a conjecture will also be of interest, and we let $\mathcal{E}_2$ be the σ-algebra generated by all such sets.[9] Summarizing:

σ-algebra	Generating sets
$\mathcal{E}_0$	$\{A\}$ for $A \in \mathcal{A}$
$\mathcal{E}_1$	$\mathcal{A}(h_t, Y')$ for $t \geq 0, h_t \in H_t, Y' \subset Y$
$\mathcal{E}_2$	$\{\{\omega\} \mid \omega \in A\}$ for $A \in \mathcal{A}$

.

[8] Recall that a conjecture A is an element of the σ-algebra $\mathcal{A}$ over the set of states Ω. An element of $\mathcal{E}$ is a set of conjectures, and hence is an element of a σ-algebra over the set $2^{\mathcal{A}}$ of sets of states.

[9] The collection $\mathcal{E}_0$ contains every set of the form $\{\omega\}$, but $\{\{\omega\} \mid \omega \in A\}$ may be uncountable, and so must be explicitly included in the definition of the σ-algebra $\mathcal{E}$. Doing so ensures, for example, that the set of Bayesian conjectures is measurable.

We then define $\mathcal{E}$ as the σ-algebra that is generated by $\mathcal{E}_0 \cup \mathcal{E}_1 \cup \mathcal{E}_2$. A credence function φ_{h_t} is a (σ-additive) measure on $\mathcal{E}$.

Using states of the world to represent possible outcomes is standard in decision theory, as is the summation of a function such as φ_{h_t} to capture beliefs, and the elimination of conjectures that have been proven wrong. The most obvious departure we have taken from the familiar framework of Bayesian updating is to allow conjectures that consist of more than one state.[10] To confirm this, Section 4.3.1 shows that if we restrict attention to singe-state conjectures, then we have the familiar framework of Bayesian reasoning. Expanding the framework to encompass multi-state conjectures is necessary if we are to capture case-based and rule-based reasoning (See Sections 4.3.2 and 4.3.3).

We have restricted attention to deterministic conjectures. One sees this in (1), where conjectures are either clearly compatible or clearly incompatible with a given history. This is obviously restrictive, as we are often interested in drawing inferences about theories that do not make sharp predictions. However, a framework in which the implications of the evidence for various conjectures is dichotomous simplifies the analysis by eliminating assessments as to which theories are more or less likely for a given history, in the process allowing us to focus attention on the resulting induction.

4.2.3 *Updating*

How does the agent learn in this model? We have already identified one avenue for learning, namely that refuted conjectures are thereafter excluded from consideration. If this were the only avenue for learning in our model, then the updating would precisely mimic Bayesian updating, and the only generalization from a standard Bayesian model would be the introduction of multi-state conjectures.

Our generalized model allows a second avenue for learning—the credence function φ_{h_t} can vary with the history h_t. Collecting information allows the agent not only to exclude falsified conjectures, but to modify the weights she attaches to her surviving conjectures. This contrasts with Bayesian updating in a standard probability model, where unrefuted states retain their original relative weights, as well as with the notion of a likelihood function, which can only decrease in value as data are gathered.

We can obviously expect φ_{h_t} to vary with h_t if the agent is initially unaware of some conjectures. Such a conjecture will be assigned a zero weight at the outset, but a positive weight at a history h_t that brings the conjecture

[10] In the process, the notion of compatibility needs to be adapted: whereas a single state ω is compatible with history h_t if $\omega \in [h_t]$, a (possibly multistate) conjecture A is compatible with history h_t if $A \cap [h_t] \neq \varnothing$.

to mind. For example, it is possible that prior to September 11, 2001 the agent had not imagined that terrorists might fly commercial airliners into buildings. This unawareness is naturally captured by setting $\varphi_\emptyset$ of related conjectures to zero. However, given a history h_t that includes this attack, conjectures that involve similar attacks in the future may have a positive weight in φ_{h_t}.

Even without unawareness, φ_{h_t} may depend on the history h_t. The competing conjectures in our model have different domains of application. Some conjectures make predictions at each period, while others only rarely hazard a prediction. Once we reach a history h_t, shouldn't conjectures that have made many correct predictions along the way be upgraded in comparison to those who have hitherto said little or nothing? In effect, shouldn't the value $\varphi_{h_t}(\{A\})$ increase as A passes more prediction tests?

For example, suppose that there are two possible outcomes ($Y = \{0, 1\}$) and that conjecture A makes predictions at each of the periods $t = 0, \ldots, 100$, while conjecture A' makes a prediction only at $t = 100$. Conjecture A may be a market analyst who arrives at time $t = 100$ having pegged the market correctly in every period, while conjecture A' may be a competing analyst who thus far has said nothing other than "can't tell".[11] It seems that the weight we attach to A at time $t = 100$ should be higher than that of A', even if at the outset the two analysts seemed equally reliable.

Rewarding conjectures (or experts) for passing more prediction tests does not require that φ_{h_t} depend on h_t. Instead, these rewards can be built into a function φ that is independent of h_t. In the example above, at time $t = 0$ the agent already knows that conjecture A' will be irrelevant for the first 100 observations, and will join the game only at period $t = 100$. The agent can then build this comparison into the function $\varphi_\emptyset$, perhaps by assigning weights $\varphi_\emptyset(A) = 100\varphi_\emptyset(A')$, and can then simply use $\varphi_\emptyset$ throughout. Thus, if at time $t = 100$ conjecture A is still in the game, it will have a much higher weight than would A', without any alteration in φ.[12] In effect, if we know that conjecture A' will take no chances until period 100 and so will then be allocated a small weight relative to whatever conjecture has in the meantime passed many prediction tests, we might as well downgrade A' at the beginning.

Consider a somewhat more involved example in which conjecture A again makes predictions at every period, and A' now makes predictions at periods $t = 0$ and $t = 100$, but remains silent in between. We may then want to assign the two conjectures equal weights at time $t = 0$, but adjust $\varphi_{h_{100}}$ in order to

[11] For example, we could have $A = [\underbrace{1, \ldots, 1}_{101}]$ and $A' = \{\omega \in \Omega : \omega_Y(100) = 1\}$.

[12] Alternatively, if A predicts incorrectly during some of the first 100 periods, it will subsequently be excluded and hence this choice of $\varphi_\emptyset$ will not interfere with further predictions.

give A credit for having made the intervening string of correct predictions, should both still be relevant at time $t = 100$. It seems as if simply adjusting $\varphi_{\varnothing}$ and thereafter holding φ fixed will not accomplish both goals. However, we can indeed incorporate all of these considerations without allowing φ to depend on h_t. The key is to note that the conjectures A and A' can both be relevant at time $t = 100$ only if they make identical predictions at time $t = 0$. But if they make the same prediction at time $t = 0$, only the sum of their weights (and not their relative weighting) has any effect on predictions at $t = 0$. We can thus freely adjust $\varphi_{\varnothing}(A)$ and $\varphi_{\varnothing}(A')$ in such a way that would not change predictions until time $t = 0$, but will give A more weight at time $t = 100$.

The more general point is that $\{\varphi_{h_t}\}_{t\geq 0, h_t \in H_t}$ is under-identified by the rankings $\{\succsim_{h_t} \subset 2^Y \times 2^Y\}_{t\geq 0, h_t \in H_t}$. Many different credence functions $\{\varphi_{h_t}\}_{t\geq 0, h_t \in H_t}$ give rise to the same ranking of subsets (at each and every history). Indeed it turns out that any ranking that can be obtained by a history-dependent $\{\varphi_{h_t}\}_{t\geq 0, h_t \in H_t}$ can also be represented by a history-independent φ:

Proposition 4.1 *Let $\{\varphi_{h_t}\}_{t\geq 0, h_t \in H_t}$ be a collection of finite measures on $(\mathcal{A}, \mathcal{E})$. Then there exists a measure φ on $(\mathcal{A}, \mathcal{E})$ such that, at each h_t and for every $Y', Y'' \subset Y$,*

$$\varphi(\mathcal{A}(h_t, Y')) \geq \varphi(\mathcal{A}(h_t, Y'')) \iff \varphi_{h_t}(\mathcal{A}(h_t, Y')) \geq \varphi_{h_t}(\mathcal{A}(h_t, Y'')).$$

It thus sacrifices no generality to work with a function φ that is unchanged as history unfolds. We accordingly hereafter drop the h_t subscript on φ and work with an unchanging φ.

When φ is independent of history, the updating rule inherent in (1)–(2) is equivalent to the Dempster-Shafer (cf. Dempster (1967), Shafer Shafer (1976)) updating of the belief function defined by φ, in face of the evidence $[h_t]$. (See Appendix B for details). This updating rule has been axiomatized by Gilboa and Schmeidler (1993) in the context of Choquet expected utility maximization.[13]

4.3 Special Cases

The unified framework is sufficiently general as to capture several standard models of inductive reasoning.

[13] The Dempster-Shafer updating rule, explained in Appendix B, is a special case of Dempster's rule of combination. We mention in passing that it does not suffer from common criticisms of the Dempster-Shafer theory, such as those leveled by Voorbraak (1991).

4.3.1 *Bayesian Reasoning*

We first show that our framework reduces to Bayesian reasoning if one restricts attention to conjectures that consist of one state each.

Bayesian reasoning has been studied in many ways in many fields.[14] The various manifestations of the Bayesian approach differ in several ways, such as the scope of the state space and the degree to which Bayesian beliefs are related to decision making, but they share two common ingredients: (i) uncertainty is always quantified probabilistically; and (ii) when new information is obtained, probabilistic beliefs are updated according to Bayes's rule.

To embed Bayesian reasoning in our framework, define the set of *Bayesian conjectures* to be

$$\mathcal{B} = \{\{\omega\} \mid \omega \in \Omega\} \subset \mathcal{A}. \tag{3}$$

Notice that $\mathcal{B}$ is an element of $\mathcal{E}$. Moreover, for every history h_t, the set of surviving or unfalsified Bayesian conjectures $\mathcal{B}(h_t)$ is given by

$$\mathcal{B}(h_t) = \left\{\{\omega\} \,\middle|\, \omega \in [h_t]\right\},$$

and it is in $\mathcal{E}$ as well.

A credence function φ is Bayesian if only Bayesian hypotheses matter in determining the weights of credence attached to a set of conjectures, i.e. if for any set $E \in \mathcal{E}$, we have

$$\varphi(E) = \varphi(E \cap \mathcal{B}). \tag{4}$$

In particular, among the conjectures contained in $\mathcal{A}$, only those in $\mathcal{B}$ are assigned positive weight by a Bayesian credence function.

We can confirm that our model captures Bayesian reasoning:

Lemma 4.1 *Let p be a probability measure on $(\Omega, \mathcal{A})$. There exists a Bayesian credence function such that for every history h_t, there is a constant $\lambda > 0$ for which, for every $Y' \subset Y$ and h_t with $p(\mathcal{B}(h_t)) > 0$,*

$$p(y_t \in Y' \mid [h_t]) = \lambda\varphi(\mathcal{A}(h_t, Y')).$$

[14] Bayesian reasoning appeared explicitly in the writings of Bayes (1763), with precursors from the early days of probability theory such as Bernoulli (1713). Beginning with the work of de Finetti and his followers, it has given rise to the Bayesian approach to statistics (see, for example, Lindley (1965)). Relying on the axiomatic approach of Ramsey (1931), de Finetti (1931; 1937), and Savage (1972), it has grown to become the dominant approach in economic theory and in game theory. The Bayesian approach has also made significant headways in computer science and artificial intelligence, as in the context of Bayesian networks (Pearl (1986)). Within the philosophy of science, notable proponents of the Bayesian approach include Carnap (1952) and Jeffrey (2004).

Proof. Let the credence function be given by

$$\varphi(E) = p(E \cap \mathcal{B}).$$

First note that $E \cap \mathcal{B}$ is in $\mathcal{A}$.

Hence, φ attaches to each set of Bayesian hypotheses a weight of credence equal to the prior probability attached to the set, and attaches to a general set of hypotheses a weight of credence equal to that of the Bayesian hypotheses it contains. Then φ is clearly Bayesian. It then remains to identify the normalization appropriate for history h_t:

$$\begin{aligned}
\varphi(\mathcal{A}(h_t, Y')) &= p(\{\omega : \{\omega\} \in \mathcal{A}(h_t, Y')\}) \\
&= p(\mathcal{B}(h_t))\frac{p(\{\omega : \{\omega\} \in \mathcal{A}(h_t, Y')\})}{p(\mathcal{B}(h_t))} \\
&= p(\mathcal{B}(h_t))p(y_t \in Y' \mid [h_t]) \\
&:= \lambda^{-1} p(y_t \in Y' \mid [h_t]),
\end{aligned}$$

giving the result. ■

Bayesian reasoning is thus a special case of our framework: every Bayesian belief can be simulated by a model φ, and Bayesian updating is imitated by our process of excluding refuted conjectures. Apart from the normalization step, which guarantees that updated probabilities continue to sum up to 1 as conjectures are deleted but has no effect on relative beliefs, Bayesian updating is nothing more than the exclusion of refuted conjectures from further prediction.

Our model captures Bayesian reasoning via an assumption that only conjectures containing a single state enter the agent's reasoning. An agent whose credence function assigns positive weight to non-Bayesian conjectures (e.g. $\varphi(\{A\}) > 0$ for some $A \in \mathcal{A} \backslash \mathcal{B} > 0$) will not be "Bayesian" by any common definition of the term. For example, suppose that $A = \{\omega_1, \omega_2\}$ and $\varphi(\{A\}) = \delta > 0$. Such an agent can be viewed as arguing, "I think that one of ω_1 or ω_2 might occur, and I put a weight $\delta > 0$ on this conjecture, but I cannot divide this weight between the two states". Intuitively, this abandons the Bayesian tenet of quantifying all uncertainty in terms of probabilities. Formally, the corresponding rankings of subsets of outcomes, $\succsim_{h_t}$, may fail to satisfy de Finetti's (1931; 1937) cancellation axiom: it can be the case that, for two sets of outcomes, B, C, $B \succsim_{h_t} C$ but not $B \backslash C \succsim_{h_t} C \backslash B$. In addition, if we use the credence function to make decisions by maximization of the Choquet integral of a utility function, the maximization will fail to satisfy Savage's "sure-thing principle" (axiom P2). As a result, upon adding decisions to our model of beliefs, we would have a converse to Lemma 4.1: the decision maker will be Bayesian if and *only if* (4) holds. (See Appendix B for a definition of Choquet integration.)

4.3.2 *Case-Based Reasoning*

Case-based reasoning is also a special case of our model.[15]

We first introduce a simple model of case-based reasoning in which case-based prediction is equivalent to kernel classification.[16] The agent has a similarity function over the characteristics,

$$s : X \times X \to \mathbb{R}_+,$$

and a memory decay factor $\beta \leq 1$. Given history $h_t = h_t(\omega)$, a set of outcomes $Y' \subsetneq Y$ is assigned the weight

$$S(h_t, Y') = \sum_{y \in Y'} \sum_{i=0}^{t-1} \beta^{t-i} s(\omega_X(i), \omega_X(t)) \mathbf{1}_{\{\omega_Y(i)=y\}},$$

where $\mathbf{1}$ is the indicator function of the subscripted event. Hence, the agent may be described as if she considered past cases in the history h_t, chose all those that resulted in some period i with some outcome $y \in Y'$, and added to the sum $S(h_t, Y')$ the similarity of the respective characteristic $\omega_X(i)$ to the current characteristic $\omega_X(t)$. The resulting sums $S(h_t, Y')$ can then be used to rank sets of possible outcomes Y'.

If $\beta = 1$ and in addition the similarity function is constant, the resulting number $S(h_t, \{y\})$ is proportional to the relative empirical frequency of y's in the history h_t. If, on the other hand, $\beta \to 0$, the maximizer of $S(h_t, \cdot)$ will be the most recent observation, $\omega_Y(t-1)$. Thus, when the similarity function is constant, case-based reasoning can be viewed as a simultaneous (and smooth) generalization of prediction by empirical frequencies on the one hand, and of prediction by recency on the other hand.

More interesting generalizations are possible when the similarity function isn't constant, and uses the information given in X to make more informed judgments.

The next observation states that the general framework presented in Section 4.2 can accommodate a special case of case-based reasoning:

[15] Analogical reasoning was explicitly discussed by Hume (1748), and received attention in the twentieth century in the guise of case-based reasoning (Riesbeck and Schank (1989), Schank (1986)), leading to the formal models and axiomatizations of Gilboa and Schmeidler (1995; 2001; 2003).

[16] See Akaike (1954) and Silverman (1986).

Lemma 4.2 *Let there be given $s : X \times X \to \mathbb{R}_+$ and $\beta \leq 1$. There exists a credence function φ such that, for every history h_t, there is a constant $\lambda > 0$ for which, for every $y \in Y$,*

$$\varphi(\mathcal{A}(h_t, \{y\})) = \lambda S(h_t, y).$$

To prove this observation, we first define case-based conjectures. For every $i < t \leq T - 1$, $x, z \in X$, let

$$A_{i,t,x,z} = \{\omega \in \Omega \mid \omega_X(i) = x, \omega_X(t) = z, \omega_Y(i) = \omega_Y(t)\}$$

and observe that it is the union of finitely many sets of the type $[h_t, Y']$. Hence $A_{i,t,x,z} \in \mathcal{A}$ and $\{A_{i,t,x,z}\} \in \mathcal{E}$.

We can interpret this conjecture as indicating that, *if* the input data are given by x in period i and by z in period t, *then* periods i and t will produce the same outcome (value of y). Notice that in contrast to the Bayesian conjectures, a single case-based conjecture consists of many states: $A_{i,t,x,z}$ does not restrict the values of $\omega_X(k)$ or $\omega_Y(k)$ for $k \neq i, t$. Let the set of all conjectures of this type be denoted by

$$\mathcal{CB} = \{A_{i,t,x,z} \mid i < t \leq T, x, z \in X\} \subset \mathcal{A}. \tag{5}$$

A credence function φ is *case-based* if, for every set $E \in \mathcal{E}$, we have

$$\varphi(E) = \varphi(E \cap \mathcal{CB}). \tag{6}$$

Thus, among the conjectures contained in the set $\mathcal{A}$, only those in $\mathcal{CB}$ are assigned positive weight by a case-based credence function.

Once the set of conjectures $\mathcal{CB}$ has been defined, the proof of Lemma 4.2 is straightforward:

Proof. Given a similarity function s and $\beta \leq 1$, let

$$\varphi\left(\{A_{i,t,x,z}\}\right) = c_t \beta^{(t-i)} s(x, z) \tag{7}$$

where $c_t > 0$ is chosen so that $\varphi(\mathcal{CB})$ is finite, say, $c_t = t^{-2}$. Let, for $E \in \mathcal{E}$,

$$\varphi(E) = \sum_{\{A_{i,t,x,z}\} \in E} \varphi\left(\{A_{i,t,x,z}\}\right).$$

Consider a history $h_t = h_t(\omega)$ and a prediction $y \in Y$. To calculate $\varphi(\mathcal{A}(h_t, \{y\}))$ observe first that, at h_t, only the conjectures $\{A_{i,t,\omega_X(i),\omega_X(t)} \mid i < t\}$ are unrefuted and yield predictions that are included in the singleton $\{y\}$. Hence, only t conjectures will affect the prediction $\{y\}$, corresponding to the t possible case-based conjectures of the form $A_{i,t,\omega_X(i),\omega_X(t)}$ (with $i = 0, 1, \ldots, t-1$). It is then immediate that $\varphi(\mathcal{A}(h_t, \{y\})) = c_t S(h_t, y)$. ■

In general, we could define similarity relations based not only on single observations but also on sequences, or on other more general patterns of observations, and could define predictions over nonsingleton sets. Such higher-level analogies can also be captured as conjectures in our framework. For instance, the agent might find history h_t similar to history h_i for $i < t$, because in both of them the last k periods had the same observations. This can be reflected by conjectures including states in which observations $(i-k+1), \ldots, i$ are identical to observations $(t-k+1), \ldots, t$, and so forth.

4.3.3 *Rule-Based Reasoning*

The model can accommodate many other forms of reasoning, often referred to as "rule-based reasoning".[17] These other modes of reasoning are again characterized by conjectures or "rules" to which they attach weights of credence. This section provides some examples.

The rule "the price of oil always rises" corresponds to the conjecture

$$A = \{\omega \in \Omega \mid \omega_Y(t) = 1 \quad \forall t\}.$$

There are many states in this conjecture, featuring different sequences of changes in the values of the level of demand and conflict.

Our framework can also encompass *association rules*, or rules that can be expressed as *conditional* statements. For example, consider the rule "if the level of conflict has risen, so will the price of oil". This rule can be described by

$$A = \left\{\omega \in \Omega \;\middle|\; \omega_{X^2}(t) = 0 \quad or \quad \omega_Y(t) = 1 \quad \forall t\right\}. \tag{8}$$

(Recall that $\omega_{X^2}(t)$ indicates whether there was an increase in the index of conflict, and $\omega_Y(t)$ an increase in the price of oil.) The rule "an increase in conflict implies an increase in the price of oil" is then read as "either there will be less conflict, or more expensive oil, or possibly both".[18]

[17] We draw the name "rule-based" from earliest models of reasoning, dating back to Greek philosophy and its study of logic, focusing on the rules of deduction and the concept of proof. The rise of analytical philosophy, the philosophy of mathematics, and artificial intelligence greatly extended the scope of rule-based reasoning, including its use for modeling human thinking, as in the introduction of non-monotonic (McCarthy (1980), McDermott and Doyle (1980), Reiter (1980)), probabilistic (Nilsson (1986)), and a variety of other new logics.

[18] Holland's (1975) genetic algorithms address classification problem where the value of y is to be determined by the values of $x = (x^1, \ldots, x^m)$, based on past observations of x and y. The algorithm maintains a list of association rules, each of which predicts the value of y according to values of some of the x^j's. For instance, one rule might read "if x^2 is 1 then y is 1" and another, "if x^3 is 1 and x^7 is 0 then y is 0". In each period, each rule has a weight that depends on its success in the past, its specificity (the number of x^j variables it involves) and so forth. The algorithm

An association rule will be excluded from the set $\mathcal{A}(h_t, Y')$ as soon as a single counter-example is observed. Thus, if history h_t is such that for some $i < t$ we observed an increase in the level of conflict that was not followed by a rise in the price of oil, the conjecture (8) will not be used for further analysis. When an association rule is unrefuted, it may or may not affect predictions, depending on whether its antecedent holds. If the antecedent of a rule is false, the rule becomes vacuously true and does not affect prediction. However, if (in this example) we do observe a rise in the level of conflict, $\omega_{X^2}(t) = 1$, the rule has bite (retaining the assumption that it is as yet unrefuted). Its weight of credence φ will be added to the prediction that the price of oil will rise, $\omega_Y(t) = 1$, but not to the prediction that it will not, $\omega_Y(t) = 0$.

Our framework also allows one to capture functional rules, stating that the value of y is a certain function f of the value of x, such as

$$A = \left\{\omega \in \Omega \;\middle|\; \omega_Y(t) = f(\omega_X(t)) \quad \forall t\right\}.$$

4.3.4 *Combined Models*

The previous subsections illustrate how our framework can capture each of the modes of reasoning separately. Its main strength, however, is in being able to smoothly combine such modes of reasoning, simply by considering credence functions φ that assign positive weights to sets of conjectures of different types.

For example, consider an agent who attempts to reason about the world in a Bayesian way. The agent has a prior probability p over the states of the world, Ω. However, she also carries with her some general rules and analogies. Assume that she employs a model φ such that

$$\varphi(\mathcal{B}) = 1 - \varepsilon$$

(where $\varepsilon > 0$) with weight allocated among the Bayesian conjectures according to

$$\varphi(\{\{\omega\} \mid \omega \in A\}) = (1 - \varepsilon)p(A)$$

(for all $A \in \mathcal{A}$) and the remaining weight ε is split among case-based and rule-based conjectures.

chooses a prediction y that is a maximizer of the total weight of the rules that predict this y and that apply to the case at hand. The prediction part of genetic algorithms is therefore a special case of our framework, where the conjectures are the association rules involved. However, in a genetic algorithm the set of rules does not remain constant, with rules instead being generated by a partly-random process, including crossover between "parent genes", mutations, and so forth.

If ε is small, then the non-Bayesian conjectures will play a relatively minor role in determining the agent's initial predictions, and will continue to do so as long as the history unfolds along a path that is sufficiently likely under the the prior p. But what happens if the reasoner faces a surprising outcome, such as the September 11 attacks or the Lehman Brothers' collapse?

If the agent had assigned the outcome zero probability, Bayesian updating will not be well-defined. In this case, the non-Bayesian conjectures will determine the agent's predictions. For example, in the face of the September 11 attack, the agent might discard Bayesian reasoning and resort to the general rule that "at the onset of war, the stock market plunges". Alternatively, the agent may resort to analogies, and predict the stock market's behavior based on past cases such as the attack on Pearl Harbor.

Even if the outcome in question had a nonzero but very small prior probability, non-Bayesian reasoning will again be relatively more important. Conditional probabilities are now well-defined and can be used, but the formerly negligible non-Bayesian conjectures will now be much more prominent. This can be interpreted as if the reasoner has a certain degree of doubt about her own probabilistic assessments, captured by the weight $\varepsilon > 0$ put on non-Bayesian conjectures. This process will be formalized in the sequel.

4.3.5 *How Would We Know and Why Would We Care?*

We have noted in Section 4.3.1 that an agent who attaches weight to non-Bayesian conjectures will generate rankings $\succsim_{h_t}$ that are observably non-Bayesian. However, Proposition 4.1 also notes that the agent's predictions may be consistent with many credence functions φ. Indeed, it is easy to see that, if the agent is asked simply to identify the most likely singleton in Y after each history, then any given sequence of such predictions can be explained by either Bayesian or other methods of reasoning.[19] Why should we care, then, about the mode of reasoning the agent employs?

The answer is that different modes of reasoning might explain a given dataset of predictions *ex post*, yet provide different predictions *ex ante*. For example, if we knew that the agent were Bayesian, we would try to use her past predictions to estimate her prior, and use it to forecast her posterior.[20] By contrast, if the agent were known to be a case-based reasoner, her past predictions would be used to estimate her similarity function. Thus, the same dataset of observations might be compatible with both assumptions about

[19] Relatedly, Matsui (2000) demonstrated that expected utility maximization and case-based decision theory lead to equivalent sets of feasible outcomes.

[20] Naturally, such a task requires additional assumptions on the structure of the prior probability.

the mode reasoning, but it might lead to different predictions under these assumptions.

This is a manifestation of a more general point: when comparing different paradigms, one often cannot expect to have a simple experiment that identifies the correct one. Within each paradigm many theories may be developed, which can, post hoc, explain given data. However, the simplest theory within one paradigm might lead to rather different predictions than the corresponding theory within another paradigm. In other words, if we augment paradigms with a method for selecting theories within them (say, the simplest theory that fits the data), the choice of a paradigm will have observable implications.

4.4 Dynamics of Reasoning Methods

4.4.1 *When is Bayesian Reasoning Fragile?*

Under what conditions will Bayesian reasoning survive as evidence accumulates, and when will the agent turn to other modes of reasoning? Our answer is that Bayesian reasoning will wither away if the agent's prior is not sufficiently informative.

Assumptions We start by assuming that at least some weight is placed on both Bayesian and case-based reasoning:

Assumption 4.1

$$\varphi(\mathcal{B}), \varphi(\mathcal{CB}) > 0.$$

There can be many other types of conjectures that get non-zero weight according to φ. The specific inclusion of case-based reasoning is a matter of convenience, born out of familiarity. We explain in Section 4.4.1 how this assumption could be reformulated to make no reference to case-based conjectures.

Next, we think of the agent as allocating the overall weight of credence in a top-down approach, first allocating weights to modes of reasoning, and then to specific conjectures within each mode of reasoning. First consider the weight of the Bayesian conjectures, $\varphi(\mathcal{B})$. We are interested in an agent who knows relatively little about the process she is observing. An extreme case of such ignorance is modeled by a uniform prior:

$$\frac{\varphi\left(\mathcal{B}(h_t)\right)}{\varphi\left(\mathcal{B}(h'_t)\right)} = 1, \tag{9}$$

for any pair of histories of the same length, h_t and h'_t. We can relax this assumption, requiring only that the probability assigned to any particular history cannot be too much smaller than that assigned to another history of the same length. Thus, one may assume that there exists $M > 1$ such that, for every t and every $h_t, h'_t \in H_t$,

$$\frac{\varphi\left(\mathcal{B}(h_t)\right)}{\varphi\left(\mathcal{B}(h'_t)\right)} < M. \tag{10}$$

We weaken this condition still further, allowing M to depend on t, and assume only that the ratio between the probabilities of two histories cannot go to infinity (or zero) too fast as we consider ever-larger values of t. Formally,

Assumption 4.2 *There exists a polynomial $P(t)$ such that, for every t and every two histories $h_t, h'_t \in H_t$,*

$$\frac{\varphi(\mathcal{B}(h_t))}{\varphi(\mathcal{B}(h'_t))} \leq P(t).$$

Assumption 4.2 is still strong—it will be violated if, as is often assumed in Bayesian models, the agent believes she faces successive *iid* draws, say, $\omega_Y(t) = 1$ in each period with probability $p > 0.5$.[21] In this case the agent knows a great deal about the data generating process, being able to identify the process up to the specification of a single parameter. In contrast, our message is that Bayesian reasoning will fade when the agent knows relatively little about the data generating process. However, sub-section 4.4.1 shows that a similar (but somewhat more cumbersome) result holds in the *iid* case as well.

We make an analogous assumption regarding the way that the weight of credence is distributed among the various case-based conjectures. It would suffice for our result to impose a precise analog of Assumption 4.2, namely that there is a polynomial $Q(t)$ such that, for any t and any pair of case-based conjectures $A_{i,t,x,z}$ and $A_{i',t',x'z'}$, we have

$$\frac{\varphi(\{A_{i,t,x,z}\})}{\varphi(\{A_{i',t',x',z'}\})} \leq Q(t). \tag{11}$$

However, suppose (analogously to (7)) that there exists a similarity function $s : X \times X \to \mathbb{R}_+$, a decay factor $\beta \in (0, 1]$, and a constant $c > 0$ such that, for every $i < t$ and every $x, z \in X$,

$$\varphi(\{A_{i,t,x,z}\}) = c\beta^{t-i}s(x, z). \tag{12}$$

In this case, the characteristics $x, z \in X$ determine the relative weights placed on the case-based conjectures involving information of a given vintage

[21] For an easy illustration of this failure, observe that the ratio of the probabilities of a string of t successive 1's and a string of t successive 0's is $(p/(1-p))^t$, and hence exponential in t.

(i e. a given value of $t - i$), with $\beta \leq 1$ ensuring that older information is no more influential than more recent information. This formulation is rather natural, but it violates (11) if $\beta < 1$, as the relevance of older vintages then declines exponentially. Fortunately, there is an obvious and easily interpretable generalization of (11) that allows us to encompass (12).

Assumption 4.3 *There exists a polynomial $Q(t)$ such that*

- *for every i, i', t, t', x, x' and z, z' with $t - i = t' - i'$, and $t' < t$,*

$$\frac{\varphi\left(\{A_{i',t',x',z'}\}\right)}{\varphi\left(\{A_{i,t,x,z}\}\right)} \leq Q(t), \tag{13}$$

- *and for every $t, x, z \in X$ and $i < i' < t$,*

$$\frac{\varphi\left(\{A_{i,t,x,z}\}\right)}{\varphi\left(\{A_{i',t,x,z}\}\right)} \leq Q(t). \tag{14}$$

Condition (13) stipulates that within a set of conjectures based on similarities across a given time span (i.e., for which $t - i = t' - i'$), the agent's weights of credence cannot be too different. Condition (14) stipulates that when comparing similarities at a given period t, based on identical characteristics but different vintages, the older information cannot be considered too much *more* important than more recent information. Typically, we would expect older information to be *less* important and hence this constraint will be trivially satisfied.

Result The following result establishes that under Assumptions 4.1–4.3, in the long run the agent puts all of her weight on non-Bayesian (rather than on Bayesian) conjectures.

For the statement of the result we need a notation for the case-based conjectures that are relevant at history h_t:

$$\mathcal{CB}(h_t) = \mathcal{CB} \cap \left(\cup_{y \in Y} \mathcal{A}(h_t, \{y\})\right).$$

Proposition 4.2 *Let Assumptions 4.1–4.3 hold. Then at each $\omega \in \Omega$,*

$$\lim_{t \to \infty} \frac{\varphi\left(\mathcal{B}(h_t)\right)}{\varphi\left(\mathcal{CB}(h_t)\right)} = 0.$$

Hence, the Bayesian component of the agent's reasoning will wither away. As we noted in Section 4.3.5, the resulting shifting weights of credence can give rise to predictions that could not be rationalized by a Bayesian model.

The Bayesian part of the agent's beliefs converges to the truth at an exponential rate as evidence is accumulated (that is, as t grows): within the Bayesian class of conjectures, the probability of the true state *relative to* the probability of all unrefuted states grows exponentially with t. How is this fast learning reconciled with Proposition 4.2? The conditional probability of the true state increases at an exponential rate not because its numerator (the weight attached to the true state) increases, but because its denominator (the total probability of all unrefuted states) decreases at an exponential rate. But this is precisely the reason that the weight of the entire class of Bayesian conjectures tapers off and leaves the stage to others, such as the case-based conjectures. As t grows, the weight of Bayesian conjectures that remain unrefuted by history h_t, $\varphi\left(\mathcal{B}(h_t)\right)$, becomes an exponentially small fraction (given Assumption 4.1) of the original weight of all Bayesian conjectures, $\varphi(\mathcal{B})$. In contrast, the number of case-based conjectures at period t is only a polynomial (in t), and hence there is no reason for the weight of those that make predictions at history h_t to decrease exponentially fast in t. The *relative* weight placed on Bayesian conjectures thus declines to zero.

It follows that a similar result would hold if we were to replace the class of case-based conjectures with any other class of conjectures that grows polynomially in t and that provides some non-tautological prediction for each h_t, provided an assumption similar to Assumption 4.3 holds. Therefore, we do not view this result as proving the prevalence of case-based reasoning. Rather, the result highlights the fragility of Bayesian reasoning. Case-based reasoning is simply a familiar example of a mode of reasoning with the requisite properties.

Recall that case-based prediction can be viewed as generalizing the prediction of the modal outcome in the past, as well as the prediction of the most recent outcome. While we again emphasize that the role of case-based reasoning in this argument could be filled by many alternatives, we find it unsurprising that an agent who does not know much about the data generating process may use simple statistical techniques, predicting outcomes that have been observed most often or most recently. Our result describes a possible mechanism by which this may happen, for reasons unrelated to bounded rationality or to cognitive or computational limitations.

Weights of Credence Proposition 4.2 is driven by the fact that there are fewer case-based conjectures than there are Bayesian ones. In order for a relatively small class of conjectures to have unrefuted representatives at each history, it must be the case that many of these conjectures make no predictions at many histories. In a sense, conjectures from the smaller class may be viewed as saving their ammunition and picking their fights selectively.

The obvious question is then: Are the Bayesian conjectures treated fairly by our assumptions on the function φ? Specifically, if, at time t, the agent compares the Bayesian conjectures to the case-based ones, she will find that each of the former (that is still in the game) has made t successful predictions, whereas each of the surviving case-based conjectures has made no predictions at all. Shouldn't the tested conjectures get more weight than the untested ones? Shouldn't the credence function φ be updated to reflect the fact that some conjectures have a more impressive track record than others?

Section 4.2.3 explained that it sacrifices no generality to work with a function φ that is never revised as history unfolds. This simply refocuses the question in terms of the a priori assignment of weights, in the process directing attention to Assumption 4.3. Should we not make the weight of case-based conjectures of the form $A_{i,t,x,z}$ decline exponentially fast in t (violating Assumption 4.3), to give the Bayesian ones a fair chance, as it were?

We believe there are some obvious circumstances in which the answer is negative. Suppose that all of the Bayesian conjectures get the same weight, satisfying an extreme version of Assumption 4.2. It then cannot help but be the case that *some* of them are still unrefuted by history h_t: by construction, there had to be states of the world that are compatible with h_t. The agent knew at time $t = 0$ that, whatever history materializes at time t, some Bayesian conjectures will be in the game. In this case, there is no reason to artificially increase the relative weight of these conjectures upon reaching history h_t, as if they were a priori selected. Adopting the equivalent but a priori convention of decreasing the weight of the case-based conjectures at an exponential or even faster rate strikes us as similarly unjustified, being tantamount to committing to a Bayesian approach that one knows is both tautologically true and without content.[22]

Another way to look at this problem is the following. Let the agent ask herself at time 0, how much weight is given (a priori) to all conjectures of a given type that will be relevant for prediction at time t. For the Bayesian conjectures the answer is independent of t: when we sum across all possible histories, we always get the same number, $\varphi(\mathcal{B})$, because the union of the relevant conjectures across all histories of length t is the set of all Bayesian conjectures, $\mathcal{B}$, for all t. For the case-based conjectures the situation is quite different: when we consider $t \neq t'$, the set of conjectures that will be relevant at some history h_t is disjoint from the corresponding set for t'. Indeed, we have observed that the total weight of all conjectures that may be relevant at time t has to tend to zero, whereas the corresponding weight for the Bayesian

[22] At the other extreme, suppose that only one Bayesian conjecture is given positive weight by φ. In this case, at time t, if this conjecture is still unrefuted, the agent might indeed wish to put an exponentially high relative weight on it, that is, to shrink the total weight of the competing case-based conjectures exponentially fast in t. Equivalently, the agent might arrange at the beginning of the game to cause the weight placed on case-based conjectures $A_{i,t,x,z}$ to decrease very quickly in t, allowing the lone Bayesian conjecture to rule the roost if it survives, while retaining the *relative* weights on the surviving case-based conjectures so that their predictions are unaffected in the event the Bayesian hypothesis is falsified. Notice, however, that this manipulation is unnecessary. If the initial weight attached to Bayesian hypotheses is large, the weight will remain large, as there are no falsified Bayesian hypotheses to melt away. In this case, Bayesian reasoning survives even without help in the form of declining case-based weights.

conjectures in a constant. From this viewpoint, the Bayesian conjectures have an inherent advantage. Thus, it seems reasonable to require that, at the very least, the vanishing sequence of weights of case-based conjectures not vanish too fast, and this is what Assumption 4.3 states.

The *iid* Case An obvious case in which Assumption 4.2 is violated occurs when the agent believes that she observes an *iid* process. Suppose, for example, that $Y = \{0, 1\}$ and the agent believes the y_t are *iid* Bernoulli random variables, i.e., $y_t \sim B(p)$. Then Assumption 4.2 holds only if $p = 0.5$, because the ratio of single states' probabilities involves exponentials of p and $(1 - p)$. Nonetheless, a conclusion very similar to that of Proposition 4.2 still holds.

Consider the state space Ω endowed with the σ-algebra Σ defined by the variables $(x_t, y_t)_{t\geq 0}$. A probability measure μ on Σ is a *non-trivial conditionally iid measure* if, for every $x \in X$ there exists $\lambda_x \in \Delta(Y)$ such that (i) for every $h_t = ((x_0, y_0), \ldots, (x_{t-1}, y_{t-1}), x_t)$, the conditional distribution of Y given h_t according to μ is λ_{x_t}; and (ii) λ_x is non-degenerate for every $x \in X$. The next assumption states that the Bayesian part of the agent's beliefs is governed by such a measure:

Assumption 4.4 *There exists a non-trivial conditionally iid measure μ such that, for every $A \in \Sigma$*

$$\varphi(\{\{\omega\} \mid \omega \in A\}) = \mu(A)\varphi(\mathcal{B})$$

Thus, this assumption states that the weight of the Bayesian conjectures, $\varphi(\mathcal{B})$, is divided among them in a way that is proportional to the measure μ.[23]

We can now state

Proposition 4.3 *Let Assumptions 4.1,4.3, and 4.4 hold, and let μ be the measure of Assumption 4.4. Then*

$$\mu\left(\lim_{t\to\infty} \frac{\varphi(\mathcal{B}(h_t))}{\varphi(\mathcal{CB}(h_t))} = 0\right) = 1.$$

Proposition 4.3 states that, μ-almost surely, the weight of the Bayesian hypotheses relative to that of the case-based ones will converge to zero. Thus, an agent who has Bayesian beliefs μ, and who puts some weight $\varepsilon > 0$ on the case-based beliefs in a way that corresponds to Assumption 4.3, will, *according to her own beliefs*, converge to be non-Bayesian. Importantly, even if the agent were right about the Bayesian part of her beliefs, she would still predict that her own reasoning will become non-Bayesian.

[23] Observe that μ is defined over subsets of Ω (that are in Σ) whereas φ is defined over subsets of such subsets, and the assumption only deals with the subsets that contain only singletons $\{\omega\}$. Observe also that Assumption 4.4 remains silent about the distribution of the x's.

The proof of Proposition 4.3 mimics that of Proposition 4.2. The key observation is that there are exponentially many histories for any given frequencies of outcomes, provided that these frequencies are non-trivial. For example, if $|X| = 1$, $Y = \{0, 1\}$ and we consider a history of length t, there is but one history in which there are 0 y's that are equal to 1, and $O(t^k)$ histories in which there are k such y's. But there are exponentially many histories in which the relative frequency of 1 is close to pt. That is, $\binom{t}{pt}$ is exponential in t if $p \neq 0, 1$. More generally, since μ is assumed to be *non-trivial* conditionally *iid* (that is, since the conditional distributions λ_x are assumed to be non-degenerate), apart from a set of μ measure zero, any history at time t has exponentially many other histories that are just as likely.

Observe that a similar result would hold in case the agent only believes that the variables y_t, given each value of x, are exchangeable. Indeed, the very definition of exchangeability, involving all possible permutations, hints at the dangers of exponential blow-up. To prove such a result, one need only make sure that sufficiently many permutations result in different histories h_t.

Along similar lines, the conclusion of Proposition 4.2 holds also if Assumption 4.2 fails but there exists $\gamma < 1$ such that, for some polynomial $P(t)$, for every t and every h_t,

$$\varphi(\mathcal{B}_t(h_t)) \leq \gamma^t P(t). \tag{15}$$

If Assumptions 4.1 and 4.3 also hold, then the relative weight on Bayesian conjectures will decline to zero.

On the other hand, an agent who is *resolutely* Bayesian will handle *iid* variables just as one would expect.

Example 1 Suppose that X is degenerate, say, $X = \{0\}$, $Y = \{0, 1\}$, and that $\varphi(\mathcal{B}) = 1$. Suppose this Bayesian's prior is a nondegenerate mix of two prior distributions. One of these predicts that each y_t is drawn from the Bernoulli distribution $B(p)$ and one from the Bernoulli distribution $B(q)$. Then if the observations are indeed *iid* draws from $B(p)$, the relatively weight that the agent places on this distribution will almost surely (according to the true distribution) converge to one. The agent will eventually predict optimally, predicting $y_t = 1$ in each period if $p > .5$, and $y_t = 0$ otherwise. ■

Agents who are convinced they should be Bayesian thus exhibit familiar behavior. In light of this, how will an agent reason who is reasonably confident that she faces an *iid* process, but is uncertain about the parameter? Much depends on what is meant by "reasonably confident", a judgment manifested in the agent's credence function.

Example 2 Suppose that X is degenerate, $Y = \{0, 1\}$, and that the weights of credence the agent attaches to Bayesian conjectures are consistent with the various y_t being drawn *iid* from a Bernoulli distribution. If the agent is sufficiently confident of her *iid* hypothesis as to attach zero weights of credence to all other conjectures, she will be familiarly and resolutely Bayesian throughout. If she hedges her bets by attaching some weight to case-based conjectures, in accordance with Assumption 4.3, then the weight she attaches to Bayesian conjectures will decline to zero. Indeed, the agent can be assured at the beginning of the process that this will happen. Alternatively, suppose the agent attaches credence to case-based hypotheses, but attaches weights that cause $\varphi(\{A_{i,t,x,z}\})$ to decline exponentially (violating Assumption 4.3). Suppose again the Bayesian prior is a nondegenerate mix of two prior distributions, one predicting that each y_t is drawn from the Bernoulli distribution $B(p)$ and one predicting draws from the Bernoulli distribution $B(q)$. Then if the weights $\varphi(\{A_{i,t,x,z}\})$ decline appropriately, the weight of Bayesian hypotheses will increase to one if the data are indeed generated by $B(p)$ or $B(q)$, but in other cases (e.g. data drawn from $B(r)$ for some $r \neq p, q$) the Bayesian prior will slip into insignificance and case-based reasoning will prevail. They agent will thus remain Bayesian if her Bayesian prior contains the correct data generating process, but will otherwise slip into case-based reasoning. ■

Example 2.5 We can provide a simple illustration. Consider again the simplest case of $X = \{0\}$, $Y = \{0, 1\}$. Assume that y_t are *iid*, where $y_t = 1$ with probability p.

Consider the set of states

$$B_{i,y} = \left\{\omega \in \Omega \;\middle|\; \omega_Y(t) = y \quad \forall t \geq i\right\}$$

for $i \geq 0$ and $y \in Y$. Hence, each collection of states $B_{i,y}$ is identified by a given period i and outcome y, and predicts that from period i on, only outcome y will be observed.

The agent attaches weights to all of the Bayesian conjectures in the set

$$\bigcup_{i \geq 0, y \in Y} B_{i,y}.$$

The weight attached to the states in $B_{i,0} \cup B_{i,1}$ is given by $\xi 2^{-i}$, evenly distributed among such states. (The factor ξ is a normalization, to ensure weights sum to unity.) There are 2^i such hypotheses, so that the weight of a single such hypothesis is 2^{-2i}. Notice that (15) holds, so that the weights attached to Bayesian hypotheses are consistent with Bayesian reasoning withering away.

If weight is attached only to Bayesian hypotheses, then obviously Bayesian reasoning will survive. If Assumption 4.3 holds, then Bayesian reasoning will disappear. We examine a middle case here.

Because there are no x values to consider, the case-based conjectures are simply

$$A_{i,t} = \{\omega \in \Omega \mid \omega_Y(i) = \omega_Y(t)\},$$

and the set of all case-based conjectures is

$$\mathcal{CB} = \{A_{i,t} \mid i < t\}.$$

The weight attached to the case-based hypothesis in $A_{i,t}$ is given by $\xi 2^{-2t}$ (obviating Assumption 4.3).

Now consider a history h_t ending with a run of either $y = 0$ of $y = 1$ of length ℓ. The total weight of case-based hypotheses is 2^{-2t}. Among the Bayesian hypotheses, there survives a hypothesis from the $B(t-\ell, 0) \cup B(t-\ell, 1)$, with weight $2^{-(t-\ell)}$. The weight placed on Bayesian hypotheses is thus at least $2^{-(t-\ell)}$, and the weight of Bayesian hypotheses relative to case-based hypotheses is at east 2^{ℓ}. As the history unfolds, with probability one there will occur arbitrarily long strings of identical values of y, at which point the relative weight of Bayesian hypotheses will be arbitrarily large. At the same time, strings will periodically be broken, restoring the Bayesian and case-based hypotheses to an equal footing. Hence, from time to time there will emerge a Bayesian hypotheses that is accepted, only to collapse at some subsequent point. In other words, even if the data are completely random, it should be expected that theories would rise and fall every so often, with case-based reasoning being more prominent between regimes of different theories.

Observe that the balance of weights between the two modes of reasoning is driven by the success of Bayesian reasoning. This reflects the intuition that people would like to understand the process they observe, and that such "understanding" means a simple, concise theory that explains the data. If such a theory exists, agents will tend to prefer it over case-based reasoning. But when all simple theories are refuted, agents will resort to case-based reasoning. ■

4.4.2 *When will Bayesianism Prevail?*

If we had worked with the stronger version of Assumption 4.2 given by (9), we would have the expected (though perhaps reassuring) result that Bayesian reasoning disappears when the Bayesian prior is so diffuse that a Bayesian could not possibly learn anything. However, Assumption 4.2 allows Bayesian priors that will in turn allow learning, and yet still give way to other sorts of reasoning. Section 4.4.1 shows that Assumption 4.2 can be weakened yet further. When will Bayesian reasoning remain useful in the long run, or even dominate other reasoning methods?

Example 3 Suppose the agent believes that she nearly knows the true state of the world. We capture this by letting there be some ω, $\varphi(\{\omega\}) = 1 - \varepsilon$ (and hence allowing Assumption 4.2 to fail). If, on top of this, the agent is also correct in her focus on state ω, then (that is, at state ω) the weight attached to Bayesian conjectures will never dip below $1 - \varepsilon$. In other words, if the agent believes she knows the truth, and *happens to be right*, her Bayesian beliefs will remain dominant. ■

Example 4 A slightly less trivial example is the following. Suppose the agent believes she faces a cyclical process, but is uncertain of its period. To capture these beliefs in a simple model, let us consider only Bayesian and case-based reasoning. In addition, let $X = \{0\}$ and $Y = \{0, 1\}$, so that all periods have the same observable features, and they only differ in the binary variable the agent is trying to predict. For $k \geq 1$, let $\omega^k \in \Omega$ be defined by

$$\omega_Y^k(t) = \begin{cases} 0 & 2mk \leq t < (2m+1)k \qquad m = 0, 1, 2, \ldots \\ 1 & (2m+1)k \leq t < (2m+2)k \quad m = 0, 1, 2, \ldots \end{cases}.$$

Thus, for $k = 1$ the process is 01010101..., for $k = 2$ it is 001100110011... and so forth.

Let the agent's beliefs satisfy

$$\varphi\left(\left\{\{\omega^k\}\right\}\right) = \frac{1-\varepsilon}{2^k}$$

and

$$\varphi_T\left(\left\{\{\omega\}|\omega \notin \left\{\omega^k\,|1 \leq k\right\}\right\}\right) = 0.$$

Thus, the agent splits all the weight of the Bayesian conjectures among the conjectures $\left\{\omega^k\right\}$ and leaves no weight to the other Bayesian beliefs.[24] Once again, Assumption 4.2 fails. The remaining weight, ε, is split among the case-based conjectures.

Next suppose that the agent is right in her belief that the process is indeed cyclical (starting with a sequence of 0's). Thus, the data generating process chooses one of the states ω^k. At this state, once we get to period $t = k$, all the

[24] Observe that these Bayesian beliefs can also be readily described as rule-based beliefs. We suspect that this is not a coincidence. When Bayesian beliefs violate Assumption 4.2, it is likely to be the case that they reflect some knowledge about the data generating process, which can also be viewed as believing in a class of rules.

Bayesian conjectures $\{\omega^{k'}\}$ for $k' \neq k$ are refuted. In contrast, the conjecture $\{\omega^k\}$ is not refuted at any t. Consequently, at ω^k, for every $t \geq k$, the total weight of the Bayesian conjectures remains $\frac{1-\varepsilon}{2^k}$. The total weight of the case-based conjectures converges to 0, resulting in the Bayesian mode of reasoning remaining the dominant one (for large t). Clearly, this will only be true at the states $\left\{\omega^k\right\}$. At other states the converse result holds, because all Bayesian conjectures will be refuted and case-based reasoning will be the only remaining mode of reasoning. ∎

Example 5 Considering the same set-up, $X = \{0\}$ and $Y = \{0, 1\}$, let us limit attention to the first T periods. Consider a Bayesian agent who has a uniform belief over the average

$$\bar{y}_T = \frac{1}{T} \sum_{t=0}^{T-1} \omega_Y(t)$$

and, given $\bar{y}_T$, a uniform distribution over all the corresponding states. Thus, the agent puts a weight of $\frac{1}{T+1}$ on the sequence $1, 1, \ldots, 1$, but only a weight of $\frac{1}{T(T+1)}$ on each sequences with $(T-1)$ 1's and a single 0, and a weight $o(T^{-3})$ on each sequence with two 0's, and so forth.

The total weight of all case-based conjectures is a convergent series. This implies that the weight of all the case-based conjectures that are relevant at T has to decline to zero at a rate that is faster than $\frac{1}{T}$. Hence, if the agent observes the sequence $1, 1, \ldots, 1$, she will put more weight on the Bayesian conjecture that can be described also by the rule "$\omega_Y(t) = 1$ for every t". However, if the agent observes one exception to this rule, the Bayesian conjecture that predicts only 1's will have a weight that is $o(T^{-2})$. The more exceptions one observes, the lower is the weight of the Bayesian conjectures.

If the rate of decline of the weight of case-based conjectures in polynomial in T, say, $o(T^{-k})$ for $k > 1$, then finitely many exceptions to the rule "y is always 1" will suffice to switch to case-based reasoning. (Observe, however, that this reasoning is likely to make similar predictions: if all but k times one has observed $y_t = 1$, the modal prediction will still be $y_T = 1$.) If, by contrast, the weight of case-based conjectures decreases exponentially fast in T, even very spotty patterns will keep the Bayesian conjectures on par with the case-based ones. ∎

In summary, for Bayesian reasoning to prevail, the reasoner's Bayesian beliefs must be sufficiently informative (i.e. must contain the truth and must not be too diffuse), and the reasoner must have sufficient confidence in those Bayesian beliefs (e.g. build quickly declining weights of credence into the case-based conjectures relevant to successive periods). Economic models typically ensure this confidence by assuming that the agent entertains only Bayesian conjectures. We emphasize that our purpose is *not* to criticize either Bayesian reasoning or models based on Bayesian reasoning. Rather, our point is that the same characteristics that make Bayesian reasoning work well for a committed Bayesian can make it fragile in the hands of a tentative Bayesian.

4.4.3 *Probabilistic Reasoning*

Our main result establishes conditions under which Bayesian reasoning is fragile. However, it does not imply that when the weight of the Bayesian conjectures becomes negligible (relative to the weight of all unrefuted conjectures), probabilistic reasoning will be forever discarded. Instead, case-based and rule-based reasoning may subsequently give way to a new probabilistic model. Specifically, if at history h_t $\varphi\left(\mathcal{B}(h_t)\right)$ is low (relative to, say, $\varphi\left(\mathcal{CB}(h_t)\right)$), it is still possible that at a certain continuation of h_t, $h_{t'}$ with $t' > t$, the agent will again form beliefs that put a high weight on singleton hypotheses consistent with $h_{t'}$. As Proposition 4.1 indicates, this process is consistent with a single, history-independent φ.

The dynamics of our model can thus capture the type of reasoning raised in Section 4.1. Given a certain history $h_{t'}$ above, the agent forms probabilistic beliefs that can be thought of as a Bayesian model *given* $h_{t'}$. Such beliefs cannot be guaranteed to assign a high probability to all eventualities. The agent may have failed to seriously consider certain black swans, and some of them will have very low probability. As a result, the agent may find herself at a point where she mistrusts her model, and resorts to case-based and rule-based reasoning in its stead. However, at some subsequent $t'' > t'$, the agent beliefs may again effectively form a new probabilistic model.

It is easier to generate such "conditionally Bayesian" models than a single, a priori Bayesian model, for two related reasons: first, a model that starts at a history h_t has to consider only a subset of the events that a comprehensive Bayesian model deals with. If the time horizon is finite, the number of states one needs to assign probability to decreases exponentially fast as t grows, which means that the probability assignment task becomes easier. Second, as t grows, there are more data on the basis of which such probability assignments may be done. Indeed, if one considers the Bayesian model, one has to assign probabilities to many states with no data at all, out of thin air as it were. By contrast, for sufficiently large t, the agent may find regularities in the data that may suggest a new probabilistic model for the remaining periods.

At the same time, any probabilistic model generated after some history h_t will eventually face the same difficulty: whatever the finite history used for its formulation, it will become negligible relative to the size of the state space as one looks further into the future. Hence, one should expect that, apart from simple statistical problems, no probabilistic model will ever be the "correct" one. Rather, the agent will be cycling between periods in which she has a satisfactory probabilistic models, and periods in which black swans are observed and model uncertainty reigns. In such periods, case-based and rule-based reasoning are needed to make predictions, and, eventually, to formulate new probabilistic models.

To illustrate this, consider again the simplest example with no predicting variables, say, $X = \{0\}$, and $Y = \{0, 1\}$. Suppose that the agent believes that the data generating process on $\{0,1\}^{\mathbb{N}}$ follows a probabilistic model given by a measure ρ (defined on the standard σ-algebra on $\{0,1\}^{\mathbb{N}}$). However, certain periods in the past might have been exceptional – say, periods of wars, financial crises, and so forth. Hence, the agent does not believe that ρ is necessarily the appropriate probability measure to be assigned to Ω. She only believes that *after a certain history*, the continuation of the process will be governed by ρ. In other words, ρ is the conditional belief on Ω given a history h_t (with conditional state space that is also $\{0,1\}^{\mathbb{N}}$).

Assume further that the agent does not presume that she can assign probabilities to the initial period, in which wars, financial crises, and the like disrupt her prediction. She does not pretend to have probabilistic beliefs over the length of time at which the process will finally stabilize and be governed by φ. Rather, she awaits to see periods of relative calm, in which $y = 1$, and she assigns weight to rules of the type "if $y_i = 1$ for the last k periods, we may finally see the periods governed by ρ".

Let $R_{k,s}$ stand for the conjecture that, after the first time in which k consecutive 1's were observed, the process will follow a state $s \in \{0,1\}^{\mathbb{N}}$. Explicitly,

$$R_{k,s} = \left\{ \omega \in \Omega \;\middle|\; \begin{array}{c} \exists t \\ \omega_Y(i) = 1 \quad t-k \leq i < t \\ \omega_Y(i) = s(i-t) \quad t \leq i \\ (\omega_Y(i))_{i<t-1} \text{ does not contain a sequence of } k \text{ 1's} \end{array} \right\}.$$

(Observe that $R_{k,s} \cap R_{k',s'}$ may be non-empty for $s \neq s'$ if $k \neq k'$. However, $s \neq s'$ does imply that $R_{k,s}$ and $R_{k,s'}$ are disjoint for every k).

Let us assume that the agent assigns to the conjectures $\{R_{k,s}\}_s$ a total weight $Q(k) = k^{-2}$ and that ρ, when applied to Ω, satisfies 4.2. The weight of the "rule-based" conjectures will be given by

$$\varphi(\{R_{k,s}\}_{s\in A}) = Q(k)\rho(A)$$

for a measurable $A \subset \{0,1\}^{\mathbb{N}}$.

Apart from these conjectures, the agent will be assumed to assign positive weight also to the case-based conjectures,

$$A_{i,t} = \{\omega \in \Omega \mid \omega_Y(i) = \omega_Y(t)\},$$

and assume that their weight is

$$\varphi(\{A_{i,t}\}) = Q(t)/t$$

that is, that the total weight of the case-based conjectures at time t is $Q(t) = t^{-2}$ and that this weight is divided equally among the periods preceding t. In particular, Assumption 4.3 holds.

Consider a history h_t. Every sequence of 1's in it initiates a rule $R_{k,s}$. However, since Assumptions 4.2 and 4.3 hold, the probabilistic reasoning embodied by the rules $\{R_{k,s}\}_{s,k\leq t}$ will give way to the case-based reasoning as in Proposition 4.2. To be precise, fix t and consider the reasoning at history $h_{t'}$ with $t' > t$. There are up to t different sets of conjectures $\{R_{k,s}\}_{s\in\{0,1\}^{\mathbb{N}}}$ that affect the agent's reasoning in a probabilistic way, but since the weight of each of them decreases exponentially fast with t', in the long run the weight of all of them combined will be negligible relative to the weight of the case-based conjectures.

However, as t' grows, new sets of conjectures $\{R_{k,s}\}_{s\in\{0,1\}^{\mathbb{N}}}$ might join the game. Assume that t is large and that the longest sequence of 1's in h_t is of length $k << t$. When, at some point, $k+1$ 1's are observed, the weight of the probabilistic reasoning in $\{R_{k+1,s}\}_{s\in\{0,1\}^{\mathbb{N}}}$ will be $Q(k+1)$, and it will overwhelm the weight of the case-based reasoning, $Q(t)$. Moreover, this phenomenon is likely to recur. Suppose, for the sake of the argument, that the true data generating process of y_t is uniform (and iid). Considering a given length k, we may ask when will a sequence of k 1's will first appear. With very high probability, this will occur at time t which is exponentially larger than k. At such a history h_t, the agent will reason mostly by the probabilistic reasoning ρ. Over time, when $t' > t$ grows, this probabilistic reasoning will decline in weight, but, with probability 1, new probabilistic models will be developed later on.

Thus, our framework may capture non-trivial dynamics between case-based and rule-based reasoning. Moreover, it can describe how probabilistic theories may be re-developed as history unfolds. Under the assumptions of Proposition 4.2, a prior distribution that has been formed at time $t = 0$ will have a negligible effect on reasoning in the long term. Yet, conditional probabilistic models might be re-formulated, capturing the agent's beliefs that she can make probabilistic predictions from a certain time on.

4.5 Concluding Remarks

4.5.1 *Methods for Generating Conjectures*

In many examples ranging from scientific to everyday reasoning, it may be more realistic to put weight φ not on specific conjectures A, but on methods or algorithms that generate them. For example, linear regression is one such method. When deciding how much faith to put in the prediction generated by the OLS method, it seems more plausible that agents put weight on "whatever the OLS method prediction came out to be" rather than on a specific equation such as "$y_t = 0.3 + 5.47x_t$".

One simple way to capture such reasoning is to allow the carriers of weight of credence to be sets of conjectures, with the understanding that within each set a most successful conjecture is selected for prediction, and that the degree of success of the set is judged by the accuracy of this most successful conjecture. The following example illustrates.

Suppose that the agent is faced with a sequence of datasets. In each dataset there are many consecutive observations, indicating whether a comet has appeared (1) or not (0). Different datasets refer to potentially different comets.

Now assume that the agent considers the general notion that comets appear in a cyclical fashion. That is, each dataset would look like

$$0, 0, \ldots, 0, 1, 0, 0, \ldots, 0, 1, \ldots$$

where a single 1 appears after k 0's precisely. However, k may vary from one dataset to the next. In this case, the general notion or "paradigm" that comets have a cyclical behavior can be modeled by a set of conjectures—all conjectures that predict cycles, parametrized by k. If many comets have been observed to appear according to a cycle, the general method, suggesting "find the best cyclical theory that explains the observations" will gain much support, and will likely be used in the future. Observe that the method may gain credence even though the particular conjectures it generates differ from one dataset to the next.

4.5.2 *Single-Conjecture Predictions*

This chapter is concerned with reasoning that takes many conjectures into account and aggregates their predictions. Alternatively, we may consider reasoning modes that focus on a most preferred conjecture (among the unrefuted ones) and make predictions based on it alone. For example, if we select the simplest theory that is consistent with the data, we obtain Wittgenstein's (1922) definition of induction.[25] If, by contrast, we apply this method to case-based conjectures, we end up with nearest-neighbor approaches (see Cover and Hart (1967) and Fix and Hodges (1951; 1952)) rather than with the case-based aggregation discussed here.

[25] See Solomonoff (1964), who suggested to couple this preference for simplicity with Kolmogorov complexity measure to yield a theory of philosophy of science. Gilboa and Samuelson (2009) discuss the optimal selection of the preference relation over theories in this context.

4.6 Appendix A: Proofs

4.6.1 *Proof of Proposition 4.1*

Define, for each h_t and for every $Y' \subsetneq Y$,

$$\varphi\left(\left\{\left[h_t, Y'\right] \cup [h_t]^c\right\}\right) = c_{h_t}\varphi_{h_t}(\mathcal{A}(h_t, Y'))$$

for every conjecture of the form $\left\{\left[h_t, Y'\right] \cup [h_t]^c\right\}$, and set $\varphi(\mathcal{F}) = 0$ where $\mathcal{F}$ is the set of all conjectures that are not of this form, and $c_{h_t} > 0$ is to be determined. Observe that the conjecture $\left[h_t, Y'\right] \cup [h_t]^c$is unrefuted (because it contains $[h_t, Y']$, and hence is consistent with the observed history)and non-tautological (because $Y' \subsetneq Y$)only at h_t. Hence, at history h_t, only conjectures of the form $\left[h_t, Y''\right] \cup [h_t]^c$ (with $Y'' \subsetneq Y$) are unrefuted and non-tautological, and the total weight that they assign to a subset of outcomes Y' is by construction $c_{h_t}\varphi_{h_t}(\mathcal{A}(h_t, Y'))$. The coefficient c_{h_t} is chosen so that the total weight assigned by φ to all conjectures converges, which would be the case, for instance, if

$$\sum_{h_t \in H_t} c_{h_t} = t^{-2}.$$

■

4.6.2 *Proof of Proposition 4.2*

We start by showing that, because the ratio of weights assigned to specific histories of the same length t is bounded by a polynomial of t, the weight of each particular such history is bounded by this polynomial divided by an exponential function of t.

Consider a period t and a history h_t. If $\varphi(\mathcal{B}(h_t)) > \eta$, then, since for every $h_t, h'_t \in H_t$, $\varphi(\mathcal{B}(h_t)) \leq P(t)\varphi(\mathcal{B}(h'_t))$, for every h'_t,

$$\varphi(\mathcal{B}(h'_t)) \geq \frac{\varphi(\mathcal{B}(h_t))}{P(t)} > \frac{\eta}{P(t)}$$

Observe that $|H_t| \geq d^t$ for $d = |X||Y| > 1$. Hence

$$\varphi(\mathcal{B}) > \frac{d^t\eta}{P(t)}$$

and $\varphi(\mathcal{B}) < 1$ implies

$$\eta < \frac{P(t)}{d^t}$$

Since this is true for every η such that $\eta < \varphi(\mathcal{B}(h_t))$, we conclude that

$$\varphi(\mathcal{B}(h_t)) \leq \frac{P(t)}{d^t}. \tag{16}$$

We now turn to discuss the weight of the case-based conjectures that are relevant for prediction at h_t. We wish to show that this weight cannot be too small. First, observe that the set of case-based conjectures is countable. Denote the total weight of the case-based conjectures whose second period is τ by S_τ. Explicitly,

$$S_\tau = \sum_{i=0}^{\tau-1} \sum_{x,z \in X} \varphi\left(\left\{A_{i,\tau,x',z'}\right\}\right)$$

Then,

$$\varphi\left(\mathcal{CB}\right) = \sum_{\tau=1}^{\infty} S_\tau .$$

Choose T large enough so that

$$\sum_{\tau=1}^{T} S_\tau > \frac{\varphi\left(\mathcal{CB}\right)}{2}. \tag{17a}$$

From now on, assume that $t \geq T$.

Consider a conjecture $A_{(t-1),t,x,z} \in \mathcal{CB}$ and assume that $\varphi\left(\left\{A_{(t-1),t,x,z}\right\}\right) < \xi$. By (13) (of Assumption 4.3) we have that, for all $t' < t, x', z'$

$$\varphi\left(\left\{A_{(t'-1),t',x',z'}\right\}\right) < \xi Q(t).$$

By (14) (of that Assumption), we know that for all $i < t' < t$, and all x', z',

$$\varphi\left(\left\{A_{i,t',x',z'}\right\}\right) < \varphi\left(\left\{A_{(t'-1),t',x',z'}\right\}\right) Q(t) < \xi \left[Q(t)\right]^2 .$$

The overall number of case-based conjectures whose second period is $t' \leq t$ is $|X|^2 \binom{t}{2}$. Since the weight of each is less than $\xi \left[Q(t)\right]^2$ we conclude that their total weight satisfies

$$\sum_{\tau=1}^{T} S_\tau < \xi \left[Q(t)\right]^2 |X|^2 \binom{t}{2}$$

and, using (17a) we obtain

$$\frac{\varphi\left(\mathcal{CB}\right)}{2} < \sum_{\tau=1}^{T} S_\tau < \xi \left[Q(t)\right]^2 |X|^2 \binom{t}{2}.$$

Define

$$R(t) = 2\left[Q(t)\right]^2 |X|^2 \binom{t}{2}$$

and observe that it is a polynomial in t.

Thus, we have

$$\xi > \frac{\varphi\left(\mathcal{CB}\right)}{R(T)}.$$

Since this holds for any ξ such that $\xi > \varphi\left(\left\{A_{(t-1),t,x,z}\right\}\right)$, it has to be the case that

$$\varphi\left(\left\{A_{(t-1),t,x,z}\right\}\right) \geq \frac{\varphi\left(\mathcal{CB}\right)}{R(t)}.$$

We observe that at h_t there are precisely t case-based conjectures that are unrefuted and non-tautological, and among them there is one of the type $A_{(t-1)t,x,z}$ (that is, the one defined by $x = \omega_X(t-1)$ and $z = \omega_X(t)$). It follows that

$$\varphi\left(\mathcal{CB}(h_t)\right) \geq \varphi\left(\left\{A_{(t-1),t,x,z}\right\}\right) \geq \frac{\varphi\left(\mathcal{CB}\right)}{R(t)}. \tag{18}$$

Combining (16) and (18) we obtain

$$\frac{\varphi\left(\mathcal{B}(h_t)\right)}{\varphi\left(\mathcal{CB}(h_t)\right)} < \frac{P(t)R(t)}{\varphi(\mathcal{CB})d^t}$$

where the expression on the right clearly converges to 0 as $t \to \infty$.

■

4.7 Appendix B: Belief Functions

This appendix is devoted to a brief introduction to Dempster-Shafer's Theory of Belief Functions, as well as its relationship to Choquet expected utility. It contains some definitions and well-known facts, as well as one result (Proposition 4.4) which is, to the best of our knowledge, new.

4.7.1 *Capacities and Qualitative Capacities*

Let there be a finite and non-empty set Y. Recall that in our model, Y denotes the outcomes that may be observed at each period.

The space of set functions on Y is defined by

$$V = \left\{ v : 2^Y \to \mathbb{R} \mid v\left(\varnothing\right) = 0 \right\}.$$

A *capacity* is a set function $v \in V$ that is *monotone* with respect to set inclusion, that is, that satisfies $v(A) \leq v(B)$ whenever $A \subset B$ (for $A, B \subset Y$), and that satisfies $v(Y) = 1$.

A binary relation $\succsim \subset 2^Y \times 2^Y$ is a *qualitative capacity* if (where $\succ$ denotes the asymmetric part of $\succsim$)

(i) $\succsim$ is a weak order;

(ii) $\succsim$ is monotone with respect to set inclusion, that is, $B \succsim A$ whenever $A \subset B$;

(iii) $\succsim$ is a non-trivial: $Y \succ \varnothing$.

A relation $\succsim$ is *persistently monotone*, or *p-monotone* for short, if, for every $S \subset T \subset Y$, and every $R \subset Y$ such that $R \cap T = \varnothing$, if $S \cup R \succ S$, then $T \cup R \succ T$. This condition states that, if an event R makes a non-null marginal contribution to another event S, R will make a non-null marginal contribution to any larger event T (in the sense of set inclusion). Thus, p-monotonicity has the flavor of a condition of non-decreasing marginal contribution, stated in the ordinal language, which only allows us to distinguish between null and non-null marginal contributions. Observe that if one has a quantitative measure of marginal contributions by a capacity v, the non-decreasing marginal contribution condition would say that, for every S, T, R as above, $v(T \cup R) - v(T) \geq v(S \cup R) - v(S)$, which is the familiar condition called *convexity*, *super-modularity*, or *2-monotonicity*.

Another way to view p-monotonicity is provided by the following lemma.

Lemma 4.3 *Let $\succsim$ be a qualitative capacity. The following are equivalent*

(i) $\succsim$ is p-monotone: For every $S \subset T \subset Y$, and every $R \subset Y$ such that $R \cap T = \varnothing$, if $S \cup R \succ S$, then $T \cup R \succ T$.

(ii) For every $A \subset B \subset Y$, for every $C \subset Y$, if $B \cap C \succ A \cap C$, then $B \succ A$.

(iii) For every $D \subset A \subset B \subset Y$, if $D \cup (B \backslash A) \succ D$, then $B \succ A$.

(iv) For every $A \subset B \subset \Omega$, for every $E \subset B$, if $E \succ A \cap E$, then $B \succ A$.

Proof. (i) implies (ii): Assume that $\succsim$ is p-monotone and let there be given $A \subset B$ and C. Define $S = A \cap C$, $T = A$, and $R = (B \cap C) \backslash A$. Then $S \subset T$, $R \cap T = \varnothing$. Since $S \cup R = B \cap C \succ A \cap C = S$ we should also have $T \cup R \succ T$ – where $T \cup R = A \cup (B \cap C)$ and $T = A$. By monotonicity, $B \succsim A \cup (B \cap C)$ and thus $B \succ A$.

(ii) implies (iii): Given $D \subset A \subset B \subset Y$, set $C = D \cup (B \backslash A)$, so that $B \cap C = D \cup (B \backslash A)$ and $A \cap C = D$. Since $D \cup (B \backslash A) \succ D$, we have $B \cap C \succ A \cap C$, and $B \succ A$ follows.

(iii) implies (iv): Given $A \subset B \subset \Omega$ and $E \subset B$, define $D = A \cap E$. We know that $E \succ D$. Clearly, $E \subset D \cup (B \backslash A)$. Hence, by monotonicity, $D \cup (B \backslash A) \succsim E \succ D$ and $B \succ A$ follows.

(iv) implies (i): Given $S \subset T \subset Y$ and $R \subset Y$ with $R \cap T = \varnothing$, define $A = T$, $E = S \cup R$, and $B = T \cup R$. Then $A \cap E = S$. We know that $S \cup R \succ S$ and thus $E \succ A \cap E$. (iv) implies that $B \succ A$, that is, $T \cup R \succ T$. ■

In all three conditions, (ii)–(iv), we have $A \subset B$ and thus, by monotonicity, we know that $B \succsim A$. The additional condition of p-monotonicity says that if there is some evidence that $B \backslash A$ might occur—as implied by the antecedent of (ii), (iii), or (iv)—then B has to be strictly more likely than A.

4.7.2 *Möbius Transforms and Belief Functions*

Given a set function $v \in V$, we can define another set function by

$$\phi_v(A) = \sum_{B \subset A} (-1)^{|A|-|B|} v(B).$$

The set function ϕ_v is referred to as the *Möbius transform of v*. We can represent a set function $v \in V$ by its Möbius transform as as follows: for every $A \subset Y$,

$$v(A) = \sum_{B \subset A} \phi_v(B).$$

Clearly, the mapping $M : V \to V$ defined by $M(v) = \phi_v$ is linear bijection from V onto itself, and so is its inverse M^{-1}. In particular, if a set of Möbius transforms C is convex, so is its corresponding set of set functions $M^{-1}(C)$ and vice versa.

A capacity v is a *belief function* if and only if its Möbius transform is non-negative. Alternatively, one may define a set function v to be *totally monotone* if

$$v(A) \geq \sum_{B \subsetneq A} (-1)^{|A|-|B|} v(B)$$

for all $A \subset Y$, and define a belief function to be a totally monotone capacity.

The bijection of the Möbius transform was first studied, to the best of our knowledge, by Shapley (1953).[26] Dempster (1967) introduced the concept of a *belief function* to capture the degree of belief in events without requiring additive probabilities (see also Shafer (1976)). In Dempster's interpretation, $v(A)$ is a measure of the total belief in an event A, whereas $\phi_v(A)$ is a measure of the direct evidence for A itself, above and beyond any evidence for (proper) subsets of A.

Möbius transforms were more generally studied by Rota (1964). Generalizations to infinite state spaces were obtained by Gilboa and Schmeidler (1995), and by Marinacci (1996). The former deals with representation using

[26] Set functions were used in the theory of transferable utility coalitional games. In this context, Shapley (1953) showed that the unanimity games form a linear basis for the space of games, and that, when a game v is described as the linear combination of the unanimity games, $\phi_v(B)$ is the coefficient of the unanimity game on B.

only "unanimity games" but cannot guarantee countable additivity of the representation (that is, of the measure that generalizes ϕ_v above). Marinacci generalizes unanimity games to games defined on filters, and guarantees countable additivity on that space.

4.7.3 *Representations*

A capacity $v \in V$ *represents* a relation $\succsim \subset 2^Y \times 2^Y$ iff, for every $A, B \subset Y$,

$$A \succsim B \qquad \Leftrightarrow \qquad v(A) \geq v(B)$$

We mention without proof:

Remark 4.1 *A relation can be represented by a capacity if and only if it is a qualitative capacity.*

We first prove the following proposition, and then explain how this identifies the binary relations $\succsim_{h_t}$ that can be represented via credence functions via (1)–(2).

Proposition 4.4 *A relation can be represented by a belief function if and only if it is a p-monotone qualitative capacity.*

Proof. Assume that v is a belief function that represents $\succsim$. By Remark 1, $\succsim$ is a qualitative capacity. To see that it is p-monotone, let there be given $E \subset F \subset Y$, and $G \subset Y$ such that $G \cap F = \varnothing$ and $E \cup G \succ E$. Hence $v(E \cup G) > v(E)$ and thus

$$\sum_{D \subset E \cup G} \phi_v(D) > \sum_{D \subset E} \phi_v(D)$$

which means that there exists $D \subset E \cup G$, $D \not\subset E$ such that $\phi_v(D) > 0$. Since $D \subset E \cup G$ we also have $D \subset F \cup G$. However, $D \not\subset F$ because $D \cap G \neq \varnothing$ and $G \cap F = \varnothing$. This means that $v(F \cup G) > v(F)$ also holds, and $F \cup G \succ F$.

Conversely, assume that $\succsim$ is a *p*-monotone qualitative capacity. We wish to construct a belief function v that represents it. We will construct a totally monotone set function v that represents $\succsim$, and then (because, by the representation, we have $v(Y) > 0$), this v can be normalized to be a belief function.

The basic idea of the proof is straightforward. Assume, first, that there are no $\sim$-equivalences (apart from the trivial ones), that is, that all equivalence classes are singletons. In this case, we order the events according to $\succsim$ and assign to them weights ϕ_v inductively. Thanks to monotonicity, all subsets of a set A appear before it in the $\succsim$ ranking, and thus, when we come to set $v(A)$, the total weight assigned to its proper subsets is already given, and we only need to make sure that $\phi_v(A)$ is high enough to make $v(A)$ larger than

$v(B)$ for any B that precedes A in the ranking. Notice that this proof does not rely on p-monotonicity of $\succsim$; indeed, in the absence of ties, p-monotonicity is implied by monotonicity.

In the general case, however, an $\sim$-equivalence class may contain several sets, and, importantly, also sets A, B such that $A \subset B$. This means that one cannot assign a value to $\phi_v(A)$ without also affecting $v(B)$, which should still equal $v(A)$. As a result the argument is a little more delicate, and makes use of p-monotonicity of $\succsim$.

Let $(A_1 = \varnothing, A_2, A_3, \ldots, A_{2^n} = Y)$ be an enumeration of 2^Y such that $A_i \precsim A_{i+1}$ for $i < 2^n$. Let the equivalence classes of $\sim$ be $(\mathcal{E}_1, \ldots, \mathcal{E}_K)$ with $\mathcal{E}_k = \{A_i\}_{i \in E_k}$ where $E_k = \{i_k, \ldots, i_{k+1} - 1\}$ (with $i_{k+1} \geq i_k + 1$). Clearly, if $A_i \in \mathcal{E}_k$ and $A_{i'} \in \mathcal{E}_{k'}$, then $A_i \succsim A_{i'}$ iff $k \geq k'$.

We will define v and ϕ_v on $\cup_{k \leq j} \mathcal{E}_k$, by induction on $j = 1, \ldots, K$, so that v represents $\succsim$ on $\cup_{k \leq j} \mathcal{E}_k$. Observe that, by monotonicity, if $A_i \in \mathcal{E}_k$, and $D \subset A$, then $D \in \mathcal{E}_{k'}$ for $k' \leq k$. Hence the values of v on $\cup_{k \leq j} \mathcal{E}_k$ define those of ϕ_v on $\cup_{k \leq j} \mathcal{E}_k$ and vice versa.

For $j = 1$, we define, for all $A \in \mathcal{E}_1$, $\phi_v(A) = 0$, which, by monotonicity, implies $\phi_v(D) = 0$ for every $D \subset A$ and thus also $v(A) = 0$.

Assume, then, that v and ϕ_v have been defined for $\cup_{k \leq j} \mathcal{E}_k$, so that v represents $\succsim$ on $\cup_{k \leq j} \mathcal{E}_k$, and consider $\mathcal{E}_{k+1}$. Let $\mathcal{E}_{k+1} = \{A_i\}_{i \in E_{k+1}}$. For $i \in E_{k+1}$, let

$$\alpha_i = \sum_{D \subset A_i, D \notin \mathcal{E}_{k+1}} \phi_v(D).$$

Thus, α_i is a lower bound on the value $v(A_i)$, obtained by the ϕ_v already assigned to subsets of A_i. All subsets $D \subset A_i$ such that $D \prec A_i$ are included in the summation above, but there may be other subsets $D \subset A_i$ such that $D \sim A_i$ (that is, $D \in \mathcal{E}_{k+1}$).

We will define $\phi_v(A_i) \geq 0$ so that, for all $i \in E_{k+1}$,

$$v(A_i) = M_k \equiv \max_{i \in E_{k+1}} \alpha_i + 1.$$

For a given $i \in E_{k+1}$, if A_i is a minimal set (with respect to set inclusion) in $\mathcal{E}_{k+1}$, set

$$\phi_v(A_i) = M_k - \alpha_i$$

and otherwise (i.e., if there exists $h \in E_{k+1}$, $h \neq i$, such that $A_h \subsetneq A_i$)

$$\phi_v(A_i) = 0.$$

We now wish to show that, for every $i \in E_{k+1}$, $v(A_i) = M_k$. Consider first i such that A_i is a minimal set in $\mathcal{E}_{k+1}$. Obviously,

$$\begin{aligned} v(A_i) &= \sum_{D \subset A_i} \phi_v(D) \\ &= \sum_{D \subset A_i, D \notin \mathcal{E}_{k+1}} \phi_v(D) + \phi_v(A_i) \\ &= \alpha_i + M_k - \alpha_i \\ &= M_k. \end{aligned}$$

Next consider i such that A_i is not a minimal set in $\mathcal{E}_{k+1}$. Define

$$\mathcal{F}_i = \left\{ A_h \in \mathcal{E}_{k+1} \mid A_h \subset A_i \right\}$$

We argue that $\mathcal{F}_i$ is closed under intersection. Suppose that $B, C \in \mathcal{F}_i$. If $B \cap C \prec A_i \cap C = C$, then, by p-monotonicity and Lemma 4.3, $A_i \succ B$, which is known to be false because $A_i, B \in \mathcal{E}_{k+1}$ (and thus $A_i \sim B$). Hence $B \cap C \sim C$ and it follows that $B \cap C \in \mathcal{E}_{k+1}$. Clearly, $B \cap C \subset A_i$.

Let

$$B_i = \cap_{A_h \in \mathcal{F}_i} A_h \in \mathcal{F}_i.$$

(Note that B_i is a minimal set in $\mathcal{E}_{k+1}$ and thus $\phi_v(B_i)$ has been defined above, while, for all $C \in \mathcal{F}_i \setminus \{B_i\}$ we have just defined $\phi_v(C) = 0$.)

We wish to show that

$$v(A_i) = v(B_i) = M_k.$$

Clearly, every $D \subset B_i$ satisfies $D \subset A_i$. Hence $v(A_i) \geq v(B_i)$. We wish to show that for $D \subset A_i$ such that $D \not\subseteq B_i$ we have $\phi_v(D) = 0$. If $B_i \subset D$, $D \in \mathcal{F}_i$ and $\phi_v(D) = 0$ follows from the definition above. Otherwise, $B_i \not\subseteq D$ and $D \notin \mathcal{F}_i$. In particular, $D \notin \mathcal{E}_{k+1}$ and this implies that $D \in \cup_{k \leq j} \mathcal{E}_k$, and, by the induction hypothesis,

$$v(D) = \sum_{G \subset D} \phi_v(G).$$

If $\phi_v(D) > 0$, $v(D) > v(B \cap D)$ and, because v is known to represent $\succsim$ on $\cup_{k \leq j} \mathcal{E}_k$, $D \succ B \cap D$. But this would imply that $A \cap D = D \succ D \cap B$, and by p-monotonicity and Lemma 4.3, $A \succ B$, which is known not to be the case. We therefore conclude that – also in the case $D \notin \mathcal{E}_{k+1}$ – we have $\phi_v(D) = 0$. This concludes the proof that $v(A_i) = v(B_i) = M_k$.

It remains to be noted that the function v thus constructed represents $\succsim$ on $\cup_{k \leq j} \mathcal{E}_{k+1}$. ■

Observe that a corollary of this proposition is that a qualitative capacity (on a finite set) can be represented by a p-monotone capacity if and only if it can be represented by a belief function.

Every $Y' \subset Y$ corresponds to an event $[h_t, Y'] \in \mathcal{E}_1$. Hence, for every history h_t and p-monotone qualitative capacity, we can define a function φ_{h_t} that assigns weight to conjectures of the form $[h_t, Y']$ (and to no other conjectures), so as to ensure that φ_{h_t} induces a belief function on 2^Y that represents $\succsim_{h_t}$. Conversely, any nontrivial, σ-additive measure on $\mathcal{E}$ induces a belief function on 2^Y, and hence represents a p-monotone qualitative capacity.

The predictions $\succsim_{h_t}$ that can be represented by a credence function via (1)–(2) are precisely those for which $\succsim_{h_t}$ is a p-monotone qualitative capacity, for each h_t.

4.7.4 *Belief Updating*

Dempster (1967) defined the combination of two belief functions, designed to merge information from two sources. A special case of such a combination is the situation in which one source states that a certain event, B, has occurred. This piece of information is modeled by the belief function v such that $\phi_v(B) = 1$.

It is well-known that Dempster's rule of combination in this case becomes

$$v(A|B) = \frac{v\left((A \cap B) \cup B^c\right) - v\left(B^c\right)}{1 - v\left(B^c\right)}$$

which is known as the *Dempster-Shafer updating rule* for a capacity v. Clearly, if v is additive, this rule reduces to Bayesian updating.

Gilboa and Schmeidler (1993) approached the problem of updating capacities axiomatically, identifying reasonable axioms that characterize this rule.

4.7.5 *Bayesian Beliefs*

It is well-known that a capacity v is additive (that is, $v(A \cup B) = v(A) + v(B)$ whenever $A \cap B = \varnothing$) iff its Möbius transform ϕ_v is concentrated on singletons, that is, $\phi_v(A) = 0$ whenever $|A| > 1$.

Assume that v is used for decision making via maximization of Choquet integration of a non-negative utility function u, as proposed and axiomatized in Schmeidler (1989). That is, decisions are taken so as to maximize

$$\int_Y u dv = \int_0^\infty v(\{i \in Y \mid u(i) \geq t\})\, dt.$$

In this case, the decision maker maximizes expected utility (specifically, satisfies Savage's axiom P2) iff v is additive.

4.8 References

Akaike, H. (1954), "An approximation to the density function", *Annals of the Institute of Statistical Mathematics*, **6**(2): 127–32.

Alquist, R. and L. Kilian, (2010), "What do we learn from the price of crude oil futures"? *Journal of Applied Econometrics*, **25**: 539–73.

Bayes, T. (1763), "An essay towards solving a problem in the doctrine of chances", *Philosophical Transactions of the Royal Society of London*, **53**: 370–418. Communicated by Mr Price.

Bernoulli, J. (1713), *Ars Conjectandi*. Thurnisius: Basel.

Carnap, R. (1952), *The Continuum of Inductive Methods*. University of Chicago Press: Chicago.

Cover, T. M. and P. E. Hart (1967), "Nearest neighbor pattern classification", *IEEE Transactions on Information Theory*, **13**(1): 21–7.

de Finetti, B. (1931), "Sul Significato Soggettivo della Probabilità", *Fundamenta Mathematicae*, **17**: 298–329.

de Finetti, B. (1937), "La prevision: Ses lois logiques, ses sources subjectives", *Annales de l'Institute Henri Poincare*, **7**(1): 1–68.

Dempster, A. P. (1967), "Upper and lower probabilities induced by a multivalued mapping", *Annals of Mathematical Statistics*, **38**(2): 325–39.

Fix, E. and J. L. Hodges (1951), "Discriminatory analysis. Nonparametric discrimination: Consistency properties". Technical report 4, project number 21-49-004, USAF School of Aviation Medicine: Randolph Field, Texas.

Fix, E. and J. L. Hodges (1952), "Discriminatory analysis. Nonparametric discrimination: Small sample performance". Report A193008, USAF School of Aviation Medicine: Randolph Field, Texas.

Gilboa, I. and L. Samuelson (2009), "Subjectivity in inductive inference", Cowles Foundation Discussion Paper 1725, Tel Aviv University and Yale University.

Gilboa, I. and D. Schmeidler (1993), "Updating ambiguous beliefs", *Journal of Economic Theory*, **59**(1): 33–49.

Gilboa, I. and D. Schmeidler (1995), "Case-based decision theory", *Quarterly Journal of Economics*, **110**(3): 605–40.

Gilboa, I. and D. Schmeidler (1995), "Canonical Representation of Set Functions", *Mathematics of Operations Research*, **20**: 197–202.

Gilboa, I. and D. Schmeidler (2001), "*A Theory of Case-Based Decisions*". Cambridge University Press: Cambridge.

Gilboa, I. and D. Schmeidler (2003), "Inductive inference: An axiomatic approach", *Econometrica*, **171**(1): 1–26.

Holland, J.H. (1975), *Adaptation in Natural and Artificial Systems*. University of Michigan Press: Ann Arbor.

Hume, D. (1748), *An Enquiry Concerning Human Understanding*. Clarendon Press: Oxford.

Jeffrey, R. (2004), *Subjective Probability: The Real Thing*. Cambridge: Cambridge University Press.

Lindley, D. V. (1965), *Introduction to Probability and Statistics from a Bayesian Viewpoint*. Cambridge University Press: Cambridge.

Marinacci, M. (1996), "Decomposition and Representation of Coalitional Games", *Mathematics of Operations Research*, **21**(4): 1000–15.

Matsui, A. (2000), "Expected utility and case-based reasoning", *Mathematical Social Sciences*, **39**(1): 1–12.

McCarthy, J. (1980), "Circumscription—A form of non-monotonic reasoning", *Artificial Intelligence*, **13**(1–2): 27–39.

McDermott, D. and J. Doyle (1980), "Non-monotonic logic I", *Artificial Intelligence*, **13**(1–2): 41–72.

Nilsson, N. J. (1986), "Probabilistic logic", *Artificial Intelligence*, **28**(1): 71–87.

Pearl, J. (1986), "Fusion, propagation, and structuring in belief networks", *Artificial Intelligence*, **29**(3): 241–88.

Ramsey, F. P. (1931), Truth and probability, In R. B. Braithwaite, ed., *The Foundations of Mathematics and other Logical Essays*, pages 156–98. Harcourt, Brace and Company: New York.

Reiter, R. (1980), "A logic for default reasoning", *Artificial Intelligence*, **13**(1–2): 81–132.

Riesbeck, C. K. and R. C. Schank (1989), *Inside Case-Based Reasoning*. Lawrence Erlbaum Associates: Hilldale, New Jersey.

Rota, G. C. (1964), "On the foundations of combinatorial theory I: Theory of Möbius functions", *Probability Theory and Related Fields*, **2**(4), 340–68.

Russell, B. (1946), *A History of Western Philosophy*. Great Britain: Allen & Unwin.

Savage, L. J. (1972) Orginally (1954), *The Foundations of Statistics*. Dover Publications: New York.

Schank, R. C. (1986), *Explanation Patterns: Understanding Mechanically and Creatively*. Lawrence Erlbaum Associates: Hilldale, New Jersey.

Schmeidler, D. (1989), "Subjective probability and expected utility without additivity", *Econometrica*, **57**(3): 571–87.

Shafer, G. (1976), *A Mathematical Theory of Evidence*. Princeton University Press: Princeton.

Shapley, L. S. (1953), A Value for n-Person Games, in *Contributions to the Theory of Games*, II, H.Kuhn and A. W. Tucker, eds. Princeton University Press: Princeton.

Silverman B. W. (1986), *Density Estimation for Statistics and Data Analysis*. Chapman and Hall, London and New York.

Solomonoff, R. J. (1964), "A formal theory of inductive inference I,II", *Information Control*, **7**(1,2): 1–22, 224–54.

Voorbraak, F. (1991), "On the justification of Dempster's rule of combination", *Artificial Intelligence*, **48**: 171–97.

Wittgenstein, L. (1922), *Tractatus Logico-Philosophicus*. Routledge and Kegan Paul: London.

5

Analogies and Theories

The Role of Simplicity and the Emergence of Norms

5.1 Introduction

Consider the prediction problem of agents who live in an uncertain environment. They might be facing a process that is *exogenous*, that is, independent of the agents' predictions, or *endogenous*, that is, fully determined by these predictions. For example, natural processes such as the weather, earthquakes, or hurricanes are exogenous. On the other hand, social processes such as the adoption of a social norm are largely endogenous, as they are fundamentally determined by the agents' predictions thereof. Many other processes are combinations of exogenous and endogenous processes. These include, for example, prices in markets such as real estate, commodities and stock exchanges, which respond both to exogenous news and to speculative trade.

How do agents reason about such processes? Do they think about exogenous and endogenous processes in the same way? This chapter attempts to address these questions in a formal way. We consider a dynamic model in which, at each period t, an agent tries to predict the value of a variable y_t, based on a set of observable variables, x_t, as well as the history of both x and y (that is, $(x_i, y_i)_{i<t}$). One common mode of reasoning is regression analysis, whereby y_t might be regressed on x_t, on its own past values, $(y_i)_{i<t}$, or some combination of these. This process belongs to a general category known as *rule-based* learning that involves a selection of theories based on observations. In philosophy, this mode of reasoning is referred to as (case-to-rule) induction, and it is based on the belief that a rule that has been valid in the past will remain valid in the future. Hume (1748) famously pointed out that this belief requires justification, thereby stating the *problem of induction*. Wittgenstein (1922) suggested that the process of induction

consists in finding the simplest theory that conforms to the observations, while Goodman (1955) claimed that the notion of simplicity is language-dependent.[1] The basic mechanism of using unrefuted theories for prediction has remained a fundamental method of inference in science, statistics, and everyday life.

Another, perhaps simpler mode of reasoning involves analogical thinking. In its simplest manifestation, when the variable x_t is ignored, y_t is predicted to be the most frequently encountered value in the past.[2] If, however, different periods $i < t$ are characterized by different values of x_i, one may wish to rely more heavily on more similar periods.[3] In artificial intelligence, this mode of reasoning is referred to as *case-based* (see Schank, 1986, Riesbeck and Schank, 1989), and it has been axiomatized in Gilboa and Schmeidler (2001, 2003). Slade (1991) and Kolodner (1992) pointed out some advantages of case-based systems over rule-based systems.[4]

Rule-based reasoning requires agents to speculate about the data generating process that governs the phenomenon of interest. It is akin to problems of model selection, and to the classical problem of statistical inference: the data generating process is assumed to be in a certain class (i.e. a set of rules), and the problem is to find which process, within this class, is the actual one. Case-based reasoning, by contrast, is closer to statistical techniques such as kernel estimation (Akaike, 1954, Parzen, 1962, and see also Silverman, 1986), which keep on using the entire database for predictions, and do not attempt to summarize the database by a concise rule. Thus, rule-based reasoning is more ambitious than case-based reasoning. Correspondingly, rule-based reasoning requires more a priori knowledge about the structure of the problem (say, the class of possible data generating processes) than does case-based reasoning. Indeed, the former is closer to parametric statistical methods, whereas the latter—to non-parametric ones. In a sense, rule-based reasoning is future-oriented, whereas case-based reasoning is past-oriented: engaging in rule-based reasoning, one attempts to come up with general theories that can describe the entire process in the future (and as a by-product, to make predictions for the next period). By contrast, case-based reasoning only tries to predict one period ahead using past observations (where the accumulation of these predictions generates a prediction for the entire process).

[1] Solomonoff (1964) showed that, in an appropriate model, the dependence of simplicity judgments on language can be bounded.

[2] Or, in a continuous model, the average value of past observations.

[3] As suggested by Hume (1748, Section IV), "From causes which appear similar we expect similar effects".

[4] Their definition of rule-based systems is, however, different from the definition we use in this chapter.

It appears that both case-based reasoning and rule-based reasoning are common in everyday life, as well as in formal statistical analysis. In the artificial intelligence literature there are attempts to combine the two modes of reasoning in order to exploit their respective advantages (see for example Rissland and Skalak, 1989, and Domingosu, 1996). However, we are unaware of theoretical work that analyzes such combinations, especially as models of human reasoning, dealing with questions such as, when do agents tend to use analogies, and when—theories? Do they converge to one such mode of reasoning in the long run, and if so, which? Or, under which conditions will case-based reasoning be asymptotically dominant, and under which conditions will long-run behavior be governed by rule-based reasoning? Specifically, are there differences between exogenous and endogenous processes in this respect?

We start with an adaptation of the model of Gilboa, Samuelson, and Schmeidler (2013, Chapter 4), which provides a unified framework for case-based, rule-based, and Bayesian reasoning. In this model, weights are assigned to "conjectures", which are subsets of states of the world. A prediction is made by comparing the total weights of conjectures that support each possible outcome. Learning in this model is done by elimination of refuted conjectures. In the simplest case, when each conjecture is a single state of the world, the model turns out to be equivalent to Bayesian reasoning, where the elimination of refuted conjectures is the counterpart of Bayesian updating. But when conjectures consist of more than one state of the world, other modes of reasoning may be captured by the model. For instance, a conjecture might reflect the belief that "period t will have the same outcome as period $i < t$", in which case the aggregation over such conjectures captures case-based reasoning.

The focus of Gilboa, Samuelson, and Schmeidler (2013, Chapter 4) is the robustness of Bayesian reasoning versus other modes of reasoning, where its main message is conveyed by comparing the Bayesian and the case-based conjectures. This chapter provides examples of rules, for which it is difficult to provide a universal definition. For instance, rules can have different domains of applicability, allowing them, in particular, to vary in their starting periods. Thus, a rule in Gilboa, Samuelson, and Schmeidler (2013) might be "Starting at time $t = t_0$, y_t will equal y_0" In this chapter, by contrast, we limit attention to particular rules that can be thought of as general theories. All theories are required to share the same domain of applicability, and, in particular, to make predictions at each and every period t, of y_t given x_t and the history that preceded it. We assume that each theory can be explicitly contemplated, described, and referred to by the agents. It is therefore natural to assume that the set of theories is countable, as only countably many theories can have a concrete, finite description.[5] We also assume that the set of theories is rich enough so that for each history it contains a theory that can describe it. An example of such a set of theories is the functions that are *computable*, that is, those that can be described by Turing machines (or computer programs) that, for each history, compute a prediction in finite time. However, the set of computable theories is but an example, and computability plays no role in the formal model. These theories are contrasted with case-based reasoning by examining the long-run behavior of the relative weights of these two modes of reasoning.

We consider deterministic conjectures, which, given each possible history, divide outcomes dichotomously into "possible" and "impossible". Correspondingly, given a history, the conjectures are dichotomously classified as "refuted" or "unrefuted" by the given history. Probabilistic predictions can be captured by aggregation over deterministic ones.[6] However, our preferred interpretation of the model is that the agents attempt to foresee long-run trends that are beyond short-term noise variables. Thus, the variables discussed—x_t, y_t—are better viewed as ranges of values for averages taken over relatively long periods, rather than instantaneous values. Correspondingly, a "theory" would be expected to predict whether the average price of oil will go up or down over the next year, but not necessarily tomorrow.

The analysis of the relative weight of rule-based vs. case-based reasoning turns out to critically depend on the process that generates the variable y_t. When the process is *exogenous*, namely when y_t is completely independent of the agent's reasoning process, we show that, under mild assumptions, rule-based reasoning will prevail if one of the theories that the agents conceive of, and assign positive weight to, happens to be correct. Moreover, rule-based reasoning may be dominant even if no single theory is correct, and the agent indefinitely replaces one general theory by another. The states of the world in which case-based reasoning asymptotically vanishes is, however, small. Using topological and measure-theoretic notions, we show that, in general, one should expect case-based reasoning to remain prominent, alongside rule-based reasoning. For example, predicting the change of seasons is purely rule-based, because it is a simple enough process to be described by one of the theories that agents can imagine *ex ante*. By contrast, the occurrence of tropical storms does not seem to follow any simple pattern, and their prediction is, at least partly, based on similarity to past cases.

[5] See, however, subsection 5.5.1, discussing the relaxation of this assumption.
[6] See the discussion in subsection 5.5.2.

Next, consider a process that is perfectly *endogenous*, as in the case where y_t is the mode of the predictions of the agents. In contrast to the exogenous case, several results indicate that in this situation rule-based reasoning would be more often encountered, relative to case-based reasoning. Specifically, in the exogenous case we prove that, in a well-defined sense, "most" states of the world are such that case-based reasoning becomes asymptotically dominant, and rule-based reasoning vanishes. In the endogenous case, by contrast, under mild richness assumptions this phenomenon does not occur at *any* state of the world. The reason is, roughly, that case-based reasoning can be described by a theory. Assuming that a majority of the agents follow (a particular) case-based reasoning, they will soon figure out that the theory that makes this very prediction does indeed hold, and they will therefore use it for prediction. More generally, rule-based reasoning is likely to be dominant in the long run, because the agents' shared prediction agrees with a certain theory that becomes the theory of choice for their predictions. Thus, when we consider equilibrium selection in a game among many agents, it is more likely to find the agents converging to simple rules than in the case where these agents predict, say, the weather. This convergence to rules may explain the emergence of social norms as the selection of equilibria in coordination games.

As mentioned above, there are many economic phenomena involving intermediate cases, where the process y_t is determined partly by agents' predictions, and partly by exogenous factors. Speculative trade is one such example. In these cases, due to the external "noise" factors, no single theory can remain valid in the long run (unless the noise factors diminish over time). Nevertheless, when the noise factors are relatively weak, it may take a very long time for the process to converge, and in the meantime the agents' reasoning will fluctuate between rule-based and case-based reasoning. In particular, the agents' reasoning may select theories that become the equilibrium prediction for a certain period, until they are refuted, and then replaced by new theories, or by periods of case-based reasoning.

The rest of the paper is organized as follows. Section 5.2 describes the basic framework. It uses the framework of Gilboa, Samuelson, and Schmeidler (2013) and defines rule-based and case-based reasoning. Section 5.3 deals with a purely exogenous process, showing that rule-based reasoning is likely to emerge in simple states of the world, but not in all states. Section 5.4 then deals with a purely endogenous process, showing that rule-based reasoning is more likely to emerge as the asymptotic mode of reasoning than case-based reasoning. Section 5.5 concludes with comments on some variations of these models. It discusses the robustness of the results with respect to various assumptions and highlights the main conclusions of the analysis.

5.2 Framework

5.2.1 *The unified model*

We adapt the unified model of induction of Gilboa, Samuelson, and Schmeidler (2013). An agent makes predictions about the value of a variable y based on some observations x. She has a history of observations of past x and y values to rely on. We make no assumptions about independence or conditional independence of the variables across periods, or any other assumption about the data generating process.

Let the set of periods be $\mathbb{T} \equiv \{0, 1, 2, \ldots, t, \ldots\}$. At each period $t \in \mathbb{T}$ there is a *characteristic* $x_t \in X$ and an *outcome* $y_t \in Y$. The sets X and Y are finite and non-empty.[7] We exclude the trivial case where $|Y| = 1$. The set of all *states of the world* is

$$\Omega = \{\omega : \mathbb{T} \to X \times Y\}.$$

For a state ω and a period t, let $\omega(t) = (\omega_X(t), \omega_Y(t))$ denote the element of $X \times Y$ appearing in period t given state ω. Let

$$h_t(\omega) = (\omega(0), \ldots, \omega(t-1), \omega_X(t))$$

denote the history of characteristics and outcomes in periods 0 through $t-1$, along with the period-t characteristic, given state ω. Let H_t denote all possible histories at period t, i.e., $H_t = \{h_t(\omega) \mid \omega \in \Omega\}$ and let H denote all histories, i.e., $H \equiv \cup_{t \geq 0} H_t$. We let (h_t, y) denote the concatenation of the history h_t with the outcome y.

For a history $h_t \in H_t$, define

$$[h_t] = \{\omega \in \Omega \mid (\omega(0), \ldots, \omega(t-1), \omega_X(t)) = h_t\}.$$

Thus, $[h_t]$ is the event consisting of all states that are compatible with history h_t. Similarly, for $h_t \in H_t$ and a subset of outcomes $Y' \subset Y$, we define the event

$$[h_t, Y'] = \{\omega \in [h_t] \mid \omega_Y(t) \subset Y'\},$$

consisting of all states that are compatible with history h_t and with the next outcome being in the set Y'.

We endow Ω with the topology generated by the sets $\{[h_t] \mid h_t \in H_t\}$. We also denote by Σ the σ-algebra generated by these sets,[8] and define λ to be the uniform measure on Σ, that is, the unique probability measure according to which

[7] Clearly, x_t may be a vector of characteristics, or explanatory variables, each of which assumes only finitely many values.

[8] Observe that, because Y is finite, this σ-algebra coincides with that generated by the sets $[h_t, \{y\}]$ for history h_t and outcome $y \in Y$.

$$\lambda\left(\left[h_t\right]\right) = \lambda\left(\left[h'_t\right]\right) \qquad \forall t, \forall h_t, h'_t \in H_t.$$

In each period $t \in \mathbb{T}$, the agent observes a history, h_t, and makes a prediction about the period-t outcome, $\omega_Y(t) \in Y$. A *prediction* is a ranking of subsets in Y given h_t.

Predictions are made with the help of conjectures. A *conjecture* is an event $A \subset \Omega$. It can represent a theory, an analogy, or in general any reasoning aid one may employ in predicting y_t. Indeed, any such reasoning tool can be described extensively, by the set of states that are compatible with it. However, not every subset of Ω may be considered by the agent. Rather, we assume that the agent only conceives of a *countable* subset $\mathcal{A}$ of 2^Ω, referred to as the set of *conjectures*. We think of a conjecture as an idea that the agent can think of in a concrete way, reason about, describe in words, and perhaps relate to others. With this interpretation in mind, it appears natural to assume that there are only countably many conjectures.[9] As a result, summation over sets of conjectures will be well-defined.[10]

Gilboa, Samuelson and Schmeidler (2013) show that the notion of conjectures is general enough to capture Bayesian, rule-based, as well as case-based reasoning. Specifically, they assume that the agent has a *model (or cedence function)*, which is a function $\phi : \mathcal{A} \to \mathbb{R}_+$, where $\phi(A)$ is interpreted as the weight attached to conjecture A for the purpose of prediction. For a subset of conjectures $\mathcal{D} \subset \mathcal{A}$, ϕ is defined additively, that is,

$$\phi(\mathcal{D}) = \sum_{A \in \mathcal{D}} \phi(A).$$

We assume that the total weight of all conjectures is finite, and, without loss of generality, that $\phi(\mathcal{A}) = 1$.[11]

The agent learns by ruling out conjectures that have been refuted by evidence. Specifically, given a history $h_t \in H_t$, a conjecture A that is disjoint from $\left[h_t\right]$ should not be taken into consideration in future predictions.[12]

Fixing a subset of conjectures $\mathcal{D} \subset \mathcal{A}$, a history $h_t \in H_t$ and a subset of outcomes $Y' \subset Y$, consider the set of conjectures in $\mathcal{D}$ that have not been refuted by h_t and that predict that the outcome will be in Y':

$$\mathcal{D}(h_t, Y') = \left\{A \in \mathcal{D} \mid \varnothing \neq A \cap \left[h_t\right] \subset \left[h_t, Y'\right]\right\}.$$

[9] For example, if conjectures are assumed to be computable (by finite algorithms), the set of conjectures is countable.

[10] See also subsection 5.5.1 for a discussion of relaxation of the countability assumption.

[11] In GSS (2010), the set of conjectures is uncountable, and ϕ is defined as a measure over subsets of conjectures, that is, subsets of subsets of states of the world. This complication is obviated thanks to the countability assumption.

[12] One may allow theories to have a few wrong predictions before being considered "refuted". For example, for $k > 1$, we may consider a theory to consist of all the states along which the theory's prediction with the potential exception of k periods. It will be clear from the following analysis that such a modification of the notion of "refutation" does not alter our results in any fundamental way.

Observe that the conjectures in $\mathcal{D}(h_t, Y')$ are various events, many pairs of which may not be disjoint. This is important to bear in mind in the following definitions, where we sum over the weights assigned to different conjectures. As Gilboa, Samuelson, and Schmeidler (2013) point out, a model ϕ is a belief function as defined by Dempster (1967) and Shafer (1976). Further, discarding refuted conjectures is equivalent to the Dempster-Shafer updating rule of belief functions.

Given a model $\phi : \mathcal{A} \rightarrow \mathbb{R}_+$, the weight assigned to Y' by the unrefuted conjectures in $\mathcal{D}$ is

$$\phi(\mathcal{D}(h_t, Y')).$$

The total weight assigned to a subset $Y' \subset Y$ by all unrefuted conjectures is thus given by

$$\phi(\mathcal{A}(h_t, Y')).$$

The agent's prediction is a ranking of the subsets of Y, with Y' considered more likely than Y'' iff

$$\phi(\mathcal{A}(h_t, Y')) > \phi(\mathcal{A}(h_t, Y'')).$$

It will be useful to have notation for the set of conjectures, in a class $\mathcal{D} \subset \mathcal{A}$, that are relevant for prediction at history h_t:

$$\mathcal{D}(h_t) = \cup_{Y' \subsetneq Y} \mathcal{D}(h_t, Y')$$

Observe that $\mathcal{D}(h_t)$ is the set of conjectures in $\mathcal{D}$ that have not been refuted and that could lend their weight to *some* nontautological prediction after history h_t (and hence $\mathcal{D}(h_t) \subset \mathcal{D}(h_t, Y)$.)

5.2.2 *Rule-based reasoning: theories*

The notion of a rule is rather general. There are *association rules*, which, conditional on the value of x_t, restrict the possible values of y_t. For example, the rule "if the Democratic candidate wins the election, taxes will rise" says something about the rate of taxation, y_t, if the president is a Democrat (i.e. if x_t assumes a certain value). Such a rule does not restrict prediction if its antecedent does not hold. By contrast, there are *functional rules*, which predict that y_t be equal to $f(x_t)$ for a certain function f, and thus provide non-trivial predictions for every value of x_t. Other rules may be time-dependent, and allow y_t to be a function of x_t as well as of t itself. Further, rules may differ in their domain. In particular, Gilboa, Samuelson, and Schmeidler (2013) provide an example of rule-based reasoning in which the rules predict a certain constant y value beginning with a given period t, and making no predictions prior to that t.

In this chapter we restrict attention to rules that can be viewed as general theories. Such theories are constrained to make a specific prediction (i.e. a single y_t) *at each and every* t, and for any possible value of x_t. It is important to highlight that our results depend on this assumption. In particular, our results do not apply to more general definitions of "theories", whereby a theory may be restricted in its domain, say, by making a prediction at only a finite number of periods, starting at a particular t, or limiting its bite to particular values of x_t. Similarly, our notion of a theory does not include paradigms, which can be viewed as general frameworks for generating specific theories. For the purposes of this chapter, a "theory" can be tested, and can possibly be refuted, at each history h_t. Observe however that the definition is general in the sense that the functions are allowed to depend on the entire history h_t, and thus on previous values (x_i, y_i) for $i < t$.

Let $\mathcal{R} \subset Y^H$ be the set of functions considered by the agent. For a model ϕ and a theory $f \in \mathcal{R}$, we will use $\phi(f)$ to denote the weight assigned by ϕ to the conjecture consisting of all the states that do not contradict f, that is, $\phi(f) = \phi([f])$ where

$$[f] = \{\omega \in \Omega \mid \omega_Y(t) = f(h_t(\omega)) \quad \forall t\}.$$

We assume that the agent satisfies the following two conditions:

(i) For every history h_t, there exists $f \in \mathcal{R}$ such that $h_t \cap [f] \neq \varnothing$;

(ii) $\phi(f) > 0$ for every $f \in \mathcal{R}$.

The first condition states that no history will ever find the agent at a loss for theories. Whatever is the history observed, h_t, the agent will be able to conceive of a theory that would have predicted precisely the observed realizations of y_i for each $i < t$. The second condition further insists that the agent gives some positive weight to each such theory, that is, that she doesn't conceive of some theories but then arbitrarily decides to rule them out. Recall that we assume that the set of all conjectures, $\mathcal{A}$, is countable, and hence so is $\mathcal{R} \subset \mathcal{A}$. Indeed, Condition (ii) directly implies that $\mathcal{R}$ is countable, as the weight of all conjectures, $\phi(\mathcal{A})$, is assumed to be finite (and normalized to 1).

We find these conditions rather intuitive. If $\mathcal{R}$ is assumed to be countable, Condition (ii) may be viewed as a notational convention: $\mathcal{R}$ is defined, without loss of generality, as the support of ϕ. Ignoring theories in $\mathcal{R}$ with zero ϕ weight can be viewed as a failure to distinguish between theories that the agent has conceived of and dismissed and theories that the agent has not been aware of to begin with. Because the analysis will not make this distinction, Condition (ii) is basically equivalent to the assumption that the set of theories that the agent conceives of is countable. Condition (i) states that, for every history, the agent can conceive of, and assign a positive weight to, at least one theory that is consistent with this history.

A natural class of theories that satisfies these conditions is the set of computable theories. A theory $f : H \to Y$ is *computable* if there exists a Turing machine (or, equivalently, a computer program in a higher-level language such as PASCAL, C++, etc.), which, for every $h_t \in H$, halts in finite time and computes $y_t = f(h_t) \in Y$. Each computable theory can thus be described by an algorithm, that is, a finite set of instructions that define the value of $f(h_t)$ for every h_t. Since each such theory can be defined by a finite description, it seems reasonable that the agent would have to conceive of it. At the same time the agent may not be able to think about other, non-computable theories, as they cannot be described in a well-defined way. Since there are only countably many computable functions, the set of computable functions appears as a natural candidate for the set of theories $\mathcal{R}$ satisfying conditions (i) and (ii) above. However, nothing in the ensuing analysis depends on the assumption of computability.

Observe that the definition assumes that a theory $f \in \mathcal{R}$ assigns a prediction for every history h_t, including histories that are inconsistent with f itself. This is reminiscent of the definition of a strategy in extensive form games. Alternatively, one may restrict the domain of a theory f only to the histories that do not contradict it.[13]

If there are no x values to be observed (that is, $|X| = 1$), then for every $f \in \mathcal{R}$, there exists a unique state of the world compatible with it. In this case, a model ϕ that puts positive weight only on theories in $\mathcal{R}$ can also be viewed as a Bayesian model (as defined in Gilboa, Samuelson, and Schmeidler, 2013), namely as a model assigning probabilities to single states.[14] However, in the more general case, a theory $f \in \mathcal{R}$ is compatible with a non-singleton conjecture, because such a theory, as opposed to a Bayesian conjecture, need not predict the values of the x_t's. Thus, a theory f can predict the outcomes of a hurricane, should one occur, but it need not commit to a prediction about its occurrence.

A model ϕ_R is (a priori) *purely rule-based* if $\phi_R(\mathcal{R}) = 1$, equivalently, $\phi_R(\mathcal{A}\backslash\mathcal{R}) = 0$ or $\sum_{f \in \mathcal{R}} \phi_R(f) = 1$. Such a model can also be viewed as a probability distribution over $\mathcal{R}$.

5.2.3 *Case-based reasoning: analogies*

Case-based conjectures are defined as in Gilboa, Samuelson, and Schmeidler (2013): for every $i < t$, $x, z \in X$, let

13 Such a restriction would not make a major difference, because the definition of a theory at histories incompatible with it will be immaterial for our purposes.

14 The resulting Bayesian prior, however, is restricted to have a countable support.

$$A_{i,t,x,z} = \{\omega \in \Omega \mid \omega_X(i) = x, \omega_X(t) = z, \omega_Y(i) = \omega_Y(t)\}.$$

We can interpret this conjecture as indicating that, *if* the input data in period i are given by x and in period t—by z, *then* periods i and t will produce the same outcome (value of y). Notice that a single case-based conjecture consists of many states: $A_{i,t,x,z}$ does not restrict the values of $\omega_X(k)$ or $\omega_Y(k)$ for $k \neq i, t$.

Let the set of all conjectures of this type be denoted by

$$\mathcal{CB} = \left\{A_{i,t,x,z} \mid i < t, x, z \in X\right\} \subset \mathcal{A}. \tag{1}$$

A model $\phi_{\mathcal{CB}}$ is a priori *purely case-based* if all weight is put on the case-based conjectures. Note that the number of case-based conjectures is countable, and it is thus possible to assign a positive weight to each and every one of them.

While there is no restriction on how the weights should be divided among the different conjectures in $\mathcal{CB}$, it seems more natural that the agent assigns higher weights to cases that are more similar to each other than to cases with no resemblance. For example, the agent might have a similarity function over the characteristics,

$$s : X \times X \to \mathbb{R}_+,$$

and a memory decay factor $\beta \leq 1$. Given history $h_t = h_t(\omega) \in H_t$, a possible outcome $y \in Y$ is assigned a weight proportional to

$$S(h_t, y) = \sum_{i=0}^{t-1} \beta^{t-i} s(\omega_X(i), \omega_X(t)) \mathbf{1}_{\{\omega_Y(i)=y\}},$$

where $\mathbf{1}$ is the indicator function of the subscripted event. Hence, the agent may be described as if she considered past cases in the history h_t, chose all those that resulted in some period i with the outcome y, and considered the aggregate similarity of the respective characteristic $\omega_X(i)$ to the current characteristic $\omega_X(t)$. The resulting sums $S(h_t, y)$ can then be used to rank the possible outcomes y. If $\beta = 1$ and in addition the similarity function is constant, the resulting number $S(h_t, y)$ is proportional to the relative empirical frequency of y's in the history h_t.

As noted by Gilboa, Samuelson, and Schmeidler (2013), for every similarity function s and decay factor β one may define a model $\phi_{s,\beta}$ by setting $\phi_{s,\beta}(A_{i,t,x,z})$, for each t, to be proportional to $\beta^{(t-i)} s(x, z)$, and $\phi_{s,\beta}(\mathcal{A} \backslash \mathcal{CB}) = 0$.[15] In this case, for every history h_t and every $y \in Y$,

[15] Observe that only the conjectures $\left\{A_{i,t,x,z}\right\}_{i,x,z}$ are used for prediction at time t. This implies that, should the weights of these conjectures be multiplied by a positive constant (for a given t), prediction would be unaffected. Hence, embedding a similarity function s in a model ϕ one has a degree of freedom for each period t.

$\phi_{s,\beta}(\mathcal{A}(h_t, \{y\}))$ is proportional to $S(h_t, y)$. Such a model $\phi_{s,\beta}$ will be equivalent to case-based prediction according to the function S.

It is worthy of note that a particular case-based conjecture is not intended to capture an entire world view. A conjecture $A_{i,t,x,z}$ only says that, conditional on $x_i = x$ and $x_t = z$, the observed values of y in these periods will be the same ($y_t = y_i$). This can hardly be viewed as a theory about the world, and as a result case-based conjectures are not meant to be tested as are rule-based ones. In fact, when the mechanism of "refutation" of conjectures in our framework is applied to case-based conjectures, it is used to *select* the relevant conjectures, focusing on the conjectures $A_{i,t,x,z}$ for which $x_i = x$ and $x_t = z$. When the reasoner knows whether such a conjecture predicted the correct y_t (i.e., whether $y_t = y_i$), the conjecture is anyway irrelevant, as it does not constrain $y_{t'}$ for $t' > t$.

A case-base conjecture can be thought of as a building block that yields a meaningful prediction mainly when aggregated with many other building blocks according to the weight function ϕ. This is similar to the status of conjectures in Bayesian reasoning: each conjecture is a single state of the world, $\{\omega\}$, and it should not necessarily be interpreted as the statement that ω will obtain. Rather, when one aggregates over all such states, using the prior as a weighting function, one obtains a meaningful prediction tool. We tend to view rule-based reasoning along similar lines: while a single rule-based conjecture, such as "$y_t = x_t$ for every history h_t", can be viewed as a theory about the way the world functions, we allow the rule-based agent to aggregate over several (or even many) such specific conjectures.

Finally, observe that there may be other modes of case-based reasoning that go beyond the conjectures in $\mathcal{CB}$. For example, an agent seeking patterns in the data may observe that the past three periods are similar to other triples of consecutive periods in the past. To capture these analogies, one would need to define more elaborate conjectures than those in $\mathcal{CB}$. Our results would not change if one expands the set of conjectures to include these more involved analogies.

5.2.4 *Open-Mindedness*

We restrict attention to rule-based reasoning and case-based reasoning of the types described above. Formally, we assume that the set of conjectures is $\mathcal{A} = \mathcal{R} \cup \mathcal{CB}$. Within this constraint, we wish to guarantee that the agent is open-minded. Thus, we will henceforth assume that the agent assigns a positive weight $\phi(A) > 0$ to each conjecture in $\mathcal{A} = \mathcal{R} \cup \mathcal{CB}$. We denote this set of *open-minded* models by Φ_+.

5.3 Exogenous Process

5.3.1 *Learning Rules*

We now turn to study the dynamics of rule-based versus case-based reasoning. We first show that, if a particular theory (in $\mathcal{R}$) happens to describe the data generating process, the agent in our model will learn this fact. This result is not too surprising: in many different set-ups one may show that, should an agent conceive of the true model and assign some credence to it, then, in the limit, the agent will converge to believing in the true model. (See the discussion following the Proposition below.) Our main interest, however, is not in the agent's belief in the true model relative to other models, but in the mode of reasoning the agent employs. The following result is therefore an important benchmark: it provides conditions under which, at such states of the world, rule-based reasoning will become the dominant mode of reasoning, and case-based reasoning will become negligible. This benchmark is to be contrasted with the analysis that follows.

For each theory $f \in \mathcal{R}$, recall that $[f]$ is the event in which f is never refuted. A state $\omega \in [f]$ is simple in the sense that a given theory, f, is always valid in it. In particular, if the set $\mathcal{R}$ consists of computable theories, for such a state ω the computation of y_t given h_t can be done in finite time, employing a program that is independent of t, justifying the adjective "simple".[16]

We define the *set of simple states* to be

$$\mathbb{S} = \bigcup_{f \in \mathcal{R}} [f].$$

We can now state

Proposition 5.1 *For every $\phi \in \Phi_+$ and every $\omega \in \mathbb{S}$,*

$$\frac{\phi\left(\mathcal{CB}(h_t(\omega))\right)}{\phi\left(\mathcal{R}(h_t(\omega))\right)} \to 0$$

as $t \to \infty$.

That is, in all simple states, the agent will converge to reason by theories and will gradually discard case-based reasoning.

The logic of this proposition is straightforward: if we consider a simple state ω, where a certain theory f holds, the initial weight assigned to this theory will serve as a lower bound on $\phi\left(\mathcal{R}(h_t(\omega))\right)$ for all t, because the theory will never be refuted at ω. By contrast, the total weight of the set of all case-based conjectures that are relevant for prediction at time t converges to zero because

[16] Observe that even in a simple state ω, the pattern of x_t's (in ω) may be rather complicated. Theories in $\mathcal{R}$ attach y values to histories h_t, but they are not supposed to predict the x values.

it is an element in a convergent series. Intuitively, because at ω theory f is correct, it retains its original weight of credence. By contrast, case-based conjectures concern only pairs of periods, $i < t$, and thus, for each new value of t, a new set of case-based conjectures is being considered. It is inevitable that the total weight of this set (which is disjoint from sets considered in previous periods) converge to zero.

Proposition 5.1 may bring to mind "merging" results as in the literature that started with Blackwell and Dubins (1962). (See, for instance, Lehrer and Kalai, 1993.) Indeed, the positive weight assigned to a theory f, at a state $\omega \in [f]$, is reminiscent of an absolute continuity condition, implying that a state that has a positive probability (according to the real data generating process) also has a positive belief (according to the agent's subjective prior). However, Proposition 5.1 is different from the merging results: whereas the latter compare the true theory to other theories, Proposition 5.1 compares the true theory to the case-based conjectures, which do not have a Bayesian counterpart. The driving force behind the merging results is that, if at ω theory f is true, other theories, which are not equivalent to f, will be proven false. By contrast, the driving force behind Proposition 5.1 is not that the case-based conjectures are found to be false; rather, it is that the case-based conjectures relevant at time t have a total weight that converges to zero—a fact that is known a priori. Relatedly, the Bayesian theories that are compared to the true f in a merging results are the same theories at each period t (and each history h_t), as opposed to the case-based conjectures of time t that are different from those at time $t' \neq t$.

5.3.2 *The Insufficiency of Rule-Based Reasoning*

Next we turn to study states that are not simple. In such states, by definition, no single theory is correct, and thus rule-based reasoning has to evolve over time: the theories that the agent finds most credible at a given point of time are bound to be refuted in due course, and leave the stage to other theories, which were considered less credible at the outset. But, beyond the relative importance of different theories, the entire mode of rule-based reasoning may change its weight relative to that of case-based reasoning. Will rule-based reasoning be more dominant than case-based reasoning, or rather will the agent discard reasoning by theories and converge to analogical thinking?

The answer will depend on the specification of the model ϕ. In particular, the main question is how the total weight of the case-based conjectures changes over time. Since the sets of such conjectures that are relevant at two distinct periods ($t' \neq t$) are disjoint, it may appear intuitive to assume that their weight is "uniform" over the different periods. However, this is impossible as the total weight of the relevant case-based conjectures at period

t must converge to zero (as explained above). The main question is, therefore, how fast should this convergence be?

In this chapter we assume that the convergence is not too fast. A rate of decay that approximates the uniform weights, yet guarantees convergence would be polynomial: assume that ϕ satisfies the following conditions: there exist $\gamma < -1$ and $c > 0$, such that, for every t, and every $x, z \in X$,

$$\sum_{i<t} \phi\left(A_{i,t,x,z}\right) \geq ct^{\gamma}. \tag{2}$$

The set of these models will be denoted by $\Phi_{+}^{p} \subset \Phi_{+}$.

It is important to emphasize that the assumption $\phi \in \Phi_{+}^{p}$ is crucial for the analysis that follows. In particular, if one were to replace it by the assumption

$$\sum_{i<t} \phi\left(A_{i,t,x,z}\right) \leq ca^{-t} \tag{3}$$

for $a > 1$ and $c > 0$, the next two propositions will not hold.

We find assumption (2) more reasonable than (3), since that latter reduces the weight of case-based reasoning in an artificial way. The key point is that as t grows, the number of analogies grows polynomially (as opposed to the number of theories that grows exponentially). To illustrate this point, consider a version of our model with a finite time horizon, T. Define two conjectures to be T-equivalent if they make the same predictions for every h_t with $t \leq T$. In this case we would be able to divide the weight of analogies, as well as the weight of theories, uniformly within each set of conjectures, and it would follow immediately that the weight of the case-based conjectures decreases in a polynomial rate, which is in line with assumption (2). By comparison, in this case the weight of theories would decrease exponentially. However, should one prefer an assumption such as (3) to (2), the ensuing analysis would have to be revised.

We now turn to distinguish between states according to their asymptotic behavior. Define

$$\Omega_{R\phi} = \left\{\omega \in \Omega \mid \exists T, \quad \phi\left(\mathcal{R}(h_t(\omega))\right) > \phi\left(\mathcal{CB}(h_t(\omega))\right) \quad \forall t \geq T\right\}$$

$$\Omega_{C\phi} = \left\{\omega \in \Omega \mid \exists T, \quad \phi\left(\mathcal{R}(h_t(\omega))\right) < \phi\left(\mathcal{CB}(h_t(\omega))\right) \quad \forall t \geq T\right\}$$

$$\Omega_{M\phi} = \left\{\omega \in \Omega \;\middle|\; \begin{array}{l} \forall T, \quad \exists t, t' \geq T, \quad \text{such that} \\ \phi\left(\mathcal{R}(h_t(\omega))\right) \geq \phi\left(\mathcal{CB}(h_t(\omega))\right) \\ \phi\left(\mathcal{R}(h_{t'}(\omega))\right) \leq \phi\left(\mathcal{CB}(h_{t'}(\omega))\right) \end{array}\right\}$$

Thus, $\Omega_{R\phi}$ is the set of states where rule-based reasoning becomes more important than case-based reasoning, from some point on. Similarly, $\Omega_{C\phi}$

is the set of states where case-based reasoning becomes, from a certain point on, weightier than rule-based reasoning. Their complement is the set $\Omega_{M\phi}$, where reasoning is bound to remain asymptotically mixed: in these states there are infinitely many periods where rule-based reasoning is at least as weighty as case-based reasoning, but also infinitely many periods where the opposite is true.

We can now state

Proposition 5.2 *Let there be given a model $\phi \in \Phi_{+}^{p}$. Then $\Omega_{R\phi}$, $\Omega_{C\phi}$, and $\Omega_{M\phi}$ are dense in Ω.*

Thus, every open set of the state space contains both states where rule-based reasoning becomes weightier forever, and states where case-based reasoning becomes weightier forever, as well as states where neither is true. In particular, after each history h_t (where $[h_t]$ defines an open set), there are continuations in which the reasoner will be mostly rule-based, or mostly case-based, and there are continuations where she will keep switching between these two modes of reasoning.

While the topological notion of denseness suggests that rule-based reasoning and case-based reasoning will be encountered just as frequently, a measure-theoretic notion indicates that the most common situation—when $\phi \in \Phi_{+}^{p}$—is that case-based reasoning takes over. To be precise, a conclusion which is the opposite of that of Proposition 5.1 holds almost everywhere:

Proposition 5.3 *For every $\phi \in \Phi_{+}^{p}$,*

$$\lambda\left(\frac{\phi\left(\mathcal{R}(h_t(\omega))\right)}{\phi\left(\mathcal{CB}(h_t(\omega))\right)} \rightarrow_{t\rightarrow\infty} 0\right) = 1.$$

To conclude, there are states, dubbed "simple", in each of which a particular theory holds. In these states, case-based reasoning will vanish. However, these are by no means the "majority" of states. Overall, the sets of states where rule-based reasoning is asymptotically weightier; where case-based reasoning is asymptotically weightier; and where neither of the above holds are all dense. In particular, no finite set of observations may determine whether the agent's reasoning will converge to be mostly rule-based, mostly case-based, or neither. Furthermore, a simple count of histories of a given length, as does the uniform measure λ, sustains that in most histories case-based reasoning is weightier than rule-based reasoning asymptotically. Admittedly, the uniform measure may not be the only way to aggregate over states. Yet, in summary of the topological and measure-theoretic results, we find that there is no reason to assume that rule-based reasoning suffices in order to describe the way agents think about exogenous processes.

5.3.3 *Discussion*

The driving force behind Proposition 5.3 is that theories make predictions at each and every history, and therefore each new observation partitions the set of theories that are still unrefuted. Thus, at time t there are exponentially many disjoint sets of theories, and only one of them will contain unrefuted theories once history h_t unfolds. This implies that the set of theories that are relevant for prediction at h_t carries a weight that, when added to the weights of exponentially many competitor sets, sums up to a given constant (the a priori weight of rule-based conjectures). If all histories of length t are to have equal weight, it follows that the weight decreases exponentially fast in t. If not, it is certainly possible that some such sets would retain a relatively high weight, but this cannot be true of most of these sets.

This result is a consequence of the conception of a "theory" as a *general* rule, that is, as a statement that has a universal quantifier ("for all history h_t..."). By contrast, analogies do not make universal statements, and thus there can be much fewer distinct analogies than distinct theories. Differently put, the fact that the number of T-equivalence classes of theories grows exponentially in T is inherent to the definition of a theory as making a prediction—and risking refutation—at each history. By contrast, analogies are silent most of the time, and thus the number of possible analogies up to time T can be only polynomially large. Hence the weight of the relevant case-based conjectures need not decrease at an exponential rate.

The results that the set of case-based conjectures does not disappear in many (Proposition 5.2) or most (Proposition 5.3) states of the world does not depend on the case-based conjectures being analogical in nature. But rather it depends on the class of case-based conjectures being small (of polynomial growth) and relevant (offering a predictions at every period). Consequently, any other class of conjectures that has these two features, which, provided it obtains a priori credence (satisfying an counterpart of assumption (2)), may also not disappear. Our focus on case-based conjectures is motivated by the fact that analogical reasoning is a simple and basic mode of reasoning which has been extensively studied in psychology and in philosophy. It so happens that when this mode of reasoning is embedded in our model, it generates a set of conjectures that does not grow too fast.

Observe that, under our assumptions, both the set of theories and of analogies are countable. If we follow a state of the world, we may find that the agent uses a sequence of theories and a sequence of analogies for making predictions along the (histories that contain) the state. Clearly, while there are only countably many conjectures of each type, the set of sequences of such conjectures is uncountable. However, the agent is not assumed to be aware of this sequence; at no point in time is she assumed to envision the entire path of her reasoning in the future. Rather, at each t the agent is aware of countably many conjectures—be they rule-based or case-based – and only an outside observer who keeps track of the agent's reasoning would have to consider uncountably many sequences of (sets of) conjectures. Thus, we find the treatment of rule-based and case-based conjecture symmetric. Importantly, the set of conjectures the agent is presumed to be aware of is countable for each class.

Having said that, it is also worth noting that the basic logic of Proposition 5.3 and the conclusion that case-based reasoning is, generally speaking, unlikely to vanish do *not* depend on the fact that there are only countably many theories or that theories are deterministic. (See sub-sections 5.5.1 and 5.5.2.) Indeed, the reasoning described above applies to sets of theories that are consistent with a history h_t, whether this set is countable or not.

5.4 Endogenous Process

In this section we consider a process that is governed by the reasoning of a set of agents. For example, consider the behavior of agents involved in a coordination game, where each agent tries to predict the social norm that will govern the behavior of others, and to match that norm in her choice of strategy.

In this section we analyze the case in which all agents share the same weight function $\phi \in \Phi$. This extreme case attempts to capture the intuition that, while people vary in their a priori judgment of theories, these judgments are correlated. Specifically, people tend to prefer simpler theories to more complex ones, and similarity judgments are also correlated across people. For example, people might disagree whether the pattern 011111... is simpler than the pattern 010101..., but practically everyone would agree that 000000... is simpler than 011001.... Along similar lines, people would tend to concur that, other things being equal, a more recent period is more relevant for prediction than is a less recent one. Hence the assumption that all agents share the same ϕ, while extreme, is an acceptable benchmark. For such a function ϕ, define

$$\Omega_\phi = \left\{ \omega \in \Omega \;\middle|\; \omega_Y(t) \in \arg\max_{y \in Y} \phi(\mathcal{A}(h_t, \{y\})) \quad \forall t \geq 0 \right\}.$$

Thus, it is assumed that the agents' predictions determine the actual outcome. As in the case of the exogenous process, the agents are not assumed to predict the values of x_t, nor to affect them.

We first note that every state of the world may unfold in an endogenous process:

Proposition 5.4 *For every $\omega \in \Omega$, there exists $\phi \in \Phi_+^p$ such that $\omega \in \Omega_\phi$.*

The proof of Proposition 5.4 is constructive: given a state $\omega \in \Omega$ the proof describes an algorithm that generates $\phi \in \Phi_+^p$ such that $\omega \in \Omega_\phi$.

Our interest is in the dynamics of reasoning of the agents along states in Ω_ϕ for $\phi \in \Phi_+^p$. To this end, we introduce the following definitions. *Rule-based reasoning is dominant* at state $\omega \in \Omega_\phi$ at period t if

$$(i) \quad \phi\left(\mathcal{R}(h_t(\omega))\right) > \phi\left(\mathcal{CB}(h_t(\omega))\right)$$

and

$$(ii) \quad \omega_Y(t) \in \arg\max_{y \in Y} \phi(\mathcal{R}(h_t, \{y\})).$$

Thus, rule-based reasoning is dominant if there is more weight put on rule-based reasoning than on case-based reasoning, and if the prediction of the rule based reasoning is indeed the prediction that the agents make (and that defines the next observation y_t). Similarly, we say that *case-based reasoning is dominant* at state $\omega \in \Omega_\phi$ at period t if

$$(i) \quad \phi\left(\mathcal{R}(h_t(\omega))\right) < \phi\left(\mathcal{CB}(h_t(\omega))\right)$$

and

$$(ii) \quad \omega_Y(t) \in \arg\max_{y \in Y} \phi(\mathcal{CB}(h_t, \{y\})).$$

Observe that, at $\omega \in \Omega_\phi$ at period t we may have neither mode of reasoning dominating either if they happen to be equally weighty, that is, if, $\phi\left(\mathcal{R}(h_t(\omega))\right) = \phi\left(\mathcal{CB}(h_t(\omega))\right)$, or if the weightier mode of reasoning does not correctly predict the outcome. This may happen, for instance, if the weight of these conjectures is split between the different predictions, so as to make the other mode of reasoning pivotal. Define $\Omega_{RB\phi}$ to be the set of states $\omega \in \Omega_\phi$ such that, for some T, rule-based reasoning is dominant at state $\omega \in \Omega_\phi$ at all $t \geq T$. Define $\Omega_{CB\phi}$ accordingly to be the states at which case-based reasoning dominates from some period on.

Proposition 5.5 *For every $\phi \in \Phi_+^p$ we have $\mathbb{S} \cap \Omega_\phi \subset \Omega_{RB\phi}$.*

Thus, for every weight function that satisfies our assumptions, the set of states in which rule-based reasoning is eventually dominant contains all the simple states that may emerge from the process. One might wonder whether in complex states case-based reasoning might be dominant in the long run. It turns out that this possibility is precluded if the set of theories satisfies a mild richness condition, namely, that one of the theories describes case-based reasoning. Formally, we say that $\phi \in \Phi_+^p$ is *theoretically closed* if the following holds: for every h_t there exists a theory $f \in \mathcal{R}$ (and thus $\phi(f) > 0$)

such that $[h_t] \subset [f]$ and, for every $t' \geq t$, and every continuation $h_{t'}$ of h_t ($[h_{t'}] \subset [h_t]$), $f(h_{t'}) \in \arg\max_{y \in Y} \phi(\mathcal{CB}(h_t, \{y\})$. In essence, the condition says that if an external observer can predict the result of case-based reasoning according to ϕ, then the agents involved should also be able to conceive of the theory the external observer formulated. The condition is slightly stronger, in that it requires that it is possible for such a theory to begin with any finite history, and proceed according to (ϕ-) case-based reasoning after that history. For example, this condition will be satisfied if the function ϕ itself is computable, and the set $\mathcal{R}$ contains all computable functions.

We can now state:

Observation 5.1 *Assume that $\phi \in \Phi_+^p$ is theoretically closed and that, for some T, $\arg\max_{y \in Y} \phi(\mathcal{A}(h_t, \{y\}))$ is a singleton for every h_t with $t \geq T$. Then we have $\Omega_{CB\phi} = \varnothing$.*

The reasoning behind Observation 5.1 is very simple (as stated in the introduction): if ω were a state that is, in the long run, governed by case-based reasoning, then, after a certain history h_t, it can be described by the theory, f, that y_t is a maximizer of the case-based part of ϕ. Theory f is therefore identical to ω, apart from histories where case-based reasoning has a non-unique maximizer, and thus the choice of y_t according to ω and according to f need not coincide. However, if case-based reasoning provides a unique prediction from some point on, this prediction can be captured by a theory.

Observation 5.1 stands in stark contrast to Proposition 5.3: in the latter, we saw that the set of states in which case-based reasoning becomes overwhelmingly important relative to rule-based reasoning is large: not only is it a dense set, it has measure 1 according to the uniform measure over all histories. By contrast, Observation 5.1 implies that, under mild assumption, this set is empty. Thus, exogenous processes are more likely to give rise to case-based reasoning than are endogenous processes.

5.5 Variants

5.5.1 *Uncountably many theories*

As stated above, if a "theory" is supposed to be conceived of, stated, and conveyed by humans, it should be describable in words, and thus there can only be countably many theories to consider. However, one might wonder how our results would change if one were to adopt a more abstract notion of a theory, according to which any function from histories to predictions could be a "theory", resulting in uncountably many of these. Will this additional freedom make rule-based reasoning more powerful? Will it be, for instance, more likely to be observed in exogenous processes?

The answer is negative. The main weakness of rule-based reasoning, exemplified in Lemma 5.1 and Proposition 5.3, remains valid: these results rely on the overall weight that rule-based reasoning might muster, and they do not depend on the set of theories being countable, or on reference to specific theories. Rather, the very fact that the overall weight of rule-based conjectures has to be divided among exponentially many histories, implies that in "most" of these histories this weight has to decay exponentially. This argument (used in the proof of Lemma 5.1) can be repeated for any set of theories, as long as each theory has to make a prediction given each and every history.[17] By contrast, the strength of rule-based reasoning, stated in Proposition 5.1, does not immediately follow in the uncountable case. For example, if the agent's belief in theories defines a uniform prediction at each history, then at each and every state of the world, including the simple ones, the weight of rule-based reasoning will decay exponentially. In order to guarantee that a result akin to Proposition 5.1 holds, one would have to add an assumption that, among the uncountably many theories, a countable subset are assigned positive weights. Similarly, replicating the results in the endogenous process case would also require that the agents (or a majority thereof) assign positive weight to specific theories, for these theories to emerge as equilibria.

5.5.2 *Probabilistic theories*

One may wish to generalize the model to deal with theories whose predictions are probabilistic. For example, a theory may assign to each history h_t a distribution over outcomes $f(h_t) \in \Delta(Y)$, rather than a specific outcome. As mentioned above, such theories can be captured by the deterministic theories in their support. Specifically, a weight $\phi(f)$ assigned to a theory f can be split among a class of deterministic theories $D(f)$ so that the total weight of these theories at history h_t equals $\phi(f)\Pr(h_t|f)$ that, is the original weight of f, $\phi(f)$, multiplied by f's likelihood at h_t. The predictions generated by such a class of deterministic theories will be the same as those generated by the original probabilistic f, and, furthermore, the same would apply to aggregation over such theories.

Observe, however, that a single probabilistic theory will typically result, in this construction, in uncountably many deterministic ones. For example, if f states that the distribution over Y is uniform for every history h_t, all

[17] The formal statement of this result, as well as the entire discussion, require a more general model, in which ϕ is not defined for individual conjectures, but is, rather, a measure of a σ-algebra of conjectures. That is, ϕ is defined on sets of sets of states of the world, as in Gilboa, Samuelson, and Schmeidler (2010).

states of the world would be in the support of f. As just noted (in Subsection 5.5.1), this would require the more general set-up of Gilboa, Samuelson, and Schmeidler (2013), where ϕ is a measure over subsets of conjectures.

As observed in Subsection 5.5.1, results such as Lemma 5.1 and Proposition 5.3 would still hold in such a model: the driving force behind them is the fact that the total weight of all theories, probabilistic or not, is divided among exponentially many disjoint histories, and only a fraction of these can have a weight that is not decreasing at an exponential rate. However, one may argue that it is inappropriate to multiply the weight of a probabilistic theory by its likelihood function: when comparing probabilistic theories, all of whom make predictions at each at every period, the likelihood function seems to be an obvious tool. But when such theories are compared with case-based predictions, which have the luxury of making predictions only at very specific periods, such a comparison might not give theories a fair chance, as it were. Consider the following example.

Suppose that $|X| = 1$ and $Y = \{0, 1\}$. A probabilistic theory states that y_t are i.i.d. with $y_t \sim B(0.5)$. After a history of length t, the likelihood function of this theory is 2^{-t}. This theory will therefore be discredited in comparison with case-based conjectures. However, a proponent of this theory might say, "It's unfair to penalize me for not being able to predict the pattern of 0's and 1's in the data. I argued that the variables are i.i.d., and when I see a sequence with no obvious pattern, I feel vindicated. You may penalize me if the average of the y_t's is far from 0.5; you may also discredit my theory if there is an obvious pattern in the data; but you shouldn't ask me to predict a particular sequence of 0's and 1's to begin with. My probabilistic theory precisely states that there is no point in making such predictions".

Thus, when probabilistic theories are concerned, it may be more reasonable to lump periods together, and apply our model to averages of relatively long chunks of periods, predicting that these averages lie in certain positive-length intervals, as suggested in the introduction.

5.5.3 *Hybrid models*

Consider the case of trade in financial markets. Financial assets are affected by various economic variables that are exogenous to the market, ranging from weather conditions to technological innovation, from demand shocks to political revolutions. At the same time, financial assets are worth what the market "thinks" they are worth. In other words, such markets have a strong endogenous factor as well. It seems natural to assume that such processes (y_t) are governed partly by the predictions $(\hat{y}_t)$ as in Section 5.4 and partly by random shocks as in Section 5.3. For instance, assume that $\alpha\,(h_t)$ is the probability that agents' reasoning determines y_t, and with the complement probability y_t is determined by a random shock. That is,

$$y_t = \begin{cases} \hat{y}_t \text{ with probability } \alpha\left(h_t\right) \\ \tilde{y}_t \text{ with probability } 1 - \alpha\left(h_t\right) \end{cases}$$

where $\hat{y}_t \in \arg\max_{y \in Y} \phi(\mathcal{A}(h_t, \{y\}))$ and $\tilde{y}_t$ is uniformly distributed over Y. Thus, if $\alpha\left(h_t\right) \equiv 1$ we consider a model as in Section 5.4, which is likely to converge to a single dominant theory, and when $\alpha\left(h_t\right) \equiv 0$ we consider a model as in Section 5.3, coupled with a non-degenerate i.i.d. measure that guarantees asymptotic case-based reasoning. Obviously, the interesting case is where $\alpha\left(h_t\right) \in (0, 1)$ (for most if not all histories h_t).

If $\alpha\left(h_t\right)$ is independent of history, so that $\alpha\left(h_t\right) \equiv \alpha \in (0, 1)$, no theory can be dominant asymptotically. Indeed, every theory that correctly predicts $\hat{y}_t$ has a fixed positive probability $(1 - \alpha)$ of being refuted at each period, and will thus be refuted at some point with probability 1. Moreover, when t is large, we know that with very high probability the number of "noise" periods is approximately $(1 - \alpha)\, t$. Over these periods we are likely to observe a complex pattern of y_t's, and thus a result similar to Proposition 5.3 holds: the total weight of rule-based conjectures decreases, on average, exponentially fast in the number of noise periods. Because the number of noise periods increases linearly in t (as it is roughly $(1 - \alpha)\, t$), this weight is also an exponentially decreasing function of t and thus it decays faster than do the case-based conjectures. Thus, case-based reasoning will be asymptotically dominant in "most" states of the world even if $\alpha\left(h_t\right) \equiv \alpha$ is very close to 1.

However, the probability of noise in an endogenous process is likely to be endogenous as well. For example, consider the choice of driving on the right or on the left in a large population. When agents are not quite sure which equilibrium is being played, it is easier for a random shock to switch equilibria. But when all the agents are rather certain that everyone is going to drive, say, on the right, it is highly unlikely that at least half of them would behave differently from what they would find optimal based on their predictions. Thus, it stands to reason that $\alpha\left(h_t\right)$ depends on h_t, and, moreover, that it converges to 1 as t grows, if a simple theory fits the data h_t. Such convergence would allow the process to be asymptotically dominated by rule-based conjectures with positive probability.

5.5.4 *Heterogenous beliefs*

The analysis in Section 5.4 assumes that all agents share the function ϕ, which is the natural counterpart of the common prior assumption in economics.

Clearly, this assumption is not entirely realistic; people vary in their similarity judgments, in their prior beliefs in theories, as well as in their tendency to reason by theories vs. by analogies. Hence one may consider an endogenous process in which the population is distributed among different credence functions ϕ.

If we consider the case of computable theories, we find that subjectivity has limits: the distinction between computable and incomputable states is an objective one. Agents may vary in the language they use to describe theories, and, correspondingly, in their judgment of simplicity. However, any two languages that are equivalent to the computational model of a Turing machine can be translated to each other. Thus, if the process follows a simple (computable) path, all agents will notice this regularity. Different agents may discard case-based reasoning in favor of the unrefuted theory at different times, but (under the assumption of open-mindedness) all of them will eventually realize that this unrefuted theory is indeed "correct". Interesting dynamics might emerge if the agents who are slow to switch to prediction by the correct theory are sufficiently numerous to refute that theory, thereby changing the reasoning of those agents who were the first to adopt the theory.

5.5.5 *Main messages*

To conclude, it might be useful to summarize the main messages of this chapter. The first is that rule-based reasoning is generally not sufficient to describe the way agents think about the world—neither at the outset nor asymptotically. The second is that, other things being equal, an endogenous process is more likely to give rise to convergence to rule-based reasoning than is an exogenous one.

We believe that these messages are relatively robust to the assumptions of our model. For example, for an exogenous process, if one relaxes the assumption that the set for rules is countable, one can no longer guarantee that rule-based reasoning becomes dominant even in a state where a particular rule holds. Thus, the assumption of countability of the set of rules is relatively favorable to rule-based reasoning, in terms of becoming dominant when valid. Conversely, the general message that rule-based reasoning does not suffice is strengthened when the assumption of countability is relaxed. At the same time, when an endogenous process is concerned, it is still possible that some rules have a positive weight (that is, that the measure over the set of rules has atoms), and these rules would be more likely to emerge as equilibria than to be a priori selected by an exogenous random process.

5.6 Appendix: Proofs

5.6.1 *Proof of Proposition 5.1*

Assume that $\omega \in [f_r]$ for some r. In this case the denominator is bounded from below by the weight assigned to the correct theory f_r. In fact,

$$\mathcal{R}(h_t(\omega)) \searrow \phi(f_r) > 0$$

as $t \to \infty$.

By contrast, $\mathcal{CB}(h_t(\omega))$ includes the ϕ-weight only of those case-based conjectures that are relevant at t, that is

$$\phi\left(\mathcal{CB}(h_t(\omega))\right) = \sum_{\{(i,x,z)|i<t,\omega_X(i)=x,\omega_X(t)=z\}} \phi\left(A_{i,t,x,z}\right)$$

Clearly,

$$\phi\left(\mathcal{CB}(h_t(\omega))\right) \leq \sum_{\{(i,x,z)|i<t\}} \phi\left(A_{i,t,x,z}\right)$$

Defining

$$\alpha_t = \sum_{\{(i,x,z)|i<t\}} \phi\left(A_{i,t,x,z}\right)$$

and observing that

$$\sum_t \alpha_t = \phi(\mathcal{CB}) < 1$$

we must have

$$\alpha_t \to 0$$

as $t \to \infty$. Hence $\phi\left(\mathcal{CB}(h_t(\omega))\right)$ also converges to zero as $t \to \infty$, and this completes the proof.

5.6.2 *Proof of Proposition 5.2*

First consider $\Omega_{R\phi}$. By Proposition 5.1, for $\omega \in \mathbb{S}$ we have $\frac{\phi(\mathcal{CB}(h_t(\omega)))}{\phi(\mathcal{R}(h_t(\omega)))} \to 0$ and thus $\mathbb{S} \subset \Omega_{R\phi}$. However, $\mathbb{S}$ is dense in Ω, because we assumed that the set of theories is rich enough to intersect any open set $[h_t]$. Hence $\Omega_{R\phi}$ is dense.

To see that $\Omega_{C\phi}$ is dense, we use Proposition 5.3 proven below. (The proof of Proposition 5.3 does not make use of the present result.) That proposition states that

$$\lambda\left(\frac{\phi\left(\mathcal{R}(h_t(\omega))\right)}{\phi\left(\mathcal{CB}(h_t(\omega))\right)} \to_{t\to\infty} 0\right) = 1$$

and that implies that the set $\left\{\omega \in \Omega \,\middle|\, \frac{\phi(\mathcal{R}(h_t(\omega)))}{\phi(\mathcal{CB}(h_t(\omega)))} \to_{t\to\infty} 0\right\}$ is dense in Ω. However, this set is a subset of $\Omega_{C\phi}$. Hence, $\Omega_{C\phi}$ is also dense.

Finally, we wish to prove that $\Omega_{M\phi}$ is dense. It suffices to show that for every h_t there exists $\omega \in [h_t] \cap \Omega_{M\phi}$. Given such a history h_{t_0}, choose $\omega_1 \in [h_{t_0}] \cap \Omega_{R\phi}$. Let $t_1 > t_0$ be such that, at ω_1, for $t \geq t_1$, $\phi(\mathcal{R}(h_t(\omega))) \geq \phi(\mathcal{CB}(h_t(\omega)))$. Then consider the history h_{t_1} defined by ω_1. Find $\omega_2 \in [h_{t_1}] \cap \Omega_{C\phi}$ and let $t_2 > t_1$ be such that, at ω_2, for $t \geq t_2$, $\phi(\mathcal{R}(h_t(\omega))) \leq \phi(\mathcal{CB}(h_t(\omega)))$. Continuing by induction, one constructs a state $\omega \in [h_t] \cap \Omega_{M\phi}$. □

5.6.3 *Proof of Proposition 5.3*

We first prove the following lemma, which suggests that, in the "vast majority" of states, the weight of rule-based reasoning decays at a semi-exponential rate. This lemma does not depend on the allocation of weights among the case-based conjectures, and it is stated for all $\phi \in \Phi_+$ (and not only for $\phi \in \Phi_+^P$).

Lemma 5.1 *Let there be given $\phi \in \Phi_+$ and let λ be the uniform measure defined on Σ. There exists $0 < \delta < 1$ such that for every $\varepsilon > 0$ there exists T_0 such that*

$$\lambda\left(\left\{\omega \,\middle|\, \phi(\mathcal{R}(h_t(\omega))) \leq \delta^{t/2} \quad \forall t \geq T_0\right\}\right) > 1 - \varepsilon.$$

5.6.4 *Proof of Lemma 5.1*

Let there be given an open-minded model ϕ. For a period t and a sequence $x_{(t)} = (x_0, \ldots, x_{t-1}) \in X^t$, consider the state space $\Omega_{x_{(t)}}$ defined by the corresponding $y_{(t)} = (y_0, \ldots, y_{t-1}) \in Y^t$ and containing $|Y|^t$ states. Thus $\Omega_{x_{(t)}}$ is a replica of Y^t and when no confusion is likely to arise we will refer to elements of $\Omega_{x_{(t)}}$ as $y_{(t)}$. Let $\lambda_{x_{(t)}}$ be the corresponding (uniform) measure on $\Omega_{x_{(t)}}$.

Choose $\frac{1}{|X||Y|} < \delta < 1$. Observe that $\lambda_{x_{(t)}}$ attaches a probability not exceeding δ^t to each element in the space $\Omega_{x_{(t)}}$.

Let W be a random variable defined on $\Omega_{x_{(t)}}$, and measuring the total weight of rule-based conjectures that are compatible with history. That is, for $y_{(t)} = (y_0, \ldots, y_{t-1})$ choose an arbitrary $x_t \in X$ and define h_t by $h_t = ((x_0, y_0), \ldots, (x_{t-1}, y_{t-1}), x_t)$. Choose ω such that $h_t(\omega) = h_t$ and define

$$W(y_{(t)}) = \phi(\mathcal{R}(h_t(\omega)))$$

Clearly, such states ω exist.

Observe that $\{\mathcal{R}(h_t(\omega))\}_\omega$ defines a partition of $\mathcal{R}$: each theory $f \in \mathcal{R}$ is compatible with precisely one state $y_{(t)} \in \Omega_{x_{(t)}}$. Hence

$$\sum_{y_{(t)} \in \Omega_{x_{(t)}}} \phi\left(\mathcal{R}(h_t(\omega))\right) = r < 1$$

and therefore

$$\begin{aligned} E(W) &= \sum_{y_{(t)} \in \Omega_{x_{(t)}}} \lambda_{x_{(t)}}\left(y_{(t)}\right) W(y_{(t)}) \\ &= \sum_{y_{(t)} \in \Omega_{x_{(t)}}} \lambda_{x_{(t)}}\left(y_{(t)}\right) \phi\left(\mathcal{R}(h_t(\omega))\right) \\ &< \delta^t r < \delta^t. \end{aligned}$$

Denoting by B_t the event $W > \delta^{t/2}$, and using Markov's inequality, we get

$$\lambda_{x_{(t)}}(B_t) = \lambda_{x_{(t)}}\left(W > \delta^{t/2}\right) < \frac{E(W)}{\delta^{t/2}} < \frac{\delta^t}{\delta^{t/2}} = \delta^{t/2}.$$

We will also use B_t to denote the corresponding event in Ω. Since we have shown that $\lambda_{x_{(t)}}(B_t) = \lambda\left(B_t | x_{(t)}\right) < \delta^{t/2}$ for all $x_{(t)}$, we also have $\lambda(B_t) < \delta^{t/2}$.

Next observe that the bounds on the probabilities of the various B_t events converge. This implies that for the given $\varepsilon > 0$ there is a large enough T_0 such that

$$\sum_{t \geq T_0} \delta^{t/2} < \varepsilon$$

and thus, for this T_0,

$$\lambda\left(\cup_{t \geq T_0} B_T\right) < \varepsilon$$

and

$$\lambda\left(\left\{\omega \,\middle|\, \phi\left(\mathcal{R}(h_t(\omega))\right) \leq \delta^{t/2} \quad \forall t \geq T_0\right\}\right) > 1 - \varepsilon. \qquad \square$$

Completion of the proof of Proposition 5.3 Consider a given $\varepsilon > 0$ and let T_0 be the period provided by Lemma 5.1. Then, on the corresponding event (whose probability is at least $1 - \varepsilon$)

$$\phi\left(\mathcal{R}(h_t(\omega))\right) \leq \delta^{t/2} \quad \forall t \geq T_0$$

and this, together with the assumption that $\phi \in \Phi_+^p$, that is, $\sum_{i<t} \phi\left(A_{i,t,x,z}\right) \geq ct^\gamma$ for $c > 0$ and $\gamma < -1$, implies that

$$\frac{\phi\left(\mathcal{R}(h_t(\omega))\right)}{\phi\left(\mathcal{CB}(h_t(\omega))\right)} < \frac{\delta^{t/2}}{ct^\gamma}$$

where the right hand side converges to 0 as t tends to ∞.

Considering a sequence $\varepsilon_n \searrow 0$, one concludes that the convergence to 0 occurs everywhere apart from a set whose λ-measure is zero. □

5.6.5 *Proof of Proposition 5.4*

Let there be given $\omega \in \Omega$. For simplicity of notation, we define ϕ without guaranteeing the normalization $\phi(\mathcal{A}) = 1$. It will be obvious from the construction, however, that $0 < \phi(\mathcal{A}) < \infty$ so that ϕ can be normalized.

We first define ϕ on the case-based conjectures. For every $t \geq 1$, let

$$\phi\left(A_{i,t,x,z}\right) = \frac{1}{(t+5)^3}.$$

(We use a "lag" of 5 periods to make sure that the rate of decay between any two consecutive periods is not too fast. Specifically, we wish to guarantee that each element in the sequence is at least half of its predecessor.)

Clearly,

$$\phi(\mathcal{CB}) \leq |X|^2 \sum_{t \geq 1} \left[t \frac{1}{(t+5)^3} \right] < \infty.$$

We now turn to define ϕ on $\mathcal{R}$. In the proof we wish to assign weights to subsets of conjectures in $\mathcal{R}$. Note that for every subset $\mathcal{R}' \subset \mathcal{R}$ and every $a > 0$ one may assign a positive weight $\phi(f) > 0$ to each $f \in \mathcal{R}$ such that $\phi(\mathcal{R}') = a$, say by considering an enumeration of $\mathcal{R}'$, $f_1, f_2, \ldots$ and setting $\phi(f_j) = a/2^j$. In the rest of this proof, we will simply say "assign a weight $a > 0$ to the subset $\mathcal{R}'$", referring to such an assignment.

If $\omega \in \mathbb{S}$, there exists a theory $f \in \mathcal{R}$ such that $\omega \in [f]$. In this case, assign $\phi(f) = 1$ and assign the weight $a = 1/4$ to the set of all the other theories, $\mathcal{R}\backslash\{f\}$. It is easily observed that, at each $t \geq 0$, $\omega_Y(t) \in \arg\max_{y \in Y} \phi(\mathcal{A}(h_t, \{y\}))$ and thus $\omega \in \Omega_\phi$ is established, while $\phi \in \Phi_+^p$ holds.

Next assume that $\omega \notin \mathbb{S}$. Denote, for $t \geq 0$,

$$\mathcal{R}_t = \mathcal{R}(h_t(\omega)).$$

$\mathcal{R}_t$ denotes the set of theories that are unrefuted by history $h_t(\omega)$. Observe that they are all relevant for prediction at period t. Clearly, $\mathcal{R}_0 = \mathcal{R}$, as $h_0(\omega)$ contains only the value of x_0 and no theory makes any prediction about the x's. Moreover, $\mathcal{R}_{t+1} \subset \mathcal{R}_t$, because any theory that agrees with ω for the first $(t+1)$ observations also agrees with it for the first t observations. Finally,

$$\cap_t \mathcal{R}_t = \varnothing$$

because $\omega \notin \mathbb{S}$. We can thus define, for $t > 1$, the set of theories that are proven wrong at period t to be

$$\mathcal{W}_t = \mathcal{R}_{t-1} \backslash \mathcal{R}_t.$$

Observe that

$$\mathcal{R} = \cup_t \mathcal{W}_t$$

and

$$\mathcal{W}_t \cap \mathcal{W}_{t'} = \varnothing$$

whenever $t \neq t'$.

Thus, at period t $\mathcal{R}_t$ consists of all theories that were unrefuted by $h_t(\omega)$, and it is the disjoint union of $\mathcal{R}_{t+1}$, namely the theories that correctly predict $y_t = \omega_Y(t)$ and $\mathcal{W}_{t+1}$, namely the theories that predict different values for y_t, and that will be proven wrong.

If we ignore the case-based conjectures, the prediction made by the theories in $\mathcal{R}_t$ is guaranteed to be the "correct" prediction $\omega_Y(t)$ if

$$\phi\left(\mathcal{R}_{t+1}\right) > \phi\left(\mathcal{W}_{t+1}\right).$$

(Observe that, as compared to $h_t(\omega)$, $h_{t+1}(\omega)$ specifies two additional pieces of information: the realization of y_t, $\omega_Y(t)$, and the realization of x_{t+1}, $\omega_X(t+1)$. However, theories do not predict the x values, and thus the theories in $\mathcal{R}_{t+1}$ are all those that were in $\mathcal{R}_t$ and that predicted $y_t = \omega_Y(t)$; the observation of x_{t+1} does not refute any additional theories.)

A simple way to construct $\phi \in \Phi_+^p$ is to make sure that the prediction at each period is dominated by the rule-based conjectures, despite the existence of the case-based conjectures. To guarantee that this is the case, we set

$$\phi\left(\mathcal{R}_t\right) = \frac{3}{(t+5)^2}$$

at each $t \geq 0$.

Observe that, for $t \geq 0$,

$$\begin{aligned}
\phi\left(\mathcal{R}_{t+1}\right) &= \frac{3}{(t+6)^2} \\
\phi\left(\mathcal{W}_{t+1}\right) &= \phi\left(\mathcal{R}_t\right) - \phi\left(\mathcal{R}_{t+1}\right) \\
&= \frac{3}{(t+5)^2} - \frac{3}{(t+6)^2}.
\end{aligned}$$

This dictates the definition of ϕ on $\mathcal{R}$: we start with $\phi(\mathcal{R}) = \phi(\mathcal{R}_0) = \frac{3}{5^2}$, and assign the weight $3\left[(t+5)^{-2} - (t+6)^{-2}\right]$ to the subset of theories $\mathcal{W}_{t+1}$. Since $\cup_t \mathcal{W}_t = \mathcal{R}$, this defines ϕ on all of $\mathcal{R}$. Clearly, $\phi(\mathcal{R})$ is finite.

Next, observe that at each $t \geq 0$, $\omega_Y(t) \in \arg\max_{y \in Y} \phi(\mathcal{A}(h_t, \{y\}))$. Specifically, at $t = 0$ we only have to compare the rule-based hypotheses. We have

$$\phi\left(\mathcal{R}_1\right)=\frac{3}{6^2}$$

$$\phi\left(\mathcal{W}_1\right)=\frac{3}{5^2}-\frac{3}{6^2}$$

so that

$$\phi\left(\mathcal{R}_1\right)-\phi\left(\mathcal{W}_1\right)=2\frac{3}{6^2}-\frac{3}{5^2}>0.$$

For each $t \geq 1$, the total weight of the case-based conjectures is

$$t\frac{1}{(t+5)^3}.$$

We wish to show that the weight of the theories that predict the "correct" continuation $\omega_Y(t)$, $\mathcal{R}_{t+1}$, is larger than that of the theories that predict other continuations, even when the latter is combined with all case-based conjectures. Indeed,

$$\phi\left(\mathcal{R}_{t+1}\right)-\phi\left(\mathcal{W}_{t+1}\right)=2\frac{3}{(t+6)^2}-\frac{3}{(t+5)^2}>t\frac{1}{(t+5)^3}.$$

This completes the proof that $\omega_Y(t) \in \arg\max_{y \in Y} \phi(\mathcal{A}(h_t, \{y\}))$ for all t, and it is easily verified that after normalization we obtain $\phi \in \Phi_+^p$ such that $\omega \in \Omega_\phi$. □

5.6.6 *Proof of Proposition 5.5*

Assume that $\omega \in \mathbb{S}$. Then there exists a theory $f \in \mathcal{R}$ such that $\omega \in [f]$. Since $\phi \in \Phi_+$, $\phi(f) > 0$ and this implies that $\phi\left(\mathcal{R}(h_t(\omega))\right) > \phi(f) > 0$ for all t. By contrast, $\phi\left(\mathcal{CB}(h_t(\omega))\right) \searrow 0$. Similarly, $\phi\left(\mathcal{R}(h_t(\omega)) \backslash \mathcal{R}(h_{t+1}(\omega))\right) \searrow 0$ because the sets $\left\{\mathcal{R}(h_t(\omega)) \backslash \mathcal{R}(h_{t+1}(\omega))\right\}_t$ are pairwise disjoint (and the sum of their weights is bounded). Hence, from some T onwards, theory f dominates prediction and $\omega \in \Omega_{RB\phi}$. □

5.6.7 *Proof of Observation 5.1*

Let there be given a theoretically closed $\phi \in \Phi_+^p$ and assume that $\omega \in \Omega_{CB\phi}$. This implies that, from some T' onwards, $\omega_Y(t) \in \arg\max_{y \in Y} \phi(\mathcal{A}(h_t, \{y\}))$. Assume, without loss of generality, that $T' \geq T$, so that for $t \geq T'$ $\arg\max_{y \in Y} \phi(\mathcal{A}(h_t, \{y\}))$ is a singleton. By theoretical closedness of ϕ, for $h_{T'}(\omega)$, there exists $f \in \mathcal{R}$ such that $\left[h_{T'}\right] \subset [f]$ and, for every $t \geq T'$, and every continuation h_t of $h_{T'}$, $f\left(h_t\right) \in \arg\max_{y \in Y} \phi(\mathcal{CB}(h_t, \{y\})$, hence $f\left(h_t\right) = \omega_Y(t)$. It follows that $\omega \in \mathbb{S}$ and $\omega \in \Omega_{RB\phi}$. Clearly, $\Omega_{RB\phi} \cap \Omega_{CB\phi} = \varnothing$, hence this is a contradiction to the assumption that $\omega \in \Omega_{CB\phi}$. It thus follows that $\Omega_{CB\phi} = \varnothing$. □

5.7 References

Akaike, H. (1954), "An Approximation to the Density Function", *Annals of the Institute of Statistical Mathematics*, **6**: 127–32.

Blackwell, D. and L. Dubins (1962), "Merging of Opinions with Increasing Information", *Annals of Mathematical Statistics*, **33**: 882–6.

Dempster, A. P. (1967), "Upper and Lower Probabilities Induced by a Multivalued Mapping", *Annals of Mathematical Statistics*, **38**: 325–39.

Domingosu, P. (1996), "Unifying Instance-Based and Rule-Based Induction", Machine Learning, **24**: 141–68.

Gilboa, I. and D. Schmeidler (2001), *A Theory of Case-Based Decisions*. Cambridge: Cambridge University Press.

Gilboa, I. and D. Schmeidler (2003), "Inductive Inference: An Axiomatic Approach", *Econometrica*, **71**: 1–26.

Gilboa, I., L. Samuelson, and D. Schmeidler (2013), "The Dynamics of Induction in a Unified Model", *Journal of Economic Theory*, **148**: 1399–432.

Goodman, N. (1955), *Fact, Fiction, and Forecast*. Cambridge, MA: Harvard University Press.

Hume, D. (1748), *Enquiry into the Human Understanding*. Oxford: Clarendon Press.

Kalai, E. and E. Lehrer (1993), "Rational Learning Leads to Nash Equilibrium", *Econometrica*, **61**: 1019–45.

Kolodner, J. (1992), "An Introduction to Case-Based Reasoning", *Artificial Intelligence Review*, **6**(1), 3–34.

Parzen, E. (1962), "On the Estimation of a Probability Density Function and the Mode", *Annals of Mathematical Statistics*, **33**: 1065–76.

Riesbeck, C. K. and R. C. Schank (1989), *Inside Case-Based Reasoning*. Hillsdale, NJ: Lawrence Erlbaum Associates, Inc.

Rissland E. L. and D. B. Skalak (1989), Combining case-based and rule-based reasoning: A heuristic approach. Proceedings IJCAI-89, 524–30.

Schank, R. C. (1986), *Explanation Patterns: Understanding Mechanically and Creatively*. Hillsdale, NJ: Lawrence Erlbaum Associates.

Shafer, G. (1976), *A Mathematical Theory of Evidence*. Princeton: Princeton University Press.

Slade, S. (1991), "Case-based reasoning: A research paradigm", *AI Magazine*, 42–55.

Silverman, B. W. (1986), *Density Estimation for Statistics and Data Analysis*. London and New York: Chapman and Hall.

Solomonoff, R. (1964), "A Formal Theory of Inductive Inference I, II", *Information Control*, **7**, 1–22, 224–54.

Wittgenstein, L. (1922), *Tractatus Logico Philosophicus*. London: Routledge and Kegan Paul.

6

The Predictive Role of Counterfactuals

6.1 Introduction

A counterfactual is a conditional statement whose antecedent is known to be false. For example, "If the Iranian hostages had been released before the US presidential election in 1980, President Carter would have been reelected" and "Even if the Iranian hostages had been released before the US presidential election in 1980, President Carter would not have been reelected" are both counterfactuals.

Counterfactuals are common in everyday parlance and they seem to play an important role in the way people reason about social, economic, and political phenomena. It is somewhat surprising that people can reason about counterfactuals and come up with arguments about them that are acceptable to others. After all, counterfactual statements cannot be empirically validated. And yet, some counterfactuals appear to be more reasonable than others. For example, one may ask what would have happened had the US government rescued Lehman Brothers in 2008, and find that some predictions make more sense than others. Moreover, the ranking of such predictions appears to be relevant to predicting the consequences of future bailout decisions. What is the mechanism that allows such reasoning? How does counterfactual reasoning help rational agents form beliefs and make predictions?

In this chapter we extend a model of belief formation to encompass counterfactuals. In the context of this model, we can ask how counterfactuals can be used for prediction. Specifically, suppose that history provides compelling evidence for the truthfulness of a counterfactual belief. In this case, this belief can be added to the set of observations, as if it were actually experienced, and thereafter used for further predictions. Our central result is that a logically omniscient agent finds no benefit in using this type of counterfactual reasoning to make predictions.

The next subsection is devoted to a clearer definition of the problems we are concerned with. It is followed by a brief description of some fields of study that deal with counterfactuals, attempting to place this note in the context of the literature. We then proceed, in Section 5.2, to present our model, building on the unified model of induction presented in Gilboa, Samuelson, and Schmeidler (2010). Section 6.3 deals with prediction with the aid of counterfactuals. The centerpiece of this section is the aforementioned impossibility result, showing that counterfactuals cannot add anything to a logically omniscient agent's predictive ability. Section 6.4 is devoted to a general discussion, and, in particular, to the extent to which counterfactuals can be valuable in enhancing the prediction of boundedly rational agents.

6.1.1 *Modeling Counterfactuals*

Our first task is to construct a model that will integrate counterfactuals with ordinary representations of non-counterfactual belief formation. Not all counterfactuals are created equal in this respect. It is helpful to consider three examples:

1. What would have happened had a person put her hand in the fire for several seconds?
2. What would have happened had President Bush, in September 2008, decided to save Lehman Brothers from bankruptcy?
3. What would have happened had the force of gravity not existed?[1]

All three counterfactual questions are similar in form and logical structure. But they differ in terms of our ability to reason about them. Question 1 is the simplest. Assuming that the person in question did not put her hand in the fire, we have no direct empirical evidence of what would have happened had she done so. But we have plenty of evidence regarding similar cases, as well as a rather good understanding of the underlying rules and mechanisms involved, so that we have no difficulty answering this question. This is the type of counterfactual question we routinely resolve when identifying the consequences of decisions in repeated, known contexts.

Question 3 is quite different. We have no empirical evidence from worlds remotely similar to ours without gravity. Everything we know in the natural sciences would have to be re-evaluated in order to answer this question. Question 3 is so difficult to reason about, that it does not pose a serious theoretical problem: the only reasonable answer is that we don't have any idea what would have happened in this case.

[1] Questions 1 and 3 are classical examples given by Hume (1748).

Question 2 represents an intermediate case. Like Question 3, we cannot claim to have a large database of similar situations whose outcomes were actually observed. The financial crisis of 2008 is a unique event in history. The crisis of 1929 may have many similar features, but the two are not identical, and other crises take us yet further afield. Moreover, financial crises are global events that cannot be isolated and studied independently of each other: the very fact that the crisis of 1929 occurred before that of 2008 had an effect on the course of the latter. To complicate things further, it is doubtful that we have figured out the rules that govern the behavior of the world economy to the same extent that we have understood the laws that govern fire and its effect on the human body. Question 2 thus cannot be answered with scientific certainty as can Question 1. Nonetheless, Question 2 is not a matter of science-fiction speculation as is Question 3. We have some ways of reasoning about the effects of financial bail-out decisions, and often allude to counterfactual bail-out cases when debating current policy.

We seek a model that can describe the generation of counterfactual beliefs, preferably in a way that is akin to the generation of non-counterfactual beliefs. As a test of reasonability, we would like the model to show how, with a reasonable choice of parameters, one gets (i) a more or less unique, deterministic answer to Question 1; (ii) complete ignorance when it comes to Question 3; and (iii) some intuitive though speculative reasoning about Question 2. Moreover, we would like the model to be able to describe how counterfactual beliefs, such as the answer to Question 2, might be updated as (factual) history unfolds, so that an agent might feel more or less confident about counterfactual statements given information that has been gathered while these statements were already known to be counterfactual.

We are then particularly interested in the way counterfactuals are used for prediction. There are situations in which counterfactuals appear to be useless, either because their consequents are too unclear, or because they do not add much to existing knowledge. For instance, Question 3 leaves too much room for speculation to be useful in prediction.[2] On the other hand, Question 1 is easy to answer, but such an answer is likely to simply confirm predictions that already follow from factual observations. By contrast, Question 2 appears to be more interesting: it seems to lie in the middle ground where it is sufficiently familiar so that something can be said about it, and yet sufficiently novel so that reasoning about it would teach us something new.

[2] Fortunately, Question 3 also does not seem to be relevant to any practical problem. We suspect that the fact that nothing can be said about it is related to its irrelevance.

6.1.2 *Related Literature*

Counterfactual reasoning comes in many forms, and it has been studied in different disciplines. The following is but a brief survey, highlighting the way our study merges with or differs from other approaches.

Philosophy Starting with the work of Stalnaker (1968) and Lewis (1973), philosophers and logicians have studied the logic of counterfactuals, distinguished among types of counterfactuals, and considered their semantics. The formal model we present here employs a state space and is thus semantic in nature. In contrast to the philosophy literature, however, we do not insist on a syntactic model of counterfactuals. Our focus is on the process by which counterfactuals help form beliefs. Finally, we deal only with one type of counterfactual, namely, with the beliefs one has at the present about the evolution of history along paths not taken.

Decision theory The point of departure for decision theory is a function that maps combinations of acts and states into consequences. This function is typically taken to be so obviously basic as to be passed over without further notice. In practice, much of the work in making a decision (or in offering expert advice in support of a decision) revolves around identifying these consequences. Doing so requires counterfactual reasoning. When crossing a road one engages in reasoning by conditional statements of the type, "If I cross the road in front of the car, I will get hit", as well as "If I wait to cross until after the car has passed, I will be safe" and so forth. Once the decision has been made, all but one of such statements will linger in the agent's mind as counterfactuals. As is common in the philosophical literature, we will often refer to such statements as "counterfactuals" even before the truth value of their antecedent has been determined.

Any model of reasoning about decision making is thus also a model of reasoning about counterfactuals. Indeed, it is here that we gain most of our intuition about counterfactuals. Our suspicion that answers to Question 1 (in Section 6.1.1) will be useful while those to Question 3 will be useless arises out of thinking about how these questions will help us make decisions. However, our interest in counterfactuals is not motivated by the observation that people often remember the reasoning behind their decisions. Instead, we are motivated by the observation that counterfactual beliefs are often revised as additional observations are gathered, even after the antecedent is known to be false, and then used as inputs for subsequent belief formation. Thus, one might say, "Given my experience in the past 20 years, I believe that, had I chosen a different career, I would have been better off", and may utter this statement in the midst of advice about current choices. Put differently, one of the special features of counterfactuals is that our beliefs in them are continually updated and revised in light of new information, even after the conditional statement has been classified as *counter*-factual.

Psychology Psychological studies suggest that counterfactual beliefs can have a significant impact on the way that actual outcomes are evaluated, and on the resulting affective reactions. In particular, the salience of alternative scenarios can play a role in the evaluation of actual ones. For example, Medvec, Maday, and Gilovich (1995) argue that Olympic bronze medal winners tend to be more pleased with their outcome than silver medal winners, because for the former the salient alternative consequence may be not to get a medal at all, whereas for the latter the salient alternative is often the gold medal. Specifically, the winner of a silver medal may engage in thinking along the lines of "Had I only done... I would have won the gold", whereas such counterfactual thoughts are less likely to burden the bronze medalist. Our focus is not on the emotional implications of counterfactual reasoning. Rather, we focus on the cognitive aspects, namely, how counterfactual reasoning is conducted and used.

Statistics Statisticians often encounter a problem of missing data. Suppose there are multiple observations of variables $\{X_i^1, \ldots, X_i^m, Y_i\}$, but certain variables haven't been measured in certain observations. Restricting attention to observations for which all variables have been measured wastes some of the information in the data, while working with all of the information gives rise to a collection of missing-variables difficulties. In response, missing data are "filled in" using techniques such as kernel estimation, and are then used for further analysis.

Counterfactuals play a similar role in forming beliefs. Indeed, one may argue that, broadly construed, each problem can embed the other. A missing datum could be viewed as an answer to the question "what would we observe if we were to measure that which we didn't?", and so questions about missing data can be couched as counterfactuals. Conversely, any counterfactual could also be viewed as an observation that one would have liked to have but doesn't. Specifically, we might observe the outcome of act a and wonder what would have resulted from other acts $b, c \ldots$ Each such act could be viewed as another observation, with different X values and with an unobserved Y value.

Despite the formal equivalence between "filling in" missing data and counterfactual reasoning, our focus here is quite different than that usually encountered in statistics. We are interested in cases in which an observation is counterfactual because the variables $\{X_i^1, \ldots, X_i^m\}$ did not occur, and therefore Y_i was not observed. It is rarely the case in statistics that the "outcome", namely the dependent variable Y, is being conjectured for values of the dependent variables that also do not appear in the data.

History Counterfactuals are essential to the study of history. For example, consider the statement, "If General McClellan had pursued his advantage at Antietem, the American Civil War have ended a year earlier". Professionals as well as laypeople analyze history by comparing actual scenarios to counterfactual ones, pointing to possible causal relationships, which are, in turn, used to learn from historical events and to make predictions. Yet, the use and interpretation of such counterfactual statements is controversial (see Bunzl (2004)). The model we present below is most closely related to this use of counterfactuals, though it is clearly too theoretical to make a substantive contribution to the historical debate. Our model provides a theoretical framework for examining how people use counterfactuals, including (but not limited to) historical counterfactuals, to form beliefs and make predictions about likely outcomes in their current situation.

6.2 The Framework

6.2.1 *The Unified Model*

We adopt the unified model of induction of Gilboa, Samuelson, and Schmeidler (2013, Chapter 4).[3] In each period, an agent makes predictions about the value of a variable y based on some observations x. She has a history of observations of past x and y values to rely on. We make no assumptions about independence or conditional independence of the variables across periods, or any other assumption about the data generating process.

Let the set of periods be $\mathbb{T} \equiv \{0, 1, 2, \ldots, T\}$. At each period $t \in \mathbb{T}$ there is a *characteristic* $x_t \in X$ and an *outcome* $y_t \in Y$. The sets X and Y are finite and non-empty.[4] The set of all *states of the world* is

$$\Omega = \{\omega : \mathbb{T} \to X \times Y\}.$$

For a state ω and a period t, let $\omega(t) = (\omega_X(t), \omega_Y(t))$ denote the element of $X \times Y$ appearing in period t. Let

$$h_t(\omega) = (\omega(0), \ldots, \omega(t-1), \omega_X(t))$$

denote the history of characteristics and outcomes in periods 0 through $t-1$, along with the period-t characteristic, given state ω.

[3] We work with a special case of Gilboa, Samuelson, and Schmeidler's (2013) model that allows us to make the argument with a minimum of technical clutter. We present the model here, leaving most issues of motivation and interpretation to the original paper.

[4] No conceptual problems arise in extending the analysis to infinite sets X, Y or $\mathbb{T}$, but we avoid a collection of technical complications by working with finite sets.

For a history h_t, define

$$[h_t] = \{\omega \in \Omega \mid (\omega(0), \ldots, \omega(t-1), \omega_X(t)) = h_t\}.$$

Thus, $[h_t]$ is the event consisting of all states that are compatible with the history h_t. Similarly, for h_t and a subset of outcomes $Y' \subset Y$, we define the event

$$[h_t, Y'] = \{\omega \in [h_t] \mid \omega_Y(t) \subset Y'\},$$

consisting of all states that are compatible with the history h_t and with the next outcome being in the set Y'.

In each period $t \in \mathbb{T}$, the agent observes a history h_t and makes predictions about the period-t outcome, $\omega_Y(t) \in Y$. A *prediction* is a ranking of subsets in Y given h_t.

Predictions are made with the help of hypotheses. A *hypothesis (or conjecture)* is an event $A \subset \Omega$. A hypothesis can represent a theory, an association rule, an analogy, or in general any reasoning aid one may employ in predicting y_t. Indeed, any such reasoning tool can be described extensively, by the set of states that are compatible with it. Let $\mathcal{A}$ denote the set of all hypotheses, and so $\mathcal{A} = 2^{\Omega}$.

The agent makes use of these hypotheses with the help of a model. Formally, a *model (or cedence function)* is a function $\phi : \mathcal{A} \to \mathbb{R}_+$, where $\phi(A)$ is interpreted as the weight attached to hypothesis A for the purpose of prediction. The function ϕ is extended to subsets of hypotheses additively.

Given a history h_t, a hypothesis A that is disjoint from $[h_t]$ (i.e. a hypothesis that has been refuted by h_t) should not be taken into consideration in future predictions. Fixing a history h_t and a subset of outcomes $Y' \subset Y$, the set of hypotheses in $\mathcal{A}$ that have not been refuted by h_t and that predict the outcome will be in Y' is:

$$\mathcal{A}(h_t, Y') = \{A \in \mathcal{A} \mid \varnothing \neq A \cap [h_t] \subset [h_t, Y']\}. \tag{1}$$

Observe that the hypotheses in $\mathcal{A}(h_t, Y')$ are various events, many pairs of which may not be disjoint.

Given a model $\phi : \mathcal{A} \to \mathbb{R}_+$, the total weight assigned to the hypotheses that are unrefuted by h_t and consistent with an outcome in Y' is thus given by

$$\phi(\mathcal{A}(h_t, Y')) = \sum_{A \in \phi(\mathcal{A}(h_t, Y'))} \phi(A).$$

The agent's prediction is then a ranking of the subsets of Y, with Y' considered more likely than Y'' if

$$\phi(\mathcal{A}(h_t, Y')) > \phi(\mathcal{A}(h_t, Y'')).$$

6.2.2 *Counterfactual Beliefs*

We now extend the unified model to capture counterfactual beliefs. Assume that history h_t has materialized, but the agent wonders what would happen at a different history, $h'_{t'}$. We focus on the case

$$[h_t] \cap [h'_{t'}] = \varnothing$$

in which, at h_t, $h'_{t'}$ is indeed counter-factual.[5]

If the agent were at $h'_{t'}$, she would simply apply (1) to identify the hypotheses consistent with $[h'_{t'}]$. But the agent is not actually at the history $h'_{t'}$: she has observed h_t, and should take this latter information into account. Hence, the agent should consider only those hypotheses that are compatible with h_t, namely, only those A's such that $A \cap [h_t] \neq \varnothing$. Therefore, the belief in outcomes $Y'' \subsetneq Y$ resulting from history $h'_{t'}$ *conditional on history* h_t is $\phi(\mathcal{A}(h'_{t'}, Y''|h_t))$, with

$$\mathcal{A}(h'_{t'}, Y''|h_t) = \left\{ A \in \mathcal{A} \;\middle|\; \begin{array}{c} A \cap [h_t], A \cap [h'_{t'}] \neq \varnothing \\ A \cap [h'_{t'}] \subset [h'_{t'}, Y''] \end{array} \right\}. \tag{2}$$

If it is the case that $[h_t] \cap [h'_{t'}] = \varnothing$ these beliefs will be referred to as *counterfactual*.[6] Observe that the hypotheses in $\mathcal{A}(h'_{t'}, Y''|h_t)$ are required to have a non-empty intersection with $[h_t]$ and with $[h'_{t'}]$ separately, but not with their intersection. Indeed, in the case of counterfactual conditional beliefs this intersection is empty.

Let us see how the definition given above captures intuitive reasoning in Questions 1–3 in the Introduction. Begin with Question 1, namely, what would happen to an agent who were to put her hand in the fire. The agent has not done so, and thus h_t specifies the choice to refrain from the dangerous act. However, when the agent (or at outside observer) contemplates a different history, $h'_{t'}$, in which the hand were indeed put in the fire, there are many hypotheses that suggest that the hand would burn. One such hypothesis is the general rule "objects put in the fire burn", which presumably received a positive ϕ value at the outset and has not been refuted since.[7] There are also many case-based hypotheses, each of which suggest an analogy between the present case and a particular past case. Since in all past cases hands put in fires

[5] We do not distinguish in the formal model between the questions "what would happen if... were not the case" and "what would have happened if... had not been the case".

[6] If $[h_t] \cap [h'_{t'}] \neq \varnothing$, then either h_t and $h'_{t''}$ are identical, or one is prefix of the other. If h_t is a prefix of $h'_{t'}$, then $\mathcal{A}(h'_{t'}, Y''|h_t) = \mathcal{A}(h'_{t'}, Y'')$, while the reverse inclusion gives $\mathcal{A}(h'_{t'}, Y''|h_t) = \mathcal{A}(h_t, Y'')$.

[7] As in Gilboa, Samuelson, and Schmeidler (2010), we do not deal here with probabilistic rules, though such an extension would obviously make the model more realistic.

burned, each of these hypotheses suggests that this would be the outcome in the present case as well. In short, there is plenty of evidence about Question 1, captured in this framework both as general rules and as specific analogies, where practically all of them suggest the natural answer.

Consider now Question 3. What would have happened were gravity not to hold? There are many possible rules one can conjecture in this context, such as "without gravity no atoms would have existed" or "without gravity, only light atoms would have existed". However, in contrast to the rule "objects put in fire burn", none of these rules has been tested in the past, and they are all vacuously unrefuted. Thus, all of the conceivable rules remain with their original (and arbitrary) ϕ value, without the empirical mechanism allowing us to sift through the multitude of rules and find the unrefuted ones. Clearly, in this question analogical reasoning will be of no help as well. The history we observed consists only of cases in which gravity held. In this sense, all these cases are dramatically different from the hypothetical case in which gravity does not hold. Thus, a reasonable analogical reasoning would suggest that there is no similarity between the past and hypothetical cases to be able to generate a meaningful belief.

Finally, we turn to the interesting case of Question 2. In September 2008 the US government decided not to bail out Lehman Brothers. At that point, the actual history h_t and the hypothetical one, in which the government decided otherwise, $h'_{t'}$, part forever: $[h_t] \cap [h'_{t'}] = \varnothing$. Yet, there are hypotheses A that are compatible with both, that is, that satisfy $A \cap [h_t], A \cap [h'_{t'}] \neq \varnothing$. One such hypothesis may be the rule "When the government bails out all large financial institutions confidence in the market is restored". Let us assume, for the sake of the argument, that such a rule is well-defined and holds in the observed history h_t. In this case, this rule will predict that, at $h'_{t'}$, confidence in the market will be restored. Alternatively, one may point to a rule that says "The government bails out a small number of institutions, and thereafter begins a crisis", predicting that a bail-out would not have averted the crisis. Along similar lines, one may also use analogical reasoning to generate the belief given $h'_{t'}$. For example, one case-based hypothesis holds that the problem of 2008 is similar to that of the previous year, and had the US government bailed out Lehman brothers, as it bailed out mortgage banks in 2007, the crisis would have been averted, as it was in 2007. Similarly, one might cite other cases in which a bailout did not avert a crisis.

Thus, counterfactual beliefs are generated by considering hypotheses that are simultaneously consistent with the observed and with the counterfactual history. In Question 1, practically all such hypotheses point to the natural conclusion: were the hand put in fire, it would burn. In our notation, $\phi(\mathcal{A}(h'_{t'}, \{noburn\}|h_t)) = 0$ whereas $\phi(\mathcal{A}(h'_{t'}, \{burn\}|h_t)) > 0$.

In Question 3, there are no useful hypotheses to consult: no similar cases are known, and, relatedly, none of the conceivable rules one might imagine has been tested. Thus, the weight $\phi(\mathcal{A}(h'_{t'}, \{y\}|h_t))$ would reasonably be the same for any prediction y. (Indeed, it might be most reasonable to have a function ϕ for which this weight is zero.)

By contrast, in Question 2, there are hypotheses with positive weights that have been tested in the actual history ($A \cap [h_t] \neq \varnothing$) and that make predictions at the counterfactual history ($A \cap [h'_{t'}] \neq \varnothing$). Some of them suggest that a bail-out would have averted the crisis, some suggest the opposite. The relative weight assigned to these classes of hypotheses would determine the counterfactual belief.

Observe that our model can also explain how the belief in a counterfactual conditional statement changes as new evidence is gathered, even after the statement's antecedent is known to be false. For example, assume that John is about to take an exam, and decides to study rather than party. Having observed his choice, we may not know how likely it is that he would have passed the exam, had he decided to party. But if we get the new piece of information that he failed the exam, we are more likely to believe that he would have failed, had he not studied. In our model, this would be reflected by the addition of a new observation to the factual history h_t, which rules out certain hypotheses and thereby changes the evaluation of the counterfactual at $h'_{t'}$.

6.2.3 *Bayesian Counterfactuals*

Gilboa, Samuelson, and Schmeidler (2010) define the set of *Bayesian hypotheses* to be

$$\mathcal{B} = \{\{\omega\} \,|\omega \in \Omega\} \subset \mathcal{A}.$$

Each of the Bayesian hypotheses fully specifies a single state of the world. A Bayesian agent will satisfy

$$\phi(\mathcal{A}\backslash\mathcal{B}) = 0,$$

that is,

$$\phi(A) = 0 \qquad \text{if} \qquad |A| > 1.$$

As discussed in Gilboa, Samuelson, and Schmeidler (2010), this reflects the Bayesian commitment not to leave any uncertainty unquantified. A Bayesian agent who expresses some credence in a hypothesis (event) A, should take a stance on how this event would occur, dividing all the weight of credence in A among its constituent states.

The following is immediate (cf. (2)) but worthy of note.

Observation 6.1 *If* $\phi(\mathcal{A}\backslash\mathcal{B}) = 0$ *then, whenever* $[h_t] \cap [h'_{t'}] = \varnothing$

$$\phi(\mathcal{A}(h'_{t'}, Y'' \mid h_t)) = 0$$

for all $Y'' \subset Y$.

Thus, a Bayesian agent has nothing to say about counterfactual questions. This result is obvious because a Bayesian agent assigns positive weight only to singletons, that is, to hypotheses of the type $A = \{\omega\}$, and no such hypothesis can simultaneously be consistent with both h_t and $h'_{t'}$. Hence, the history that has happened, h_t, rules out any hypothesis that could have helped one reason about the history that didn't happen, $h'_{t'}$. Intuitively, this is so because the Bayesian approach does not describe how beliefs are formed, by reasoning over various hypotheses. Rather, it presents only the bottom line, that is, the precise probability of each state. In the absence of the background reasoning, this approach provides no hint as to what could have resulted from an alternative history. Indeed, Bayesian accounts of counterfactuals either dismiss them as meaningless, or resort to additional constructions, such as lexicographic probabilities.

6.3 Counterfactual Predictions

We now ask how counterfactuals can help make predictions, essentially by adding information to the agent's database.

Imagine an agent has observed history h_t. In the absence of counterfactuals, she would make predictions by comparing weights of credence $\phi(\mathcal{A}(h_t, Y'))$, for various values of Y'. Now suppose she endeavors to supplement the information at her disposal by asking, counterfactually, what would have happened at history $h'_{t'}$, where $[h_t] \cap [h'_{t'}] = \varnothing$.

The agent first uses her counterfactual beliefs to associate a set of outcomes Y'' to the counterfactual history $h'_{t'}$. She then adds the counterfactual information $[h'_{t'}, Y'']$ to her data set. This counterfactual information may allow her to discard some hypotheses from consideration, thereby sharpening her predictions.

What set of outcomes Y'' should she associate with history $h'_{t'}$? To consider an extreme case, suppose that $\mathcal{A}(h'_{t'}, Y'' \mid h_t)$ is nonempty only for $Y'' = \{y_0\}$. Thus, the agent is certain that, had $h'_{t'}$ been the case, y_0 would have resulted. The counterfactual question posed by $h'_{t'}|h_t$ is then analogous to Question 1 in Section 6.1.1, with an obvious answer. In this case, she can add the hypothetical observation $[h'_{t'}, \{y_0\}]$ to her database, and continue to generate predictions based on the extended database, as if this observation had indeed been witnessed. This "extended database" cannot be described by a history, because no history can simultaneously describe the data in h_t and in $h'_{t'}$ (recall that $[h_t] \cap [h'_{t'}] = \varnothing$). However, the agent can use both the actual history h_t and the hypothetical observation $[h'_{t'}, \{y_0\}]$ to rule out hypotheses and sharpen future prediction.

More generally, assume that the conditional beliefs $\phi(\mathcal{A}(h'_{t'}, Y'' \mid h_t))$ are positive only for a subset of outcomes $Y_0 \subset Y$ and subsets thereof, i.e.,

$$\phi(\mathcal{A}(h'_{t'}, Y_0|h_t)) > 0 \tag{3}$$

$$\phi(\mathcal{A}(h'_{t'}, Y''|h_t)) > 0 \Rightarrow Y'' \subset Y_0, \tag{4}$$

so that the agent is absolutely sure that, had $h'_{t'}$ materialized, the outcome would have been in Y_0. Thus, no other subset of Y competes with outcomes in Y_0 for the title "the set of outcomes that could have resulted had $h'_{t'}$ been the case". We are then dealing with a counterfactual analogous to question 2 in Section 6.1.1) (with the previous paragraph dealing with the special case in which $Y_0 = \{y_0\}$). In this case the agent adds to the database the hypothetical observation that $h'_{t'}$ results in an outcome in Y_0.

Now the agent uses the information that history h_t has occurred, and the counterfactual information that history $h'_{t'}$ would have resulted in an outcome from Y_0, to winnow the set of hypotheses to be used in prediction. In particular, the hypotheses used the the agent include:

- All hypotheses that are consistent with h_t but not with $h'_{t'}$. Indeed, since $h'_{t'}$ did not materialize, it cannot make a claim, as it were, to rule out hypotheses that are consistent with observations.
- All hypotheses that are consistent with each of h_t and $h'_{t'}$, provided that they are consistent with the counterfactual prediction Y_0 (satisfying (3)–(4)).

In other words, define the new set of hypotheses relevant for evaluating the set of outcomes Y' at history h_t, given counterfactual information $[h'_{t'}]$, to be

$$\mathcal{A}(h_t, Y'|h'_{t'}, Y_0) = \left\{ A \in \mathcal{A} \;\middle|\; \begin{array}{c} \varnothing \neq A \cap [h_t] \subset [h_t, Y'] \\ A \cap [h'_{t'}] \subset [h'_{t'}, Y_0] \end{array} \right\}. \tag{5}$$

The agent then uses ϕ to rank the sets $\mathcal{A}(h_t, Y'|h'_{t'}, Y_0)$, for various values of Y', and then to make predictions.[8]

[8] We have added the result of a single counterfactual consideration to the reasoner's database. Adding multiple counterfactuals is a straightforward elaboration.

Our model allows us to consider agents who are not Bayesian, but are nonetheless rational. This is important, as Observation 6.1 ensures that there is no point in talking about counterfactual predictions made by Bayesians. Indeed, we view the model as incorporating the two essential hallmarks of rationality: the consideration of all states of the world, capturing beliefs by a comprehensive, a priori model ϕ containing all the information available to the agent, and the drawing of subsequent inferences by deleting falsified hypotheses. An agent who is rational in this sense need not be Bayesian, which is to say that the agent need not consider only singleton hypotheses. In this case, counterfactuals are potentially valuable in making predictions.

Our result is that counterfactual reasoning adds nothing to prediction:

Proposition 6.1 *Assume that* $[h_t] \cap [h'_{t'}] = \varnothing$ *and that* Y_0 *satisfies (3)–(4). Then, for every* $Y' \subset Y$,

$$\phi(\mathcal{A}(h_t, Y')) = \phi(\mathcal{A}(h_t, Y'|h'_{t'}, Y_0)). \tag{6}$$

Predictions made without the counterfactual information (governed by $\phi(\mathcal{A}(h_t, Y'))$ *thus match those made with the counterfactual information (governed by* $\phi(\mathcal{A}(h_t, Y'|h'_{t'}, Y_0))$*).*

Thus, the counterfactual information has no effect on prediction. The (immediate) proof of this result consists in observing that, for Y_0 to include all possible predictions at $h'_{t'}$, it has to be the case that, among the hypotheses consistent with h_t, the only ones that have a positive ϕ value are those that are anyway in $\mathcal{A}(h_t, Y'|h'_{t'}, Y_0)$.[9]

This result has a flavor of a "cut-elimination" theorem (Gentzen, 1934–5):[10] it basically says that, if a certain claim can be established with certainty, and thereby be used for the proof of further claims, then one may also skip the explicit statement of the claim, and use the same propositions that could be used to prove it to directly deduce whatever could follow from the unstated claim. Clearly, the models are different, as the cut-elimination theorem deals with formal proofs, explicitly modeling propositions and logical steps, whereas our model is semantic, and deals only with states of the world and the events that do or do not include them. Yet, the similarity in the logic of the results suggests that Proposition 6.1 may be significantly generalized to different models of inference.

[9] Formally, it is obvious that $\mathcal{A}(h_t, Y'|h'_{t'}, Y_0) \subset \mathcal{A}(h_t, Y')$, since the first condition in the definition of $\mathcal{A}(h_t, Y'|h'_{t'}, Y_0)$ is precisely the definition of $\mathcal{A}(h_t, Y')$. Suppose the hypothesis A is in $\mathcal{A}(h_t, Y')$ but not in $\mathcal{A}(h_t, Y'|h'_{t'}, Y_0) \subset \mathcal{A}(h_t, Y')$. Then, from (5), it must be that $A \cap [h'_{t'}]$ is not a subset of $[h'_{t'}, Y_0]$. But then, from (3)–(4), it must be that $\phi(A) = 0$.

[10] We thank Brian Hill for this observation.

6.4 Discussion

6.4.1 *Why do Counterfactuals Exist?*

Proposition 6.1 suggests that counterfactuals are of no use in making predictions, and hence for making better decisions. At the same time, we find counterfactual reasoning everywhere. Why do counterfactuals exist? We can suggest three reasons.

Lingering decisions Section 6.1.2 noted that counterfactuals are an essential part of connecting acts to consequences, and hence in making decisions. The counterfactuals we encounter may simply be recollections of this prediction process, associated with past decisions. Before the agent knew whether h_t or $h'_{t'}$ would materialize, it was not only perfectly legitimate but necessary for her to engage in predicting the consequences of each possible history. Moreover, if the distinction between h_t and $h'_{t'}$ depends on the agent's own actions, then it would behoove her to think how each history would evolve (at least if she has any hope to qualify as rational). Thus, the agent would have engaged in predicting outcomes of both h_t and $h'_{t'}$, using various hypotheses. Once h_t is known to be the case, hypotheses consistent with both histories may well still be vivid in the agent's mind, generating counterfactual beliefs. According to this view, counterfactual beliefs are of no use; they are simply left-overs from previous reasoning, and they might just as well fade away from memory and make room for more useful speculations.

New information We assumed that counterfactual outcomes are "added" to the database of observations only when they are a logical implication of the agent's underlying model. However, one might exploit additional information to incorporate counterfactual observations even if they are not logical implications of the model ϕ. For example, as mentioned above, statisticians sometimes fill in missing data by kernel estimation. This practice relies on certain additional assumptions about the nature of the process generating the data. In other words, the agent who uses ϕ for her predictions may resort to another model, $\hat{\phi}$, in order to reason about counterfactuals. The additional assumptions incorporated in the model $\hat{\phi}$ may not be justified, strictly speaking, but when data are scarce, such a practice may result in better predictions than more conservative approaches. In fact, our results suggest that such a practice may be useful precisely because it relies on additional assumptions.

It is, however, not clear that adding such "new information" is always rational. Casual observations suggest that people may support their political opinions with counterfactual predictions that match them. It is possible that they first reasoned about these counterfactuals and then deduced the necessary political implications from them. But it is also possible that some of these counterfactuals were filled in in a way that fits one's pre-determined political views. Our analysis suggests that the addition of new information to a database should be handled with care.

Bounded rationality We presented a model of logically omniscient agents. While logical omniscience is a weaker rationality assumption than the standard assumptions of Bayesian decision theory, it is still a restrictive and often unrealistic assumption. Our agent must be able to conceive of all hypotheses at the outset of the reasoning process and capture all of the information she has about these hypotheses in the function ϕ. Nothing can surprise such an agent, and nothing can give her cause to change her model ϕ as a result of new observations. Given the vast number of hypotheses, this level of computational ability is hardly realistic, and it accordingly makes sense to consider agents who are imperfect in their cognitive abilities. For such an agent, a certain conjecture may come to mind only after a counterfactual prediction Y_0 at $h'_{t'}$ is explicitly made, and only then can the agent fill in some parts of the model ϕ. According to this account, counterfactual predictions are a step in the reasoning process, a preparation of the database in the hope that it would bring to mind new regularities.

In this bounded-rationality view, discussions about counterfactuals are essentially discussions about the appropriate specification of ϕ. An agent may well test a particular possibility for ϕ by examining its implications for counterfactual histories, leading to revisions of ϕ in some cases and enhanced confidence in others. The function ϕ lies at the heart of the prediction model, so that counterfactuals here are not only useful but perhaps vitally important to successful prediction. In a sense, this view of counterfactuals takes us back to Savage (1954), who viewed the critical part of a learning process as the massaging of beliefs that goes into the formation of a prior belief, followed by the technically trivial process of Bayesian updating. The counterpart of this massaging in our model would be the formation of the function ϕ. Whereas in most models of rational agents this function simply springs into life, as if from divine inspiration, in practice it must come from somewhere, and counterfactuals may play a role in its creation.

6.4.2 *Extension: Probabilistic Counterfactuals*

The counterfactual predictions we discuss above are deterministic. It appears natural to extend the model to quantitative counterfactuals. In particular, if the credence weights $\phi(\mathcal{A}(h'_{t'}, Y'|h_t))$ happen to generate an additive measure (on sets of outcomes Y'), they can be normalized to obtain a probability on

Y, generating probabilistic counterfactuals along the lines of "Had $h'_{t'}$ been the case, the result would have been $y \in Y$ with probability $p(y|h'_{t'}, h_t)$".

Probabilistic counterfactuals of this nature can also be used to enrich the database by hypothetical observations. Rather than claiming that one knows what would have been the outcome had $h'_{t'}$ occurred, one may admit that uncertainty about this outcome remains, and quantify this uncertainty using counterfactuals. Further, one may use the probability over the missing data to enhance future prediction. However, under reasonable assumptions, a result analogous to Proposition 6.1 would hold. For instance, if the agent makes predictions by taking the expected prediction given the various hypothetical observations, she will make the same probabilistic predictions as if she skipped the counterfactual reasoning step.

6.4.3 *A Possible Application: Extensive Form Games*

Consider an extensive form game with a choice of a strategy for each of the n players. Assume for simplicity that these are pure strategies, so that it is obvious when a deviation is encountered.[11] Should a rational player follow her prescribed strategy? This would depend on her beliefs about what the other players would do, should she indeed follow it, but also what they would do if she were to deviate from her strategy. How would they reason about the game in face of a deviation?

For concreteness, assume that player I is supposed to play a at the first node of the game. This is part of an n-tuple of strategies whose induced play path is implicitly or explicitly assumed to be common belief among the players.[12] Player I might reason, "I should play a, because this move promises a certain payoff; if, by contrast, I were to play b, I would get ..."—namely, planning to play a, the player has to have beliefs about what would happen if she were to change her mind, at the last minute as it were, and play b instead.

This problem is related, formally and conceptually, to the question of counterfactuals. Since player I intends to play a, she expects this to be part of the unfolding history, and she knows that so do the others. However, she can still consider the alternative b, which would bring the play of the game to a node that is inconsistent with the "theory" provided by the n-tuple of strategies. Differently viewed, we might ask the player, after she played a, why she chose to do so. To provide a rational answer, the player should reason about what would have happened had she chosen to do otherwise. The answer to this counterfactual question is, presumably, precisely what

[11] When one considers mixed (or behavioral) strategies, one should also consider some statistical tests of the implied distributions in order to make sure that the selection of strategies constitutes a non-vacuous theory.

[12] See Aumann (1995), Samet (1996), Stalnaker (1996), Battigalli and Siniscalchi (1999).

the player had believed would have happened had she chosen b, before she actually made up her mind.

Our model suggests a way to derive counterfactual beliefs from the same mechanism that generates regular beliefs. For example, consider the backward induction solution in a perfect information game without ties. Assume that for each k there is a hypothesis A_k "All players play the backward induction solution in the last k stages of the game". These hypotheses may have positive ϕ values based on past plays of different games, perhaps with different players. Suppose that this ϕ is shared by all players.[13] For simplicity, assume also that these are the only hypotheses with positive ϕ values. At the beginning, all players believe the backward induction solution will be followed. Should a deviation occur, say, k stages from the end of the game, hypotheses A_l will be refuted for all $l \geq k$. But the deviation would leave $A_{k-1}, \ldots, A_1$ unrefuted. If the player uses these hypotheses for the counterfactual prediction, she would find that the backward induction solution would remain the only possible outcome of her deviation. Hence she would reason that she has nothing to benefit from such a deviation, and would not refute A_k. Note that other specifications of ϕ might not yield the backward induction solution. Importantly, the same method of reasoning that leads to the belief in the equilibrium path is also used for generating off-equilibrium, counterfactual beliefs, with the model providing a tool for expressing and evaluating these beliefs.

6.5 References

Aumann, R. J. (1995), "Backward induction and common knowledge of rationality", *Games and Economic Behavior*, **8**: 6–19.

Battigalli, P. and M. Siniscalchi (1999), "Hierarchies of conditional beliefs and interactive epistemology in dynamic games", *Journal of Economic Theory*, **88**: 188–230.

Bunzl, M. (2004), "Counterfactual History: A User's Guide", *The American Historical Review*, **109**: 845–58.

Gentzen, G. (1934–1935), "Untersuchungen Uber das logische Schliessen", *Mathematische Zeitschrift*, **39**: 405–31.

Gilboa, I., L. Samuelson, and D. Schmeidler (2010), "Dynamics of Inductive Inference in a Unified Model", *Journal of Economic Theory* **148**, 1399–432.

Hume, D. (1748), *An Enquiry Concerning Human Understanding*. Oxford: Clarendon Press.

Lewis, D. (1973), *Counterfactuals*. Oxford: Blackwell Publishers.

[13] Such a model only involves beliefs about other players' behavior. To capture higher-order beliefs one has to augment the state space and introduce additional structure to model the hierarchy of beliefs.

Medvec, V., S. Madey, and T. Gilovich (1995), "When Less is More: Counterfactual Thinking and Satisfaction Among Olympic Medalists", *Journal of Personality and Social Psychology*, **69**: 603–10.

Samet, D. (1996), "Hypothetical knowledge and games with perfect information", *Games and Economic Behavior*, **17**: 230–51.

Savage, L. J. (1954), *The Foundation of Statistics*. New York: John Wiley and Sons; Second Edition 1972, Dover.

Stalnaker, R. (1968), "A Theory of Counterfactuals", in Nicholas Rescher, ed. *Studies in Logical Theory: American Philosophical Quarterly, Monograph 2*. Oxford: Blackwell Publishers, 98–112.

Stalnaker, R. (1996), "Knowledge, belief and counterfactual reasoning in games", *Economics and Philosophy*, **12**: 133–63.

Index

The manufacturer's authorised representative in the EU for product safety is Oxford University Press España S.A. of el Parque Empresarial San Fernando de Henares, Avenida de Castilla, 2 – 28830 Madrid (www.oup.es/en or product.safety@oup.com). OUP España S.A. also acts as importer into Spain of products made by the manufacturer.

www.ingramcontent.com/pod-product-compliance
Ingram Content Group UK Ltd.
Pitfield, Milton Keynes, MK11 3LW, UK
UKHW020923170926
475595UK00031B/36
9780198738022